Awaken
the Power
Within

ALSO BY ALBERT AMAO SORIA

Beyond Conventional Wisdom

The Dawning of the Golden Age of Aquarius

The Renaissance of Mind Healing in America

Healing Without Medicine

Awaken the Power Within

IN DEFENSE OF SELF-HELP

ALBERT AMAO SORIA, PhD

A TarcherPerigee Book

tarcherperigee

An imprint of Penguin Random House LLC
375 Hudson Street
New York, New York 10014

Most TarcherPerigee books are available at special quantity discounts for
bulk purchase for sales promotions, premiums, fund-raising, and educational
needs. Special books or book excerpts also can be created to fit specific needs.
For details, write: SpecialMarkets@penguinrandomhouse.com.

Library of Congress Cataloging-in-Publication Data

Names: Amao, Albert, author.
Title: Awaken the power within : in defense of self-help / Albert Amao.
Description: New York : TarcherPerigee, 2018. |
Identifiers: LCCN 2018009196 (print) | LCCN 2018012424 (ebook) |
ISBN 9780525504566 (e-book) | ISBN 9780143132592 (paperback)
Subjects: LCSH: Self-actualization (Psychology) | BISAC: SELF-HELP /
Personal Growth / Success. | SOCIAL SCIENCE / Research.
Classification: LCC BF637.S4 (ebook) | LCC BF637.S4 A5863 2018 (print) |
DDC 158/.9—dc23
LC record available at https://lccn.loc.gov/2018009196

Printed in the United States of America
1   3   5   7   9   10   8   6   4   2

BOOK DESIGN BY KATY RIEGEL

Let those who dwell in the dust

wake up and shout for joy.

—Isaiah 26:19 (NIV)

ACKNOWLEDGMENTS

I would like to express my heartfelt gratitude to

American scholar on positive thinking Mitch Horowitz

for his spiritual support.

Contents

Part One: Self-Help and Positive-Thinking Movements

Part Two: Self-Help and Self-Healing

Part Three: The Oneness of Life

Foreword

THIS IS ONE of the most illuminating and unconventional books about self-help that you will ever read. Author Albert Amao Soria either/or thinking on nearly every page. He rejects the false and intellectually withering choice of "take it or leave it," which often clouds our political, cultural, and social dialogues.

Rather, Albert examines the question of what really *works* in self-help, at once rejecting overdone promises that emanate from certain quarters of the field (and he names them), while at the same time eschewing the practice of lumping together all self-help under the overused label of "snake oil," as do many academic and journalistic critics. Rather, Albert writes from three fresh and original points of view:

1) As an author, Albert has personally experimented with the therapeutic philosophies he critiques in this book. This gives him rare insight into the agencies and pitfalls they present. Born into an impoverished urban family in Peru, Albert movingly writes of how his life took an unexpected and fruitful path because he had access to self-help literature as a boy. Specifically, he read works of New Thought, which deals with the question of mind causation.

2) He is deeply sympathetic to the needs and wishes of the individual self-help reader—he does not mock, distance himself from, or place himself above the "motivation junkie," as Barbara Ehrenreich and other critics sometimes term the dedicated seeker. Rather, in understanding the drive and dignity of the therapeutic and spiritual inquirer, Albert can clearly evaluate, as a sociologist and critic, what programs are promising (such as Napoleon Hill's *Think and Grow Rich*), and what modalities rest on oversold claims and are bound to leave readers dejected and confused.

3) Finally, Albert writes as a dedicated, lifelong spiritual seeker. He is not only deeply serious about conventional self-help philosophies, but is a student and searcher within mystical, metaphysical, and occult lines of thought. I first met him at a summer conference of the Theosophical Society in America, where I was delivering a talk on my first book, *Occult America*. At the time, Albert was completing his previous book, *Healing Without Medicine*, an evaluation of placebo and mind-therapeutic phenomena. As you will see, Albert locates some of the deepest and most effective aspects of self-help practice within the continuum of traditional esoteric thought. This is historically accurate. I've argued that you cannot fully understand today's self-help culture without realizing how it arose, in its earliest iterations, from mystical and occult movements, which today would seem as culturally out of place as magician's robes at a business motivational conference; but the thought lineage is nonetheless there, particularly with regard to the positive-mind movement and its key contention that *thoughts are causative*.

You need not share Albert's interests in the esoteric (as I do) in order to profit from his insights. Whatever your intellectual and therapeutic tastes, this book gives you a deepened perspective on the culture of self-help and self-improvement, now an $11 billion yearly industry; a better understanding of what works and what does not; and a new sense of the hopes and needs of self-help readers, who are rarely seen or understood in critical literature.

To evaluate an ethical, spiritual, or therapeutic philosophy, and to grasp its values, weaknesses, and strengths, one must—as

Albert does—bring a participatory element to the investigation. William James believed this deeply and lived and worked by this ethic. I attempt to, as well. Albert's role as a critical observer-participant allows him to open windows that many conventional observers are unaware of. His revealing perspective will not only add to your own but may, depending on your outlook, enrich your personal experiments into self-development.

—Mitch Horowitz
New York City

Mitch Horowitz is a PEN Award–winning historian whose books include Occult America *and* One Simple Idea: How Positive Thinking Reshaped Modern Life. *Former vice president and executive editor at TarcherPerigee, his latest book is* The Miracle Club: How Thoughts Become Reality.

Introduction

The truth will set you free.
—JOHN 8:32 (NIV)

WHAT I AM sharing in this book is to a large extent based on my own personal experience in the school of life. I recognize that my views are not all-encompassing or exhaustive, and I do not mean they constitute the truth, but they are the fruit of my search for the truth in many paths and schools. I am writing this book as a sociologist, a social observer, and a seeker. The depth and experiences of my own search through spiritual, ethical, and self-help ideas have not solved all my problems in life, but my search has provided me with the understanding that humans have the inner strength and wisdom to confront life challenges squarely to reach their goals.

In my personal case, I can testify that authentic self-help, including positive thinking and *positive action*, has worked wonderfully for me. Born in a poor Latin American country into a very impoverished family with both parents practically illiterate, I was the oldest of five children. I started working when I was six years old, shining shoes and selling newspapers to help my family. Nobody then would have believed that I would be able to finish high school.

Since my parents were having difficulty making ends meet, without any consent from them I immigrated to Lima, the capital of Peru, where there were more opportunities for work. I had very humble jobs until, thanks to my maternal aunt's intercession, I was employed in a governmental institution as a janitor. That, for me, was a great promotion, which allowed me to earn some money and attend high school at night and help my family. I made the firm decision, against all odds, to finish high school. The prospect of going to university was a faraway dream at that time. Nevertheless, I resorted to inspirational and positive literature and tried to emulate what other successful people had accomplished; only in that way was I able to navigate through hardships and endure difficult times.

In Peru, a poor country, state universities are free of tuition and fees; however, in order to be admitted, a student has to take a proficiency test. Only those who rank the highest on the test are chosen to be admitted, according to the limited number of vacancies determined by the university. With a high score, I was lucky enough to be selected at the National University of San Marcos in Lima, to get the degrees of bachelor, master, and finally doctor of philosophy in sociology. All these things were possible because, when I was a teenager, I had access to New Thought literature and positive-thinking philosophy. As Ralph Waldo Emerson said, *"Once you make a decision*, the universe conspires to *make* it happen." Indeed, once I decided, took action, and persevered, everything fell into place as if by magic. That is my personal experience in this field. The rest is history.

The main purpose of this book is to examine the rationale of the self-help culture in America, which, though based largely on a distorted concept of the term "self-help," has become a predominant feature in the lifestyle of this nation. It analyzes the accuracy of self-help and positive-thinking claims and attempts to distinguish between authentic and inauthentic self-help; it also attempts to uncover the real reasons people flock to inauthentic self-help programs. Millions of people buy books, audiotapes, and videos and attend motivational seminars and workshops without finding solutions to their problems. In the end, they become despondent and hopeless.

First of all, we need to define what we understand by the

concept of authentic self-help, which has been misunderstood and misused. By definition, the word "self-help," as its name indicates, refers to helping or motivating oneself without relying on others, not to being coached by somebody else. As per Merriam-Webster's dictionary, self-help is "the action or process of bettering oneself or overcoming one's problems without the aid of others; especially: the coping with one's personal or emotional problems without professional *help*"[1] (emphasis original).

These definitions are very clear in indicating that self-help is the assistance of oneself without the aid of another person. In other terms, it is the endurance and courage of an individual to deal by oneself with challenges in life. Thus, I postulate that authentic self-help is guidance from the inner self; the key is to learn to listen to the inner voice of the higher self. Most of the time, this voice speaks to us in the most difficult crises we face in life: we feel the hunch, the gut feeling, the inspiration given by the "small, quiet voice" indicating the route to take to the solution of the problem confronted. However, sometimes we don't listen because we are so preoccupied or mesmerized by the challenge we are confronting.

In a few words, the notion of self-help should be understood as self-reliance. American Transcendentalists, represented by Ralph Waldo Emerson, Henry David Thoreau, Margaret Fuller, and others, firmly believe in the power of the individual and in the intrinsic goodness of people. They consider that social organizations such as the mass media, religions, and political parties have domesticated and corrupted the minds of individuals, disempowering them. We live under the spell of the illusion created and maintained by the predominant social classes. This book tries to demonstrate that some of the conventional wisdom we live by is untested and has no scientific basis at all.

My entire journey in esoteric, occult, and mystical schools and organizations has led me to understand that the concept of reliance on the inner self is the way to go; it is the main source of power and wisdom available to humans, as will be demonstrated in the last chapter of this work. Honestly, there is nothing new in the above statement; all the masters and sages of life have declared that truth. However, that wisdom is highly appreciated when one realizes that fact through one's own experience.

The domestication process has become so ingrained in people's minds that many are not willing to change their way of life. Most of the time, they become upset and disturbed when their cherished beliefs are challenged. They want to continue living in their comfort zone, although not according to the truth. The herd mentality is powerful enough that they don't want to wake up from their mesmeric state of mind.

The arguments of this book are based on psychological, metaphysical, and philosophical investigations, as well as on modern scientific discoveries. The primary goal is to empower human beings, restoring their innate power. Based on Eastern and Western sacred scriptures and contemporary scientific discoveries, I attempt to demonstrate that "all the power that ever was or will be" is inside human beings; there is no need to look outside for help.

Historically, religion, education systems, and conventional wisdom have been used by the dominant classes or groups as a means of social control and to make people subservient to their interests, creating a herd mentality. In a Western consumerist society such as modern America, some pseudoreligions and pseudo-positive-thinking and sham self-help movements have turned our modern culture into a quick-fix society, creating social alienation. As a sociologist and cultural critic, I find myself morally obligated to shed some light on this predicament.

The issue is that some New Age "gurus" and false motivational speakers, life coaches, a few evangelical religious preachers, and some sensationalist authors seeking to gain fame and success have turned many of these programs strictly into exercises of business entrepreneurship. These organizers enroll people in their programs under the pretext of helping them, but the underlying motivation is strictly business and a desire for profit. The same thing can be said regarding most practitioners of complementary and alternative therapies. Likewise, many religious leaders, false preachers, and unprofessional healers pretend to heal people in the name of the Holy Spirit or something else with unverifiable techniques, which are merely placebos.

From time to time, self-help books appear on the market that propose easy and quick solutions to all the problems of life, offering ideas and techniques similar to the old "snake oil"—a panacea for healing all kinds of ailments. They advocate enlightenment in a short period of time and offer various "magical solutions" to all human suffering. Many books and occult and esoteric schools on the Internet offer enlightenment and occult knowledge that promise to put their students into positions of power and advantage over others. There are programs and seminars that propose to make one a millionaire or help people to earn easy money just by using their expensive systems, and the list goes on and on. I acknowledge that there may be authentic mystical and occult schools, but these do not need to publicize themselves; they do not proselytize, and they do not seek followers. The earnest will find them.

I am not in the business of debunking, but someone has to clear the air of the foggy environment of American culture. If I mention names it is because in any serious investigation those involved must be identified, but there is no intention whatsoever to discredit or minimize their intellectual capacities or diminish anyone's efforts in publishing a book, which is indeed a very difficult enterprise. Unfortunately, when somebody publishes a book or any writing, it becomes public information and is subject to being reviewed, commented on, or criticized. Likewise, this book that you hold before you will be reviewed, commented on, or criticized sooner or later. That is how knowledge develops and humans advance the unveiling of the real nature of reality.

Someone advances one idea, others will refute or accept it, and somebody else will summarize and complement or surpass it with knowledge available at that time, and the process of achieving wisdom goes on. Thus, we should acknowledge and credit the one who puts forth an idea in the public domain, because it is the starting point for discussion as others comment and contribute to that initial idea. I am fully convinced that nobody, no school of thought nor any discipline, holds the absolute truth; all knowledge and all systems of thought are historical. In a process similar to that by which scientific knowledge advances and new discoveries will give new glances and override previous ones. *C'est la vie.*

During the last few decades, many pseudo-self-help and -positive-thinking books and materials have come out promising to alleviate human suffering. Sad to say, most of the time, they do not yield the wondrous results they offer; instead of helping people, they lead to depression and frustration as people feel that something is defective or wrong with them when the techniques do not succeed. Why is that?

Contemporary people are becoming very compliant with modern services that technology offers, and we are becoming a quick-fix society; individuals seek shortcuts or gimmicks to achieve rapid results. In my research on collective psychology, I found that most people expect to have their wishes fulfilled without much effort and—most important—as soon as possible. This could be one of the reasons they flock to these programs seeking quick-fix solutions to their daily life difficulties. They are willing to give money and time in exchange for these programs. Even worse, they become repeat customers in the hope of getting some relief for their afflictions. As people do not find what they are looking for, they blame themselves, or, in other cases, they feel despondent and victimized.

For instance, in the year 2007, the book and video named *The Secret,* made by Australian television writer and producer Rhonda Byrne, became bestsellers thanks to promotion by Oprah Winfrey via her TV show. People flocked to read the book and see the video expecting to find the "secret" (a magic technique) that would help them become financially successful, find the partner of their dreams, become happy, enjoy health and longevity, and so forth.

The so-called secret is the Law of Attraction, which has been part of the American New Thought philosophy for a century.[2] The book and video *The Secret* were effectively advertised as something mysterious, as old occult knowledge held by only a few people. Credit should be given to all the speakers on the video; their teaching and message are actually uplifting and positively formulated. The issue is that the whole point of the video, which was encapsulated under the Law of Attraction, was nothing new. *The*

Secret became a sensation due to marketing, not because it holds any new or secret knowledge.

I remember that when the video *The Secret* was released, it came with such fanfare as to suggest that some real occult secret would be disclosed and consequently all of the viewer's dreams might come true. The advertising was crafted to be very appealing to those inclined toward metaphysics and New Thought literature. I was invited to watch the video at the home of a New Age person who advertised herself as a life and financial coach. I had to pay seven dollars to be admitted. There were about twenty people in her living room, eager to learn about the secret. The host had been one of the first to manage to buy the video. She showed the same movie for several weeks. The film consisted mainly of interviews of modern New Age personalities who stressed the notion of the Law of Attraction and the idea that thoughts create reality. It seems that the author of the video and the book tried to sell the well-known Law of Attraction as top secret, as something mysterious and new.

What a disillusion when I realized that the same teachings had already been widely disseminated in the public domain through the seminars of Esther and Jerry Hicks, who presented the philosophy of a nonphysical being named Abraham. Esther Hicks channeled the message of Abraham in public lectures, which were recorded by her husband and sold on audiocassettes. She gave lectures on these subjects all over the country. She regarded the Law of Attraction as the most powerful law in the universe. However, in order for something to be manifested, the Law of Attraction has to be complemented by two other laws: the Law of Deliberate Creation and the Law of Allowing. That's it.

A couple years later, I attended a weekend workshop on the book *The Power of Now: A Guide to Spiritual Enlightenment* (1997), authored by Eckhart Tolle. The workshop was supposed to provide some elements to achieve peace of mind and "enlightenment." At that time, I had never heard about Tolle and his message. The weekend workshop was very simplistic and boring; I learned nothing new. When I asked the presenter where Tolle got the idea of the "power of Now," he replied he did not know; all he knew was that Tolle was very heavily into Zen Buddhism.

However, *The Power of Now,* again with the patronage and sponsorship of Oprah Winfrey, ranked number one on the *New York Times* bestseller list. The book offers a formula for permanent peace of mind, happiness, enlightenment, and a blissful life. Incidentally, the subtitle of the book, *A Guide to Spiritual Enlightenment,* suggests anyone can reach spiritual enlightenment. According to this book, people should never have any problems or distress; as long as a person is in the "now," everything will be okay. These ideas seem to be mental anesthetics similar to physical painkillers and, like them, do not solve any real problems, although they may temporarily alleviate symptoms. I will fully elaborate on this subject in pages ahead.

Is it not logical to deduce that, if the claims indicated above were true, life on earth would be a paradise right now? Most people would be living free of any problems and lying on Caribbean beaches. Money would come to people's pockets without any effort; food, monthly rent, and children's university tuition would all be free, and all debts would simply disappear. Since this is not the case, something must be missing in these recipes.

The positive side of my experiences is that they provided me with the motivation to write this book you are holding in your hands, to separate the wheat from the chaff, to separate the foggy, deceitful environment from authentic self-help culture.

An example of an authentic self-help book is Napoleon Hill's masterpiece, *Think and Grow Rich,* originally published in 1937; therein he set practical principles for personal achievement and success in thirteen proven steps to what he calls the "*secret.*" Hill's formula of success is oriented toward practical action and self-empowerment. The value of this work resides in the fact that it is the result of the interviews he conducted with accomplished millionaires of his time. The principles of Hill's secret have been tested by many others, who later became very prosperous in their personal endeavors. In the preface of the book, Hill commences his perennial message as follows:

In every chapter of this book, mention has been made of the money-making *secret* which has made fortunes for more than five hundred exceedingly wealthy men whom I have carefully analyzed over a long period of time.

The secret was brought to my attention by Andrew Carnegie, more than a quarter of a century ago. . . .

This book contains *the secret*, after having been put to a practical test by thousands of people in almost every walk of life[3] (emphasis added).

The *"secret"* is that anyone putting into practice the principles set up by Hill, which include the importance of *practical action* to achieve one's goals, has a great probability of success. However, the unstated idea of pseudo-self-help programs is the notion that a person lacks the required inner resources to deal with challenges in life, that he or she needs the assistance of someone else to manage his or her own destiny. Contrary to that thesis, the fundamental hypothesis of this work is to demonstrate the old mystical adage, *All the power that ever was or will be is within you, right now, right here.* This premise is nothing new; it was taught by Jesus Christ when he said: "The kingdom of heaven is within you" (Luke 17:21, NIV). It is believed that in the Occidental world, Catholic and Protestant churches have disempowered Christian people by making them believe that they need somebody else or their "particular religion" to deal with problems in life and to be saved.

Thus, the goals of this book can be formulated as follows:

1. To raise awareness about pseudo-self-help programs that take advantage of credulous people.
2. To demonstrate that in modern times, most self-help programs have become commercialized and are used as means to gain profit.
3. To unmask the falseness of the overreaching claims made by pseudo–New Age "gurus" and practitioners of commercialized positive-thinking and self-help programs.
4. To assert that each individual is the creator of his or her own reality and circumstances and is the only one who can change them.

This work attempts to provide the reader with solid grounds for viewing the claims of self-help and positive-thinking programs in a completely new way; it will clarify misconceptions about life and the role of humankind in this world. Along those lines, I hope this work will ignite a motivation in the reader for self-empowerment and self-reliance, which are the starting points for gaining control over one's life.

Modern people are hungry to find authentic outlets conducive to spiritual fulfillment. That may be one of the reasons for finding in America a wide range of exotic creeds and strange beliefs. During the last few decades, there has been a reaction against the dogma and victimization of people by several spurious religious organizations. This could explain why many Americans quickly embrace foreign religions and exotic ideas that do not create the sense of guilt and unworthiness that Christianity often does. Those who are interested in modern American practical spirituality based on the New Thought movement cannot afford to ignore this work.

Time and again, everything is reduced to the magical word "beliefs." Beliefs are the essence of religious creed. Everybody struggles to prove that his or her beliefs are authentic and to conduct his or her life according to those beliefs. Beliefs are the most powerful means for bringing both miracles and misery in life. Hence, one's belief system is the stronghold needed to manifest one's personal reality and social environment. The Bible says, "According to your faith let it be done to you" (Matthew 9:29, NIV). The idea here is to determine which beliefs are the most rational, practical, and useful for the betterment of humankind. The only validity of any concept is in its usefulness. Any belief or knowledge that is impractical in bringing about awakening and expansion of consciousness for the human welfare is unworthy and useless.

PART ONE

Self-Help and Positive-Thinking Movements

CHAPTER I

Overview of
the Self-Help Movement

Nowadays, there are many different self-help techniques and programs; each one has its own theories, beliefs, methods, and practitioners. The modern concept of self-help has come to be some assisted self-guided techniques, rather than self-reliance and self-improvement. The movement encompasses a wide variety of self-help programs, including books, videos, audiobooks, seminars, personal coaching, and support groups. Through these programs, the client supposedly learns certain techniques to better deal with life's problems, including methods of dieting, fitness exercises, stress management, achievement of excellence, acquiring wealth, improving relationship with one's partner, and so on.

Currently, there are hundreds of books on the market debunking and demeaning the self-help business in America; some of their authors postulate that some self-help methods make people helpless and codependent rather than benefit them. The fundamental impasse of modern self-help materials and programs is that they have become coaching businesses as they consider normal human problems to be dysfunctions and offer or sell sham solutions.

Why is this happening? In modern times, in a materialistic

and consumerist society, mainstream religions are losing ground in providing spiritual meaning, emotional support, and significant experiential knowledge to their adherents. Here come the false preachers and "gurus" to fill the vacuum selling their "panacea" products to gullible people. Steven Starker, a sociologically minded scholar, and a psychologist by profession, posits that the "self-help book is a firm part of the fabric of American culture, too pervasive and influential to be ignored or lightly dismissed, and certainly worthy of investigation."[1] Incidentally, one of the purposes of this work is to shed some light about this concern expressed by many social scientists.

During the last decades, several self-help programs have tried to fill this vacuum. However, most of them are based on a *greed syndrome*. This greed syndrome is defined as the natural instinct of humans to take advantage of their fellow humans. This condition of avarice seems to be a characteristic of human nature that goes back to the beginning of civilization. Precisely, one of the features of ancient religions was to set limits on the greed syndrome through the idea of moral judgment by a powerful deity. It can be said that all religions, in addition to setting moral rules for human behavior, are based on limiting the voracity of greediness of humans.

Starker, a professor of psychology at the Oregon Health Services University, wrote an excellent work in 1989 entitled *Oracle at the Supermarket: The American Preoccupation with Self-Help Books*. He deals with the history of self-help and provides one of the best analyses of self-help books available. It is deplorable that mainstream academia and scholarship have not given much attention to this work. Although many years have passed since its publication, it has only two reviews on Amazon.com. One reason for this could be the strange and unattractive title, *Oracle at the Supermarket*. The words "oracle" and "supermarket" do not match at all; one wonders what an oracle has to do with a supermarket and, in this particular case, with self-help. The key to understanding this word combination is that Starker uses the term "oracle" as a substitute for "self-help books" for the following reasons:

As is well known, the oracle of ancient Greek culture offered wisdom, knowledge, prophecy, and healing to questing pilgrims. I
submit that these functions have been usurped, in America, by the
self-help book, which provides inspiration, education, and hope to
millions. . . . The wisdom of self-help is dispensed, today, not only
at local libraries and bookstores, but even at suburban supermar-
kets. Readers are provided advice on diet, exercise, sex, divorce,
religion, personal growth, and virtually all other aspects of living,
often with step-by-step instructions.[2]

Starker commences his book with the following words: "The
quest for enlightenment is a ubiquitous and noble part of human
culture, calling to mind images of ancient scrolls, arduous pilgrim-
ages, blind soothsayers, bearded prophets, Indian gurus, encoun-
ters with the oracles of Delphi, and a certain forbidden, but
inescapably tempting, apple."[3] Starker's position is that self-help
books are replacing spiritual guides, ministers, and practical professional assistance. The commercialized, fake literature of this
field goes on to offer wisdom and enlightenment; thus, there is no
need to seek them in foreign lands or from "enlightened gurus" as
the self-help material offers them right here.[4]

One interesting thing that Starker found in his research is that,
of books published in the period of 1983–1984, approximately
3,700 titles begin with the words "How to." Among the titles were
*How to Achieve Security, Confidence, and Peace; How to Achieve
Total Success; How to Avoid Stress Before It Kills You; How to Be a
Better Parent; How to Be More Creative; How to Be Slimmer, Trim-
mer and Happier;* and *How to Beat Death.*[5]

In modern times, most "self-help" programs are in essence
coaching devices; that is, the practitioner assumes the role of parent, priest, or advisor. These programs serve as palliatives or mental narcotics, creating codependency, which involves emotional or
psychological reliance on the practitioner, much like an addiction.

The problem is that, if one takes away the psychological "help"
for addicted people, one creates a vacuum, and the consequences
could be worse than the original problem. It is believed that most
self-help and motivational consumers are repeat customers who

keep coming back whether the program worked for them or not, creating a sense of victimization.[6] When the need is not met by a specific book or service, the seeker will resort to the next book or the next provider or practitioner, who will provide the answers, the comfort, the cure, the solution to his or her emotional or psychological ailments.

Regarding the therapeutic or cognitive component of these methods, it can be said that self-help and "positive thinking" have a psychological and cognitive therapy component inherent in them. Indeed, everything in life can be therapeutic: the advice of a friend, reading a book or a poem, walking in the forest, fishing, and so on. In my case, playing tennis is therapeutic: chasing the ball around, hitting the ball hard, screaming when I miss-hit a shot, expressing content when I make good passing shots, and so on; it is a great mechanism for releasing emotions and getting relief from stressful situations.

Some people turn for personal advice to a close friend or mentor, others to fortune-telling (tarot or astrology); if the dilemma is profound and existential, people search for "reliable and insightful knowledge." In other instances, the quest for an answer begins at the local library, bookstore, or New Age seminar or workshop, and the search ends with a practitioner who advertises his or her services in New Age magazines and local newspapers. Most of these ads appeal to people because they promote spiritual and metaphysical means of reaching wholeness. Interestingly, most of these practitioners have been in the same predicament as the seekers and are in no better position to coach them. Some of these self-help practitioners or coaches provide medical, psychological, financial, and spiritual advice without having the proper credentials.

In modern times, some use the label of "self-help" for manipulation and commercialization rather than for assisting those in need. Self-help critics have found many self-help claims to be misleading and incorrect. Paradoxically, the more people read this kind of literature, the more they think they need it. This can be properly called "indirect coaching." Writer and investigative reporter Steve Salerno severely criticizes all deceitful self-help techniques, which he calls "SHAM," an acronym for "self-help and actualization movement." Salerno has authored an interesting book with an insightful title, *SHAM: How the Self-Help Movement Made America Helpless.*

I have been very close to individuals who use these programs; they search and spend their money on most of the self-help programs available on the market, usually beginning with one technique that appeals to them. They might feel somewhat better at the beginning and then relapse later on—their situation returns to what it initially was. Many also attend workshops and conferences where another salesperson is offering "snake oil"; they then become interested in that and participate in that program. Since they do not find the solution to their emotional issues in one program, they seek another guru to solve their problems, and the search becomes endless.

In 2005, Salerno stated that "self-improvement in all its forms constitutes an $8.56 billion business."[7] He further mentioned that "Market data now expects the industry to be perched at the $12 billion threshold by 2008."[8] In another part of the book, he asserts that "corporations spend billions of dollars each year on SHAM speakers."[9] It seems that corporations use them as a way to reward their employees seeking maximum productivity.

Furthermore, I have a problem with the proposition of easy methods in prosperity Gospels because they create false expectations that can be detrimental for an individual. Precisely due to the sensationalistic and commercialized theology of self-help and positive thinking, New Thought organizations may not be growing; some present these kinds of techniques in a manner similar to a cotton candy dream, without adding the most important complement, which is positive action and effort.

For instance, I was acquainted with a person who used to work for a car assembly plant; he was making decent money. He was very religious and attended a Protestant church on a regular basis. When the assembly plant closed, he received payment for a few months and a good severance, which allowed him to be free from worry for a couple of years. Although he was trained in techniques to search for a job, he was unable to find one for a few years. He was in his middle forties; as a religious person, he started praying for guidance while time passed by and his savings were drying up. Then he started reading "motivational books" to find inspiration in finding a new job. Somehow, he read a couple of motivational books from an evangelical minister and became convinced that he could start a business, although he did not have any experience as a business-man or a specific plan. The idea was to import parts of cars from China and to assemble them in America. He took the project very seriously, but he neglected the competitive factor of the already established companies doing similar business. Nevertheless, he firmly believed that he would make good money and become a prosperous entrepreneur, because the books he read promised that. "Just think positively and believe that you can make it; trust in the Providence" was the mantra. Although this assertion may be true, they did not mention that years of work and dedication would be required.

He sought investor partners to sell his idea; he also visited commercial banks asking for financial support for his project. As one might think, none of them gave a damn about his ideas, be-cause of his lack of experience and a solid plan. Finally, he became depressed and eventually ended up in a mental hospital for some months. Since he was very loyal to his church, the minister some-how helped him to marry a divorced woman with children; she was professional and self-sufficient. His faith saved him.

The moral of this case is that it is not enough to have good ex-pectations and to think positively as my friend did. Time, dedica-tion, and persistence are also required for one to eventually see results. As Napoleon Hill asserted, "There is no such thing as something for nothing!"[10]

That is one of the reasons I have some concern about those ir-responsible prosperity Gospels that indiscriminately sell the idea that anyone can become rich or reach any goal in a short of period of time without positive action and effort. It sounds like common sense, but there are some individuals who believe in their evangelic ministers or a well-known life and business coach who use their credentials to exert some influence on those who are uninformed.

Remarkably, self-help has turned into a New Age religion in

America, as people expect transformative magic from these programs much like they once would have expected from divine intervention. Minister Joel Osteen, an American evangelist preacher, has successfully associated religion with self-help and motivational programs.

The self-help movement has morphed into being a quasireligion, in which false prophets embellish their teachings based on religious scriptures to support their bogus claims. Pseudo-self-help creates dependency on New Age gurus or false prophets, who preach that their programs will alleviate all the customers' ailments and personal problems. When their techniques do not work, they inevitably blame the people, claiming they did not properly focus or correctly apply their teachings.

As a sociologist, I am interested in finding out how so many Americans have become engulfed in this predicament. The golden thread that will lead this work is the following:

People flock to these programs from a place of unworthiness and a sense of inferiority. The indirect and direct coaching business creates codependency and a vicious circle, leading to depression and helplessness.

Why do people rush to easy, quick-fix solutions? There are many explanations for this; one is that some people have been brainwashed by the negative mass media and evangelical preachers who expound ideas that their religion and their interpretation of the sacred scriptures is the only truth. The psychological explanation could be that humans wittingly or unwittingly seek the principle of less effort and the path of least resistance. False "coaches" create needs as they raise false expectations and aspirations on needy people. They assert that anybody can have, be, or do whatever he or she wants and achieve lofty goals, without considering the physical or intellectual limitations of individuals. They put forward these ideas and suggestions with the intention of selling their "easy-fix programs" or specific religious ideologies.

American pop culture has become profoundly permeated with the notion of the self-help business; every year Americans spend millions of dollars on books, videos, seminars, workshops, and the like that promise to fix their daily problems. This may be the reason well-known journalist Tom Tiede appropriately labeled the United States the "Self-Help Nation." The long title of his book tries to encapsulate the American social dilemma: *Self-Help Nation: The Long Overdue, Entirely Justified, Delightfully Hostile Guide to the Snake-Oil Peddlers Who Are Sapping Our Nation's Soul.* Indeed, America is deeply engaged with ideas of self-help and self-improvement programs. This is a typical American ideology, which is derived from the New Thought movement (positive-thinking philosophy). It is indeed an American brainchild.

The notion of self-improvement, personal freedom, and prosperity dates back to the creation of this country by our forefathers; it can be traced to "Ben Franklin's do-it-yourself pragmatism."[11] A sociological analysis of the history of America reveals that, unlike the European and foreign monarchies of the past, where wealth, social rank, and nobility titles were inherited, the United States of America is *the country of self-made men and women.* Since its creation as a nation, America has been viewed as the land of freedom and opportunity, where creativity, inventiveness, and hard work are the basis of American progress and development. This can be verified by the fact that many men with humble origins have become presidents, and other men and women have become millionaires after starting with nothing.

Here comes the ideology of "individual effort" and the belief that anyone who works hard, sticks to his or her personal goals, and shows endurance can eventually attain his or her dreams. That is the magical formula. Every immigrant coming to this country comes with the expectation of having a better standard of living and becoming successful. America was and still is the land of opportunity, where anyone can become successful in any area of life, as long as he or she is determined to make the needed effort and persist in it to reach his or her goals. *This is the trademark of the United States of America.*

This country is a free nation where entrepreneurship and individual initiative coupled with action are fostered; they have made this country extremely prosperous and currently a leading nation in the whole world. This is not a hollow statement at all; it can be verified by examining the lives of some presidents of this country who grew up in poverty and humble conditions to become presidents of the United States. As an example, I can mention Abraham Lincoln, who was born in a one-room cabin to a carpenter and had a humble childhood. Likewise, President Harry S. Truman had a modest upbringing. President James A. Garfield was born into poverty. He grew up in a log cabin in Ohio with four siblings. He worked various odd jobs from carpenter to janitor to get himself through college.[12] The list goes on; lack of space does not allow me to include them all.

The key to prosperity for any nation is based on the quality of education provided to its children. In the United States' educative system, the ideas of self-improvement and hard work can be traced back to the mid-1800s. Since then, children have been exposed to the notion that hard work and individual effort will yield good rewards. The notion of prosperity has been inculcated in children's minds beginning in elementary school, which eventually became the American ideology.

American educator William Holmes McGuffey (1800–1873) is well known for writing a series of elementary school books popularly known as the *McGuffey Readers*. These schoolbooks offered basic lessons in many subjects. "They became standard texts in nearly all states, eclipsing all rival textbooks for half a century and reaching by 1925 a reputed total sale of more than 122 million copies."[13] It was in these textbooks that the ideology of being "success-minded" and hardworking was instilled in children's minds.

Starker indicates that the first of McGuffey's "readers appeared in 1836. These illustrated books were widely distributed and read, going through numerous reprintings. More than 120 million copies of his *Eclectic Reader* were sold, and for many years, nearly all American schoolchildren learned to read from it."[14] McGuffey's fundamental message was to praise and exalt "individual effort." Starker quotes the following extract from McGuffey's lesson:

TRY, TRY AGAIN

If you find your task is hard
Try, try again;
Time will bring you your reward.
Try, try again;
All that other folks can do.
Why with, patience, should not you?
Only keep this rule in view:
Try, try again.[15]

While McGuffey's message was the mantra "Try, try again," there was another, more direct message with which American children were instructed. This initially came from a sermon delivered by Reverend Charles S. Wing and was subsequently taught in Sunday schools: "I think I can; I think I can." This mantra-like chant was published in a little story called "Thinking One Can." It appeared in the *New York Tribune* on April 8, 1906.[16] Later, a different, illustrated version of the same story was disseminated in the children's book *The Little Engine That Could*.

The underlying narrative of the "little engine" has been told and retold many times since then. The leitmotif of this story is as follows: A stranded train is unable to find an engine willing to take it over a high mountain to its destination. Only the little blue engine is willing to try and, while repeating the mantra "I think I can; I think I can," achieves the seemingly impossible task. The message of the story is to teach children the value of self-motivation and self-confidence. In the year 2007, the National Education Association named this book one of its "Teachers' Top 100 Books for Children."[17] Furthermore, in recent years, the same story has been featured in animated films.

There is a popular theme in American mythology that one can be whatever one wants to be or have whatever one wants to have. Author Ted Baxter wrote a book entitled *You Can Be Whatever You Want to Be: I Did It and You Can Do It Too at Any Age,* which is utter nonsense. Not every human being was born to be Michelangelo, who was a sculptor, painter, architect, poet, and engineer; or Leonardo da Vinci, who was a sculptor, architect, musician, mathematician, and engineer; or Mozart, who was a prodigy. Not everybody has the height of basketball star Michael Jordan (six feet six inches) to be proficient in that sport, and so on. Every human being is a unique person with unique abilities, but we cannot be whatever we want. The beauty of life is in its diversity and disparity.

The sociohistorical explanation for the idea that one can be whatever one wants to be has a historical context. After the Second World War, America emerged worldwide as a leading country industrially, financially, and economically. America started flourishing as a modern capitalist country; as industry and finance grew, people found job opportunities and had access to education. People of all backgrounds began to see their dreams, such as having a house, car, TV, radio, and the like, accomplished. The American standard of living improved a great deal. But those who were privileged enough to receive an education due to their parents' fortune were in a better position than others who did not have the same luck.

The concept of the American dream holds that everyone who works hard can become wealthy and live a lavish lifestyle. This is exactly the notion that was sold to the American people throughout our childhoods and was disseminated through education, movies, and mass media such as TV, radio, magazines, and newspapers. Conversely, the negative side of American hyper-individualism involves placing blame on those who have not succeeded, implying that their lack of success is their own fault and not that of an unfair, rigged economic system.

The notion of self-empowerment puts the Self or the "I Am" back on his throne. German philosopher Ludwig A. Feuerbach well understood the problem. In a letter addressed to Georg Friedrich Hegel, he stated that Christianity, since its inception as a religion, has created a dualism of good versus evil while ascribing evil to humankind. This dualistic notion seems to be the influence of the Zoroastrian religion on early Christianity. In Zoroastrianism, twin brothers Ormuzd and Ahriman are in eternal conflict, representing the concepts of good and evil.

From the above deliberations there can be distinguished two types of "self-help"; one being genuine self-help, referring to authentic methods of inspiration and assisting people by means of advising, supporting, and providing encouraging ideas conducive to making the individual self-sufficient; and the other being *coaching-help*, which is used by some people as a means of profit making.

Coaching-help has become a huge business that generates big profits for the coaches. I use the term "coaching-help" for the marketed techniques that create codependency in which the individual becomes entrapped in a vicious cycle. A "smart" person, after experiencing some degree of success, becomes inspired to make money teaching others and giving them ideas for becoming successful, gaining friends, finding their ideal partner, and so on. The idea is to make money getting people to believe that one is helping them. Coaching-help under this circumstance is more a business than real help.

The principle of the coaching business is based on the premise that somebody considers him- or herself superior to others and feels that he or she is in a position to provide advice and give tips or instructions as to how people should behave and think in order to get what they want. The coach is usually someone who knows how human psychology operates and takes advantage of it to manipulate people's minds, creating false dreams, fears, and expectations. Similarly, fortune-tellers know human flaws, hopes, and fears and know how to manipulate them.

The common denominator among all these questionable self-help programs is twofold: 1) they promise a quick-fix solution, and 2) they offer to make life problem-free. The underlying notion is that people should reach their cherished goals rapidly and without much struggle. People usually respond to these promises from a place of worthlessness with the hope that someone has goodwill toward them.

Interesting enough, during the last few decades many books

have appeared decrying the increasing amount of pseudo-self-help literature, confirming my concerns expressed above. I will examine only the most important ones.

Sociologist and cultural critic Micki McGee states in her book *Self-Help, Inc.: Makeover Culture in American Life* that she views the self-help business as a makeover, or reinvention, of oneself. She clearly states, "At the heart of this project [the self-help program] is the notion that no one, try as they may, can invent themselves."[18]

This means that the idea of self-help, according to McGee, involves a person reinventing him- or herself. This immediately brings to mind the teachings of nineteenth-century French magician and father of modern Occidental occultism Éliphas Lévi, who gave the injunction that the magnum opus—the great work—of a magician is to reinvent himself.[19] This is in essence a good intention, but not everybody is up to it; forcing people to do something beyond their means creates psychological problems.

McGee postulates that most Americans rely on pseudo-self-help literature for advice on how to deal with an increasingly unstable and competitive work environment. To verify that statement, she conducted a survey of the self-help books on the *New York Times* bestseller lists during the period of 1973 through 1997 and found a "correlation between the numbers of self-help books in print and the declining economic circumstances and opportunities for working Americans."[20] That correlation is partially correct, because pseudo-self-help books (alternative medicine, inspiration and spirituality, business coaching, personal development) continue to be bestsellers in contemporary times. The idea is that, when a common need is detected, a book or some other product comes to the market offering a solution to it. This is evidenced by the fact that many books are in print advising how to lose weight, how to find the partner of your dreams, how to find the perfect job, and so on. This is an interesting thesis that deserves proper consideration.

McGee's fundamental question is, "Why doesn't self-help help?" She finds that America is a nation that relies heavily on self-help and makeover traps, where people are caught up in endless cycles of self-invention in a society that is constantly changing.[21] McGee observes that the notion of reinvention propounded by would-be self-help programs does not work but instead keeps people's situations the same. She writes, "What this examination of self-improvement culture will show is that although the idea of individual self-determination remains a potent political force, the versions of false self-invention offered in the preponderance of popular self-help literature typically maintain the status quo."[22] However, her generalization is an overreaching statement, as she does not distinguish genuine self-help books, which are few indeed, from those sham ones.

The concept of a "makeover," in the sense McGee uses it, implies a remodeling of the human personality similar to the occult idea of "self-transformation." This spiritual alternative could be impractical in a materialistic and quick-fix society, where material success is the most important goal for the average American.

It should be considered that the self-help component does not happen in a void or vacuum; we are social creatures, and we live in a sociocultural society. Humans are conditioned educationally, culturally, and emotionally, from the time they are born, by the family and social environment in which they live. For instance, a sense of unworthiness can come from a Christian background in which people are indoctrinated from the time they are little with the idea that they are sinners just because they have come into this world. Some Protestant preachers claim that because Jesus died on the cross for our sins, we consequently have to pay for them with suffering and tears. The huge contradiction of this tenet is that, if Jesus died for everyone's sins, then the debt is paid for, and no additional suffering should be required. Even worse, according to the Calvinist doctrine of "predestination," only certain eligible people will be saved by the grace of God; the majority will not receive salvation no matter what they do; they are damned forever. Those ideas are deeply embedded in the subconscious mind of a person raised in this environment. It is no wonder that adults in Christian countries have a deep sense of inferiority and unworthiness.

It is also important to note that the tenets of genuine self-help and self-improvement literature have their roots in the esoteric and occult schools of mystery. A thorough explanation of this statement would require another full book. My interest here is to point out the influence of esoteric and occult literature on modern culture. This subject has been studied by author Mitch Horowitz in his excellent book *Occult America: The Secret History of How Mysticism Shaped Our Nation*, which is highly recommended to those readers interested in the subject.

My position is that genuine self-help serves as a motivational or inspirational element to stimulate the beginning of an action. In other words, it is an internal motivation for one to do something by him- or herself. However, there are people who, under the pretext of providing self-help, take advantage of others and turn their needs into a business, creating codependency. According to the journalist Tom Tiede, the underlying suppositions of indirect coaching are "You are dumb; I am smart because I went to university and have a degree," or "You are dumb; I am smart because I am successful."[23] He further considers many self-help books deceptive and manipulative.

To counteract the negativity of the mass media we need to be mindful and alert about the intrusion of collective negative suggestion. Many suggestible people may get sick from the insistent advertisement of pharmaceutical products, which usually implies that anyone is subject to getting sick. These ads are endorsed by medical doctors and assented to by common opinion; therefore, what the pharmaceutical industry promotes eventually becomes a socially accepted idea. This I call "nocebo suggestion." Alertness and mindfulness can prevent people from becoming vulnerable to collective suggestions, especially during difficult and stressful times.

In addition to the above, in a modern capitalist society, where marketing and profits are the most important thing, it does not matter by what means revenues are achieved. Similarly, in the coaching business, materials including books, recordings, seminars, workshops, e-books, and so on, are marketed under the guise of self-improvement and self-help, producing profitable returns. This enterprise includes expansion to countries abroad; we export American values, lifestyles, ideas, and so forth to the world. Since the United States of America as a nation has become so successful economically and financially, the American lifestyle, including New Age ideology, is mimicked by many young people from other cultures as a way to become successful (though it should be mentioned that American success mainly benefits only the top one percent of individuals, and average American individuals, especially the middle class, have largely become impoverished during the last decades). One of the reasons Arab countries resent America is the imposition of our values and culture on their young people. This invasion comes through the movies, videos, music, and all mass media. We are literally destroying the traditional lifestyles of many cultures around the world.

The self-help business is also utilized by Protestant ministers, who, using their pulpits, are very successful in imposing pseudo-self-help ideas on their churchgoers. They are skillful enough to base the concept of self-help on biblical passages; in some cases, their televised sermons are seen abroad in different countries; they secure audiences and markets for their books. No wonder their books become bestsellers.

Along these lines, coaches, motivational speakers, and some New Age gurus often associate "Christian spirituality" with prosperity and self-improvement. Although these attributes (prosperity and self-improvement) were the conditions that paralleled the rise of a capitalism economy, they do not, however, have anything to do with spirituality. This can be verified by the fact that Jesus and many Christian saints preached poverty, humbleness, and humility as virtues of a good Christian.

The mass media have played an important role in this indoctrination and propagation of American values and culture through books, movies, TV, and music. Anyone who has traveled around the world is aware how deeply American values have become pervasive around the planet. In hotels, restaurants, and important places abroad, the music played in the background is usually American. Moreover, American restaurants such as McDonald's, Burger King, Pizza Hut, and Papa John's, among others, can frequently be seen in the main cities of overseas countries.

These are only a few examples; a list of American businesses that have become pervasive in foreign countries would go on for pages. The English language is becoming universal because it means opportunity, money, and success anywhere an individual resides.

One can ask, what is wrong with self-help culture? American self-help and self-improvement were created by those seeking prosperity on this new continent. Authentic self-help means to motivate someone and give him or her emotional incentive to take a positive step. The problem is when people use these programs for business purposes to fatten their bank accounts. They neglect the real purpose of self-help. Nevertheless, the adage "Don't throw the baby out with the bathwater" applies here; self-help can motivate and inspire people—give an inner jump start to begin a new project or goal.

The well-known author Barbara Ehrenreich, in her book *Bright-Sided: How the Relentless Promotion of Positive Thinking Has Undermined America*, consistently criticizes the modern "positive-thinking gurus" including Norman Vincent Peale, Rhonda Byrne, Joel Osteen, and Oprah Winfrey, among others, and I fully agree with her. However, I completely disagree when she associates positive thinking with consumerism and capitalism. The term "positive thinking" is a psychological device, which is independent from the use that some people give to it.

In the introduction of the above-mentioned book, Ehrenreich describes repeatedly the beneficial effects of positive thinking; however, she ends up indicating that positive thinking could be detrimental for people. I think she is confusing positive thinking with blind optimism and consumerism in a capitalist economy. Again, positive thinking is a mental attitude to squarely confront problems in life and to keep the mind on the positive side rather than in despair. The pitfall is that many have corrupted the term "positive thinking" with blind optimism and inactiveness. That is precisely one of the purposes of this work, to *"separate the wheat from the chaff."*

Furthermore, Ehrenreich blames positive thinking ideology for the growth of a consumerist society in America. She says:

The consumer culture encourages individuals to want more—cars, larger homes, television sets, cell phones, gadgets of all kinds—and *positive thinking* is ready at hand to tell them they deserve more and have it if they really want it and are willing to make the effort to get it. . . . Perpetual growth, whether of a particular company or an entire economy, is of course an absurdity, but *positive thinking* makes it seem possible, if not ordained.[24] (emphasis added)

She also blames positive thinking for the 2008 American stock market crash, suggesting that optimism and positive thinking generated the Great Recession. The truth of the matter is that those really responsible for it were the top executives of the financial institutions. They created false expectations for people under the slogan of the "American Dream." Moreover, Ehrenreich states that the invasion of Iraq was out of a "reckless optimism,"[25]—this is nonsense. The truth is the invasion of Iraq was due to reckless decision-making by the leaders on power. "Optimism" does not have anything to do with it. Unfortunately, the consequences of that decision will be paid by the American middle class for many years to come. What irony!

Furthermore, it should be distinguished from a mental discipline (such as positive thinking) by those who use this psychological device for business purposes to fatten their bank accounts. Thus, I do not agree with blaming positive thinking for the growth of a consumerist society; instead it should be blamed for the capitalist system and the greed syndrome of the huge companies. In a consumerist society the big corporations manipulate consumers through the mass media, creating unnecessary and superficial needs. They encourage people to buy their products and services through well-crafted commercials and ads. This practice has nothing to do with positive thinking as a psychological discipline.

Moreover, positive thinking without the individual inner strength is nothing. This will be fully elaborated on in later chapters in this book. Finally, everything has its limitations, even positive thinking, as a self-help device. We cannot ask something that cannot be delivered.

The pseudo-self-help movement in America has become similar to an evangelical theology. People become dependent on these programs and come to require a tutor or coach to conduct their lives. Self-help gurus and coaches are taking the role of minister or priest. The interesting thing is that more and more people read self-help literature seeking inspiration and motivation to solve their daily life problems. Steve Salerno indicates that the more people read this literature, the more they think they need it, and they become addicted to it.

Salerno mercilessly rebukes the self-help coaches and "gurus," including Dr. Phil, Laura Schlessinger, Tony Robbins, and others. He labels them as a bunch of money-grabbing charlatans and demagogues. He opted for using the term SHAM, which refers to something false that is presented as the truth. These false prophets claim to be able to heal all of society's psychological dramas and problems with their seemingly endless streams of contrived "mumbo-jumbo" techniques. In short, Salerno does an excellent job debunking most of the "sacred cows" of the self-help movement.

In summary: The purpose of genuine self-help programs is to assist individuals in becoming self-sufficient and to acknowledge that there is an inner source of strength in every individual that can help them endure difficult moments in life. At the risk of redundancy, the following needs to be stressed: The problem in modern times is that self-help culture has become commercialized and has lost its authentic notion of self-help. The fake "positive-thinking gurus" inflict a sense of victimization among their clients, making people believe they need them. Self-help authors and practitioners seek to become *New York Times* bestsellers and accumulate money and prestige; those are the ones who have "undermined America." When self-help culture loses sight of making the individual self-sufficient, it loses all its meaning as self-help. Consequently, false self-help programs may cripple people's ability to deal with problems on their own.

Authentic self-help books and products, as well as support groups, can play an effective role in ameliorating daily life problems; they can serve as a means of releasing or discharging emotions. Nevertheless, placebo effects can never be wholly discounted in these programs. The keynote for the self-help philosophy was provided by Benjamin Franklin, who used the proverb "God helps those who help themselves" in his *Poor Richard's Almanack*.

CHAPTER 2

Overview of Positive Thinking

Positive thinking is our national creed.
—MITCH HOROWITZ[1]

POSITIVE THINKING IS a direct offshoot of the New Thought movement that started in the middle of the nineteenth century in New England. In modern parlance, positive thinking and New Thought are considered synonymous. The use of positive thinking by Protestant ministers is yet another indication of the way New Thought has become prevalent in modern Americans' outlook on life.

"Positive thinking" can be defined as the mental attitude that selectively admits thoughts, words, feelings, and images that are conducive to instilling confidence in oneself. In other words, positive thinking rests on personal self-assurance and the expectation that everything will work out in the long run. It is a mental attitude of expecting good and favorable results from any enterprise, as long as the actions to bring about that outcome are conducted in good faith. It is above all an optimistic mental attitude. This approach can be useful in making one feel good about oneself and self-assured about the trend of events in one's life. The underlying idea is that if something does not work as expected, the experience of it will provide a good lesson for future endeavors. It is a motivational message that temporarily makes an individual feel more in control.

The criticism of positive thinking results from a misunderstanding of it; critics usually associate it with wishful thinking. Some believe that positive thinking is a technique to mentally formulate a desire and expect that it will come true by itself, or visualize one's dream job and have the job somehow appear, or think one is a millionaire and then magically one will grow rich, and so on. These conceptualizations by definition are utterly wrong. *Positive thinking is a means of keeping the mind focused on constructive, uplifting, and altruistic thoughts* while disregarding the negative ones. As a result, things somehow usually unfold in a favorable manner. As the name suggests, positive thinking is about thinking confidently.

The difference between positive thinking and religious faith is that faith is a belief heightened to the highest degree by the assumption of a providential intervention. In a broader concept, "faith" can be defined as a body of beliefs in a deity, saint, or superior being, ascribing supernatural powers to them. In that sense, desires based on genuine religious faith are the most powerful means for crystallization. For instance, an authentic belief in the intervention of an all-powerful deity enhances the placebo effect of self-healing.

Steady faith, or unwavering belief, is a subtle mental power that has some effect on the outcome expected by the believer. Every human being has a belief system; it may be religious or political, or involve being a sports fanatic or having revolutionary convictions, social beliefs, and so forth. Those beliefs, conscious or unconscious, are part of a person's outlook on life.

Initially, New Thought was conceptualized as a mind power circumscribed to the field of healing by changing the frame of mind of the sick person; however, its narrative, in time, has been applied to broader aspects of life, such as success, personal relationships, harmonious marriage, financial prosperity, and so on. In general, the practitioners of this ideology resort to the Bible and other worldwide sacred scriptures to support their philosophy.

Recounting the whole story of the New Thought movement would require several volumes. I have already delineated the history of this movement as related to the origins of mind healing in my book *Healing Without Medicine: From Pioneers to Modern Practice.*

There are several books on the market regarding positive thinking and its implications on American ideology in general. Among these are two remarkable and highly recommended works that trace the influence of New Thought and positive thinking in this country. One was penned by Anne Harrington, Harvard professor and chair of the history of science department, and is titled *The Cure Within: A History of Mind-Body Medicine* (2008). The other was written by Mitch Horowitz, former vice president and editor in chief of TarcherPerigee, and is titled *One Simple Idea: How Positive Thinking Reshaped Modern Life* (2014). Both authors comprehensively examine occult philosophy and metaphysical thinking as expressed in New Thought philosophy and discuss how these have deeply influenced American modern life, from healing modalities to social and political activities, becoming part of American culture.

The titles of these two books are self-explanatory, and they are closely related. Interestingly, both authors write about the same topic but from different perspectives: Harrington approaches the subject as an academic in a detached, intellectual manner and is very careful not to take sides. She is largely interested in exploring the origin of New Thought, its impact as a method of healing, and the way positive thinking has been medicalized (becoming part of preventive medicine and treatment). On the other hand, Mitch Horowitz is a living example of how positive thinking and determination work. He states:

> Hence, it is from inside that I approach this book—as someone who has worked with positive-thinking ideas not only in my personal life but for much of my professional life, as well. As I write this, I am vice-president and editor-in-chief at a publishing house that specializes in self-help, New Age, positive thinking.[2]

He correctly indicates that positive thinking has practically become a modern American creed. "It forms the foundation of business motivation, self-help, and therapeutic spirituality, including within the world of evangelism."[3] As with the development of our capitalist system, it can be said that American optimism parallels positive thinking. The logical sequence is that optimism generates positive expectations, and these in turn produce hopeful thoughts and feelings (or a positive outlook). The opposite view, pessimism, generates gloomy thinking and consequently negative expectations.

In the book *One Simple Idea*, Horowitz traces the roots of positive thinking and how they have become the fabric of American thought and ideology today. According to him, positive thinking has become pervasive in modern American religion, politics, and popular culture. Ronald Reagan, Bill Clinton, Donald Trump, and others have highly praised this ideology. Protestant ministers and evangelists such as Joel Osteen, Robert H. Schuller, Thomas D. Jakes, and others constantly resort to the ideas and slogans of positive thinking in their sermons, which they then coat with evangelical and biblical stories to increase the effectiveness of their teachings. The subtle message of these evangelical preachers in their televised sermons seems to be that God or Jesus wants you to be rich, happy, and prosperous, but in the meantime, send your money to the church. These preachers are very skillful as motivational speakers; they have the persuasion technique to convince their audiences and sell their books.

In passing, I should note that I disagree with the premise of Harrington's chapter "The Power of Suggestion," as she considers the healing performed by suggestion to be temporary and not significant, meaning that the patient usually relapses. Harrington feels that the use of placebos, exemplified by Norman Cousins, is the most effective among all methods of mental healing. Cousins was a celebrated American political journalist who cured himself from an apparently incurable disease using massive doses of vitamin C and laughter.

Harrington's position is stated below:

> The narrative's conclusion is clear: suggestion's cures are at the best palliative and at worst fool's gold. The patient under the influence of suggestion has not actually been cured by her doctor, but

has instead brought on all the changes herself, using her own mind—and these changes remain, in a sense, only mental.[4]

In my book *Healing Without Medicine*, I mention that healings, whether with traditional or nontraditional medicine, are prone to relapse. This is also the case in cures performed by placebo. I have already pointed out that all healing without medicine is self-healing, and in some cases, even healing with medicine is self-healing because of the placebo effect. We cannot disregard the extraordinary power of the human body to regain its wellness and stay well. This is a sine qua non statement: usually, the healer's role is to activate the inner capacity of the sick person to regain his/her balance. Hence, *any healing achieved, whether by suggestion or placebo, is self-healing*. I will further elaborate on this issue in the pages ahead.

It is interesting that Harrington on several occasions mentions French medical doctors Hippolyte Bernheim and Jean-Martin Charcot, both of whom used hypnosis as their method of treatment. Bernheim was a member of the Nancy School of hypnosis; this school was the first to use hypnosis as a therapeutic method by giving suggestions to individuals.

I agree with Harrington when she asserts faith or religious beliefs to be the most potent instruments for healing.[5] However, she disregards "suggestion" as a permanent means for restoring health; instead she considers "placebo" to be the valid therapy. I posit that placebo is an indirect suggestion.

Regarding the extraordinary healing of Norman Cousins, who regained his health from an almost paralytic condition, Harrington questions herself: "Was the placebo effect, then, the faith cure of our time and indeed the key to making sense of all faith cures, past and present?" She answers in the affirmative. For Harrington, the "placebo effect" is basically the healing power of faith.[6] She goes on to corroborate her response: "The second event that began to transform the placebo from a suspect instrument of suggestion to a catalyst for the miracle cures of positive thinking was the rise of the new field of psychoneuroimmunology."[7]

Harrington's contribution to the movement of positive thinking is her thorough research of the medicalization of self-help and positive thinking, but she completely ignores the modern commercialization of these methods. She also says that the placebo effect has roots in discontent with modern medicine.[8] My contention is that placebos have existed since the beginning of civilization; they are the means by which shamans, medicine men, witches, clergymen, and quacks used to heal people in the past and still do today.

The mid-nineteenth and twentieth centuries experienced a boom in New Thought organizations and churches in America and abroad. Earlier, American philosopher Ralph Waldo Emerson (1803–1882) set the tone for a new way of thinking that emerged in this country. The term "New Thought" appears to have originated with Emerson's lecture "Success," published in 1870, in which he wrote: "to redeem defeat by *new thought*" (emphasis added). Currently, there are hundreds of New Thought organizations and churches thriving around the world.[9]

Everything started in New England, in the mid-1860s, when Phineas P. Quimby (1802–1866) began performing mind or mental healing by changing the frame of mind of the ill person. Some people who were cured by Quimby became his disciples and began practicing mind healing in New England, creating a new way of thinking in America. The key idea was to give priority to the mind rather than to the body. This notion began an ideological revolution in the thinking of the United States after the end of the American Civil War.

Quimby became very famous in New England as the doctor who healed without medicine. Due to his pioneering work on mind or mental healing, he came to be considered the father of the New Thought movement (NTM). Nowadays, there are many churches and organizations under the umbrella of the NTM, such as Religious Science, Divine Science, Unity, and others around the world.

One aspect that needs to be stressed is the fact that the NTM, positive thinking, and the Law of Attraction, among other self-help programs, are the brainchildren of American thinkers. The impact of this ideology can be seen in all areas of the American outlook and way of life. These teachings are pervasive in New Age motivational seminars, twelve-step programs, recovery programs, mind-body therapies, and so on.

Emerson propounded an ideological emancipation from European intellectual influence in America. His celebrated essays "Nature," "The American Scholar," and especially the renowned "Self-Reliance"[10] set the tone in the search for an authentic American way of thinking. In "Self-Reliance," first published in 1841, Emerson openly rejects conformity and passive acceptance of common opinion (which I understand as "conventional wisdom"). Emerson is the first American who postulated, "Trust yourself," meaning rely on your inner self and do not take the ideas of common society for granted. He repetitively emphasizes self-reliance, believing in your personal intuition and experiences, creating your own self-esteem, acting independently, and so on. He is also the author of the following statement: "Always do what you are afraid to do." Here we see the seminal concept for ideas such as "You can do it," "It is up to you," and "Trust in yourself," which are basic notions for the formulation of self-help, positive thinking, and self-transformation.

Emerson found that people are usually influenced by the predominant society's ideas, which are not necessarily beneficial for people. Individuals can easily become engulfed in the masses' opinions. When a man blindly adheres to thoughts or opinions of conventional wisdom, he develops a herd mind. I have written elsewhere that "conventional wisdom" means uncritical acceptance of information and knowledge gained from education, parents, teachers, and mass media. Humankind appears to have a natural tendency to spontaneously accept and pursue what is dictated by conventional wisdom. This attitude has been labeled the "herd instinct," that is, the natural tendency to follow what others think and do. Emerson emphasized the notion of differentiating the concepts of authenticity versus social alienation, genuineness versus the feeling of being disconnected and isolated from the values of one's own community.

Regarding the above concerns, Jungian psychologist Edward F. Edinger considers contemporary social alienation to be due to the isolation of modern humans and lack of meaning in life. He wrote,

"One of the symptoms of alienation in the modern age is the wide-spread sense of meaninglessness. Many patients seek psychother-apy not for any clearly defined disorder but because they feel that life has no meaning."[11] On the other hand, psychiatrist Thomas S. Szasz eloquently argued, in his book *The Myth of Mental Illness*, that modern psychotherapists are replacing the role of the traditional priest: people, in the past, used to go to church to confess their sins and find relief for their emotional problems; in modern times they go to psychotherapists for the same purpose.

Thus, it can be said without any shadow of doubt that Emerson is the theoretical forefather of the New Thought, positive-thinking, and self-help movements. He was the inspiration for most of the New Thought pioneers, especially Prentice Mulford and Ernest Holmes. Emerson also taught about the need for each individual to avoid conformity and encouraged people to follow their own instincts and ideas. Emerson argued that inside each person there is a genius. He wrote: "To believe your own thought, to believe that what is true for you in your private heart is true for all men—that is genius." In Emerson's thought, the need to trust oneself and the value of self-worth are extremely important.

Later, Hindu philosopher Jiddu Krishnamurti (1895–1986), who immigrated to America, came up with ideas similar to what Emerson called "self-reliance." Krishnamurti taught that there should not be a subordinate relationship between a spiritual mas-ter and his or her disciples. Two of his favorite statements resem-ble Emerson's: "I maintain that Truth is a pathless land, and you cannot approach it by any path whatsoever, by any religion, by any sect," and "You yourself have to be the master and the pupil. The moment you acknowledge another as a master and yourself as a pupil, you are denying truth."[12]

Emerson recommends that an individual be willing to open his mind to his intuitions and personal experiences. He reiterates the value of self-worth. Once one succumbs to the predominant common opinion, one becomes indoctrinated and unable to think for oneself and to affirm one's identity as a particular individual with one's own ideas. An individual who exerts his or her capacity to think is able to affirm his or her real identity. For Emerson, it is extremely important to empower people and increase their self-esteem based on their intrinsic value as human beings rather than on prestige or external circumstances. He stresses the notion, "Be yourself."

Horowitz makes an insightful contribution to the history of this new, emergent ideology of healing, as he explains how the label New Thought was adopted by the new thinkers to differentiate their position from the term "Christian Science," which Mary Baker Eddy had copyrighted for the exclusive use of her organization. Another interesting insight Horowitz brings to the history of the New Thought movement and positive thinking is the reinstatement of the New Thought author Prentice Mulford (1834–1891), who had been almost forgotten in the list of the movement's pioneers. Horowitz correctly identified Mulford as the "missing link"[13] between early New Thought, which was limited to healing purposes, and modern New Thought, which has become the *American prosperity Gospel*. In passing, it is noteworthy that Mulford and William W. Atkinson (1862–1932) were the ones who popularized the phrase "Law of Attraction," based on the notion that thoughts are similar to magnets, with attraction properties.

According to Horowitz's assessment, Mulford drew most of his metaphysical ideas from Swiss theologian Emanuel Swedenborg (1688–1772) through New Thought pioneer Reverend Warren Felt Evans (1817–1889). Evans was a disciple of Quimby and one of the first writers of New Thought philosophy. Evans was an ordained Methodist minister until 1863;[14] later on, he abandoned that ministry and joined the Church of the New Jerusalem, also known as New Church (Swedenborgian Church). Evans came to Quimby to be cured of nervous problems; after he was healed, he started practicing mental healing as taught by Quimby.

Prentice Mulford seems to have borrowed his ideas of success and prosperity directly from Emerson's essay "Success." Mulford adapted and elaborated on Emerson's notion of prosperity and came up with the term "science of success," which he used in his writings.

Mulford is well known in New Age circles for his book *Thoughts Are Things*, which was published in 1889. The historic context in which Mulford wrote that book was an America that was a strongly religious nation. It was extremely odd for ordinary people to accept the idea that "thoughts are things." At the end of the nineteenth century, the only people who consented to such notions were people familiar with esoteric and occult literature. Even nowadays, ordinary and educated people do not believe this concept. The truth of the matter is that thoughts are things in the mental plane and are prone to becoming real (or actualized) in the physical plane as long as they are fed with strong emotions and unwavering desire.

So how did Mulford come up with the idea that "thoughts are things"? It can be explained by the fact that, in addition to the influences of Emerson, Evans, and Swedenborg, Mulford may have had access to occult literature or some kind of relationship with an esoteric organization. It is documented that he attended séances and spiritualist meetings.[15] It is not accidental that Arthur Edward Waite, a notorious English scholar, magician, and member of the occult school called the Hermetic Order of the Golden Dawn, wrote a preface and an introduction to Mulford's book *The Gift of the Spirit*.

Mulford's abstract concept of "thoughts are things" is brought down to earth and elucidated by Napoleon Hill. He started the introduction to his book *Think and Grow Rich* with the following words:

> Truly, "thoughts are things," and powerful things at that, when they are mixed with definitiveness of purpose, persistence, and a burning desire for their translation into riches or other material objects.[16]

Also important to this discussion is Ernest S. Holmes (1887–1960), an American New Thought writer and founder of the spiritual movement known as Religious Science. He is the author of the seminal work *Science of Mind*, which is a textbook for members of the Religious Science Church, and he also wrote several other metaphysical books. Holmes synthesized the best of the New Thought and combined it with the best of the world's major religions. The metaphysical principles described in *Science of Mind* inspired and influenced future generations of New Thought and metaphysics students and teachers. Holmes's influence beyond New Thought can be seen in the self-help movement as well.

In his early life, Holmes was also profoundly inspired by Emerson.[17] He was tremendously impressed with the idea of self-reliance, a concept extremely important for emerging American intellectuals who needed to break their cultural and ideological dependence on European influence. In Holmes's autobiographical section of *Science of Mind*, he indicates that Emerson was his first major intellectual discovery, in 1907. He states, "Reading Emerson was like drinking water to me. . . . I have studied him all my life."[18]

Horowitz aptly notes, "Not only did Holmes devise a fully fleshed-out theology, but he also inspired the most formative self-help philosophy of the twentieth century."[19] The next person to enter the arena of mind power and self-help was Norman Vincent Peale (1898–1993), who popularized the New Thought concept of positive thinking. Peale was originally ordained as a Methodist minister, then changed his affiliation to the Reformed Church of America and became a famous preacher in New York City. He has been wrongly credited as the progenitor of the positive-thinking movement known as "self-help." Historically, the basic ideas of self-help, as I indicated above, originated with Emerson and were adopted by Holmes.

Although, Peale was a friend of Ernest Holmes; he was very reluctant to make any allusion to the New Thought movement, from which Peale took many ideas; even the name of "positive thinking" has New Thought roots. As Harrington documented, the slogan "positive thinking" was originally coined by Charles Fillmore[20] (1854–1948), cofounder of the Unity Church of Christianity, one of the largest New Thought communities in the United States.

Based on the above, there are reasons to believe that Peale became familiar with the idea of positive thinking as a means of self-help, which initially had esoteric origin. As Professor Harrington accurately noted, "Peale did more than anyone else *to dissociate the basic New Thought message from its original, somewhat esoteric roots* and make it feel as American as baseball and apple pie"[21] (emphasis added). This seems to be the case; Peale used Prentice

Mulford's slogan "thoughts are things" when he wrote, "It has been said that 'thoughts are things,' that they actually possess dynamic power."[22]

Initially, Peale became interested in Freudian psychotherapy and even opened a clinic in the "basement of the Marble Collegiate Church, where Peale was a pastor,"[23] with his psychoanalyst friend Dr. Smiley Blanton for treatment of religious-psychological dysfunctions. He and Blanton coauthored a book titled *The Art of Real Happiness* in 1950. Peale soon became interested in New Thought literature; he attended Ernest Holmes's lectures. Furthermore, Peale was a high-ranking (thirty-third-degree) Scottish Rite Freemason[24] and thus had access to esoteric literature. Furnished with the teachings of Holmes and the ideology of New Thought, Peale became convinced of the power of the mind and popularized the teaching of positive thinking in America. Hence, most of Peale's development regarding positive thinking derived from New Thought philosophy.

Furthermore, Peale's ideas also were strongly influenced by French pharmacist and psychologist Émile Coué (1857–1926), father of applied psychology, who came to New York to give lectures about his self-help therapies. Coue was a former student of the Nancy School of hypnosis; based on that teaching, he became the main proponent of self-hypnosis, which was then called autosuggestion. Coue's methods of psychotherapy and self-improvement were based on positive affirmations and autosuggestion. His book *Self-Mastery Through Conscious Autosuggestion*, originally published in 1922, was extremely popular in America, as was his slogan/affirmation, "Every day, in every way, I am getting better and better."

It should also be mentioned that Hill's book *Think and Grow Rich*, printed in 1937, was a landmark in the prosperity and positive-thinking ideology.

Along these lines, the best contribution of Peale to American metaphysics resides in the fact that he popularized the concept of positive thinking, an optimistic attitude toward difficulties in life. He also promoted some occult and esoteric teachings under his concept of positive thinking, especially the philosophy of the New Thought movement. That kind of knowledge was considered part of the "occult culture" and not acceptable for the American Christian milieu of his time. However, due to his ministerial position, he did get away with it.

It is deplorable that Peale was never up-front about his sources; he never gave credit for his ideas to Emerson, Holmes, Evans, Coué, or William James, even though the notion of positive thinking as self-help was already well known many years before he published his masterpiece, *The Power of Positive Thinking*. Peale's first chapter, titled "Belief in Yourself," is Emerson's trademark. Emerson often said, "Believe in yourself; our strength grows out of our weakness." Some other chapter titles of Peale's books are abstracts from the New Thought philosophy. The secret of "prayer," which is the cornerstone of Peale's book, comes directly from New Thought philosopher Charles Fillmore, who advocated the power of prayer as the cornerstone of his philosophy as well as that of the Unity Church, which he cofounded. Here is how Peale defined the concept of prayer:

> I believe that prayer is a sending out of vibrations from one person to another and to God. All the universe is in vibration. . . . When you send out a prayer for another person, you employ the force inherent in a spiritual universe . . . and in this process you awaken vibration in the universe through which God brings to pass the good objectives prayed for.[25]

When I read this paragraph, it seems like I am reading a passage of the "Principle of Vibration," which is part of the Hermetic book named *The Kybalion*. According to this principle, everything we know in the visible and invisible realms exists at different rates of vibration. Peale describes prayer in terms of vibration and energy, which were Hermetic and esoteric concepts at that time. Statements such as "All the universe is vibration" or the idea that one person can "send energy" to another were unheard-of in the Protestant and evangelical milieu of Peale's time. *The Kybalion* treatise was originally published in 1908, and its authorship is ascribed to William W. Atkinson, an early pioneer of the New Thought movement. I will further elaborate on this in

upcoming pages. Concerning Peale's scholarship, Tom Tiede eloquently describes it as follows:

> Peale did not invent optimism, nor was he ever tried and convicted
> of selling elixir lineament, but he was the founding father of the
> modern self-help hippodrome. He may have never read Thomas
> More—indeed, his writings suggest *he never read anyone*—yet he
> became famous and wealthy.[26] (emphasis added)

The contents of Peale's book are mainly about his personal religious experiences. The book has come under serious scrutiny for
not meeting the standards of a reliable book because he does not
document the sources of his information; it lacks a bibliography
and does not have footnotes or endnotes to authenticate his statements. There is no specific information about the personalities
mentioned in the book; they are kind of anonymous. Since the
book has religious overtones, it seems Peale wrote it mainly to ad-
dress his church followers and expected his readers take his arguments and statements for granted, similar to the way they treated
religious text.

Undoubtedly, the success of Peale's *The Power of Positive Thinking*, published in 1952, is due in good part to his high position as
minister of a large Protestant church, where his Sunday sermons
had large audiences. Moreover, Peale had the advantage of having
access to the power of the mass media; he hosted a weekly radio
program and then a TV show. All of these were effective means of
obtaining publicity, giving him influence over large groups of
people. Usually, acolytes, members, and churchgoers buy books
written by their preacher. In addition, Peale had a powerful political position in the Republican Party; he was a strong supporter of
President Richard Nixon, with whom he had a good relationship.
President Ronald Reagan awarded Peale the Presidential Medal of
Freedom, which is the highest award that can be given to a civil-
ian. Peale openly opposed the election of John F. Kennedy as president because Kennedy was Catholic.

Human fate is sometimes ironic. Mary Baker Eddy took the

teachings of her mentor, Phineas P. Quimby, and never acknowledged him; Peale earned such popularity with the ideas of the New Thought pioneers yet never mentioned this movement. Peale became famous with the publication of *The Power of Positive Thinking*, which has been a megaseller since it came onto the market. The rest is history.

The issue here is to find a sociological explanation for how Peale's *The Power of Positive Thinking*, M. Scott Peck's *The Road Less Traveled*, Tolle's *The Power of Now*, and Byrne's book and video *The Secret* have become bestsellers with bogus teachings and unfounded information. Is it that Americans have fallen victim to the self-help and positive-thinking business?

First, the last two books, *The Power of Now* and *The Secret*, were highly endorsed by Oprah Winfrey on her TV show, which reached a large audience.[27] In the larger context, the explanation could be as follows: After World War II, positive thinking and the prosperity Gospel became part of the American character as a result of industrialization and people's migration from rural areas to urban cities seeking opportunities for success. In addition, an entire generation of baby boomers started searching for opportunities for prosperity. The social market was ready for motivational programs to enhance human potential and methods of achieving success in self-help seminars and programs and in mind-body therapies. All of these were used by corporations and large companies to increase productivity. The idea was extended to personal issues, such as helping people gain friends, have happy marriages, and be successful in any endeavor. Moreover, this ideology was spread to other countries of the world via motion pictures, TV, and mass communication; people worldwide saw America as the land of opportunity, freedom, and prosperity.

Harrington states that positive thinking is based on the words "Believe in yourself! Have faith in your abilities!"[28] These words ring a bell, as they are typical of Emerson's teaching. The underlying message for generations of young Americans has been that hard work and determination are the means of achieving the American Dream.

Along with Peale's *The Power of Positive Thinking*, Peck's *The Road Less Traveled: A New Psychology of Love, Traditional Values and Spiritual Growth* (1978) has been extremely successful and a bestseller for many years. In the introduction to the twenty-fifth-anniversary edition of *The Road Less Traveled*, Peck has the honesty to acknowledge that his book became a bestseller five years after its publication, mainly due to the Alcoholics Anonymous (AA) organization. He also recognizes that without AA's support, his book would likely not be recognized. In Peck's own words:

> Since I was an unknown author, *The Road* was published without fanfare. Its astonishing commercial success was a very gradual phenomenon. It did not appear on the national bestseller lists until five years after its publication in 1978—a fact for which I am extremely grateful. Had it been an overnight success, I doubt very much that I would have been mature enough to handle sudden fame. In any case, it was a sleeper and what is called in the trade a "word-of mouth book." Slowly at first, knowledge of it spread by word of mouth by several routes. One of them was Alcoholics Anonymous. Indeed, the very first fan letter I received began: "Dear Dr. Peck, you must be an alcoholic!" The writer found it difficult to imagine that I could have written such a book without having been a long-term member of AA and humbled by alcoholism.
>
> Had *The Road* been published twenty years previously, I doubt it would have been even slightly successful. Alcoholics Anonymous did not really get off the ground until the mid-1950s (not that most of the book's readers were alcoholics).[29]

The question here is, why did the book become so successful five years after its publication and thanks to AA support? Why did it appeal so strongly to people with cravings? It seems the key answer resides in the three words with which the book starts: "Life is difficult." These three simple words are extremely effective coming from a prominent psychiatrist to emotionally needy people.

Nevertheless, the contribution of Peck lies in the fact that he makes people understand that we are imperfect, with problems, that life presents humans with many challenges, and that the key to success is to face these tests and trials with discipline and stoicism. In this way Peck gave some rationality to those AA members about their predicament. His credential as a psychiatrist educated at Harvard University was a good enticement for people to rely on his writings.

Peck's entire book revolves around three words—"*discipline*," "*responsibility*," and "*love*"—with strong religious overtones. In some parts of the book, Peck sounds like a religious preacher similar to Peale. The main postulate, that "life is difficult," is common knowledge to everybody; one does not need to go to college to be aware of it. In another part of the book, Peck asserts, "I have come to conclude that evil is real"; I think that is common understanding. However, his definition of "evil" is very interesting; he writes that "evil" is "laziness carried to its ultimate, extraordinary extreme." "Evil" could be defined more appropriately as cruelty and deliberately inflicting pain on others without any sense of conscience. Peck further affirms, "As I have defined it, love is the antithesis of laziness."[30] I thought the antithesis of love was hate. Oh well! One would expect a more substantial and serious answer to these questions coming from a doctor educated at Harvard University.

We have to credit Peck for being honest; he mentions that the three words "life is difficult" are a paraphrase of Buddhism's First Noble Truth, which is "Life is suffering." Based on this, Peck states that "life is a series of problems," then exhorts humans to take "personal responsibility." That is overly simplistic advice. We have been told since kindergarten that we have to take responsibility for our actions. "Discipline" and "responsibility" are the magic words, the solution for life's daily problems, according to Peck. What about suffering? He explains it by quoting, out of context, Carl Jung, who wrote, "Neurosis is always [a] substitute for legitimate suffering."[31] It should be kept in mind that suffering is the best teacher; it gives people lessons to learn that in time turn into wisdom. Common sense suggests that if there were no suffering, there would not be joy, and vice versa. *C'est la vie.*

The hint to understanding why Alcoholics Anonymous members

flock to this book is its simplicity; statements such as "Life is difficult" and "Life is full of problems," asserted by a psychiatrist, appear to somehow rationalize human suffering through addiction. In other words, the subtle message here could be interpreted as "It is okay for you to be in this predicament because life is difficult," or "It is okay to mitigate your suffering with alcohol." It is well known that addiction to alcohol is extremely difficult to overcome.

Then syndicated journalist Tom Tiede comes onto the stage to severely rebuke Peck's book, criticizing it as a simplistic work written by a prominent psychiatrist, claiming that "Peck uses his professional credentials for spiritual purposes."[32] According to Tiede, Peck's work is centered entirely on the idea that "life is difficult, that life is a series of problems."[33] And Peck advises his readers to have the discipline to solve life's problems. What a discovery! Tiede further asserts that Peck speaks much like a religious preacher when he says he will "take believers on 'the journey of spiritual growth.'"[34]

More than that, I think Peck is also playing the role of prophet, because the last paragraph of his book ends with prophetic words. After talking about the grace of God and stating that we live in the eye of God, he concludes:

> It is probable that the universe as we know it is but a single stepping-stone toward the entrance to the kingdom of God. . . . I sometimes tell [my patients] that the human race is in the midst of making an evolutionary leap. "Whether or not we succeed in that leap," I say to them, "is your personal responsibility." And mine. This universe, this stepping-stone, has been laid down to prepare a way for us. But we ourselves must step across it, one by one. Through grace we are helped not to stumble, and through grace we know that we are being welcomed. What more can we ask?[35]

When Peck uses the phrases "evolutionary leap" and "entrance to the kingdom of God," he seems to be referring to what I call the "transitional period" from the Fishes (Piscean) Age to the Water-Bearer (Aquarian) Age. In my last book, *The Birth of a New Consciousness and the Cycles of Time*, I posited that we are in this transitional period of entering the Water-Bearer Age, a cosmic age of brotherhood, universal understanding, and wisdom. According to my calculation, the transitional period covers the time from 2010 to 2298, after which we will finally and fully enter the golden age of the Water-Bearer (Aquarius).

Coming back to Tiede, after he took on many self-help "gurus," including M. Scott Peck, Laura Schlessinger, Susan Forward, Norman Vincent Peale, Leo Buscaglia, and others, he ended up suggesting the typical American value propounded by Ralph Waldo Emerson: *self-reliance*.[36]

Following the prosperity philosophy established by advocates of New Thought, we later saw a boom in popular and successful self-help programs in America, notably those of Dale B. Carnegie (1888–1955), who developed courses in self-improvement, salesmanship, corporate training, public speaking, and interpersonal skills. Carnegie is well known as the author of the bestseller *How to Win Friends and Influence People* (1936), which remains popular today. He was followed by Joseph Murphy with his bestseller *The Power of Your Subconscious Mind,* then by Napoleon Hill with *Think and Grow Rich,* and finally by Napoleon Hill's most devoted disciple and follower, Bob Proctor, with *You Were Born Rich.*

However, and there is always a "however," some authors lately have expressed dissatisfaction with the positive-thinking ideology and have presented strong counteractive arguments in their books debunking positive thinking.[37] So what is the truth about it?

The simple idea that thinking positively will make one successful in life is not a guaranteed winning formula. An individual has to take action toward the desired aim; in addition, he or she must show determination and persistence toward achieving that goal. Positive thinking will help as an incentive and as a mental support to navigate through difficult times. That is all it can do; we cannot ask for something that cannot be delivered. I will continue this discussion in the next chapter.

Chapter 3

Making Sense of Self-Help and Positive Thinking

Ne te quaesiveris extra.
("Do not seek outside yourself.")[1]

M UCH LIKE THE earlier self-help books and material, most self-help programs on the market today are regarded by modern authors and scholars as ineffective. Mitch Horowitz encapsulates this skepticism as follows: "Most serious people regard positive thinking as a cotton-candy theology or a philosophy for dummies."[2] These critics argue that, instead of being too optimistic, in order to succeed in life, one has to plan, be self-critical and analytical, and work on what one is aiming for rather than hope for miracles. This legitimate concern was well articulated by British author and professor of public understanding of psychology Richard Wiseman, who wrote the following:

Self-help gurus and business coaches preach the same simple mantra: if you want to improve your life, you need to change how you think. Force yourself to have positive thoughts, and you will become happier. Visualize your dream self, and you will enjoy increased success. Think like a millionaire, and you will magically grow rich. In principle, this idea sounds perfectly reasonable. However, in practice, the approach often proves surprisingly ineffective, with research showing that people struggle to continually think happy thoughts, that employees remain unmoved by imagining their perfect selves, and those dreaming of endless wealth fail to make millions.[3]

This argument seems fairly reasonable; however, we cannot throw out the baby with the bathwater. Positive thinking and authentic self-help programs, along with positive action, are fundamental components of achieving success. Positive thinking falls into the category of self-help, and as such, it can be helpful in activating "healing forces of faith, hope, and courage, while moderating the potentially harmful effects of helplessness and despair."[4] There is an intrinsic value in them.

The above is confirmed by Wiseman's research on human behavior, which reveals that positive *thinking* is not good enough; one must take positive *action*. This, the ability to motivate oneself, to take action, is precisely the difference between successful people and average ones.[5]

The problem is when these programs are misapplied by New Age "gurus" and entrepreneur coaches and used as a means to take advantage of other people, with the exclusive purpose of making money. When they are commercialized, they lose their authentic value as self-help. That is why some authors find problems with them.

Along these lines, psychologists and therapists have expressed their opinions that in some cases, self-help programs and positive thinking may be detrimental. This might be true for individuals with negative psychological determinants such as feelings of worthlessness, victimization, and low self-esteem; these are factors that hinder people from attaining their desired goals. For people with chronic depression and despondency, raising expectations with positive-thinking and self-help programs can be counterproductive. The problem is that such people are trying to reach something for which they are not prepared or fit, physically and emotionally. Forcing them into something beyond their individual capabilities and expectations may do more harm than good.

There are New Age metaphysical writers and mentors who, under the guise of being spiritual teachers, advise their audiences with conformist and condescending ideas such as "You are perfect as you are"; "You don't need anything else"; "Just be yourself"; "You don't need to become someone different to be happy"; and so forth, propounding the idea of a status quo. This is the opposite of the notion of self-improvement. However, evolution is the law of nature and human potentiality. It is said that, whatever nature left out, man has to improve. This is in accord with the old metaphysical adage "Nature unaided fails."

As everything has its limitations, positive-thinking and self-help programs will not work on their own or act like magic; one cannot expect that everything will go well just from imagining a desired goal and then sitting on a couch. These programs can help up to a certain point as long as one is willing to take the steps needed to reach one's objective with determination and personal will. The notion that a person can have everything and can do whatever he or she wants is just absurd.

However, recent developments in quantum physics, neuroscience, and the study of placebo effects in human behavior provide objective reasons to believe that thoughts and firm determination can exert concrete influence on the trend of circumstances. The main problem with these programs is that they are usually advertised as quick fixes and in a sensationalistic manner, creating false expectations. It is well known that any worthwhile system requires time and dedication to yield significant benefits.

The most dangerous drawback is that, when people do not get what these programs offer, they feel defeated and think that something is defective with them. They become depressed and sometimes resort to drugs or medication to overcome these feelings. So these motivational programs can have a negative effect on some people. In some cases, they can lead to failure and disillusionment and not only backfire against people but seriously worsen their mental health. [6]

The best way to evaluate the impact of these programs is to obtain the opinions and comments of people who have bought the books or other materials. The reviews on Amazon.com are an interesting place to start. As usual, there are favorable and unfavorable comments. Some people find Eckhart Tolle's book *The Power of Now* interesting and inspiring. Others seem to be frustrated and upset, as in the case of a person who identified as Blue Moon. This person states, "I practiced [the teachings] time to time, only to end up blaming myself because I couldn't stay positive or focused more than a few days." Others complain about the fact that they tried to put the teachings of the book into practice and have not found them to be much help.

Another reason for the failure of these approaches to work in some people is what psychologists call "psychological resistance." Psychological resistance is the phenomenon of people directly or indirectly sabotaging the crystallization of their desires—they are psychologically determined to fail. Resistance can also arise because people are subconsciously determined to sabotage any positive change. These individuals may foster patterns of self-punishment, self-victimization, and feelings of unworthiness.

Others oppose changing their behavior because most of the time, they don't want to get out of their comfort zones. In some cases, they even refuse to discuss, remember, or think about presumably traumatic past experiences because they are emotionally painful; these people may require psychotherapy as opposed to self-help programs.

One example of psychological resistance can be found in the writings of the Apostle Paul, who acknowledges the following: "For I know that good itself does not dwell in me, that is, in my sinful nature. For I have the desire to do what is good, but I cannot carry it out. For I do not do the good I want to do, but the evil I do not want to do—this I keep on doing" (Romans 7:18–19, NIV).[7] As many have noticed, the Apostle Paul also had a deep sense of unworthiness; he acknowledged, "Christ Jesus came into the world to save sinners—of whom I am the worst" (1 Timothy 1:15, NIV).

Psychologist Dr. Roger Callahan pioneered the concept of "psychological reversal" with the development of the therapeutic method known as "thought field therapy." He states that some people are psychologically reversed (PR); this is like wanting to go to one's destination while driving a car that keeps slipping into reverse gear. It is like an internal saboteur. When psychological reversal is present, it can block significant and permanent progress in all areas of one's life. It often means that a person continues doing things that are not necessarily in his or her best interest, rather than the things the person says he or she wants to do. This self-sabotage can set off a cycle of blame and shame.

To counteract psychological reversal, Callahan proposes what is called reverse psychology, which is a technique that advocates a belief or behavior that is the opposite of what is desired, with the expectation that this approach will persuade the subject to do what actually *is* desired. It is a method of trying to make individuals do what one wants by asking them to do the opposite of what they expect. Since they are determined to do the opposite, they will actually choose the desired action. This technique relies on the psychological phenomenon of reactance, in which a person has a negative emotional reaction to being persuaded and thus chooses the option that is being advocated against.

In psychological parlance, reactance is understood as reaction to rules or regulations that threaten to eliminate behavioral freedoms. It can occur when someone is pressured to accept a certain view or behavior contrary to his habitual way of life. It is a mental attitude to "protect" oneself against something one thinks is threatening one's comfort zone.

Coming back to the modern teachings of positive thinking, Peale asserts in his book that practicing his teachings (prayers and affirmations) will give the reader absolute self-confidence and deliverance from suffering; this promise is similar to the pseudo-self-help ideology. If this were true, societies would not need social workers, psychologists, psychiatrists, religious ministers, mental health counselors, and so on. Nonetheless, Peale's techniques seem to be a disguised form of autosuggestion, similar to the Silva Method mind control technique. The Silva Method uses self-hypnosis, meditation, affirmations, and visualization for self-improvement purposes. Incidentally, prayers are kinds of affirmations conducive to self-suggestion as the person repeats the same declaration or prayer over and over again, similar to a mantra.

Peale's ideas were challenged by professionals in various fields, such as scientist Robert L. Park, who wrote the book *Superstition:*

Belief in the Age of Science (2008). Psychologist Albert Ellis (1913–2007), founder of Rational Emotive Behavior Therapy (cognitive therapy), equated Peale's techniques with those of Émile Coué, who is the father of conditioning psychology and the main advocate of the theory that people can self-heal with positive affirmations.[8]

Critics of Peale's *The Power of Positive Thinking* assert that the book does not meet professional standards; many of his examples and stories cannot be verified. Most of the testimonials that Peale quotes as supporting his statements are unnamed and unknown. Therefore, there is uncertainty whether some of them were invented or really happened, as Peale does not provide the sources of his information.

Critics also consider that Peale gives readers false self-confidence and promises of deliverance from pain and suffering based on the use of repetitive affirmations and praying, a technique similar to autosuggestion (self-hypnosis). Commonly, people who flock to these kinds of programs are seeking shelter from their emotional problems and are avoiding facing reality as it is.

Many professionals from different fields have expressed opinions contrary to Peale's conception of positive thinking. For instance, Bob Knight, a successful basketball coach with many years of experience in this field and the coauthor, along with Bob Hammel, of *The Power of Negative Thinking: An Unconventional Approach to Achieving Positive Results* (2013), claims that his coaching philosophy is to instill discipline by "preparing to win" rather than hoping to win. This means understanding the downside and drilling his teams to prevent the things that could go wrong. According to Knight, "negative thinking" will actually produce more positive results, in sports and in daily life. He is of the opinion that victory is often attained by the team that is prepared to successfully tackle any unforeseen event.

Furthermore, Knight challenges Peale's *The Power of Positive Thinking*, indicating that discipline produces more positive results, in sports and in daily life, than Peale's deceptive method. A realistic view is needed in order to make things happen; a person has to prepare and plan to win. Discipline is finding the right thing to do and doing it to the best of one's ability, rather than just dreaming the desired goal will come about by itself.

Psychiatrist Tony Humphreys wrote a book with a title similar to Knight's book: *The Power of Negative Thinking* (1996). He proposes giving his readers self-awareness and understanding through a guide for personal healing, growth, and development. Humphreys's book has been translated into twelve foreign languages. This work successfully refutes many of Peale's and Dale Carnegie's (*How to Win Friends and Influence People*) ideas.

Another example is psychiatrist Julie K. Norem, who authored *The Positive Power of Negative Thinking* with the purpose of refuting Peale's concept of positive thinking. As we can see, all these works provide evidence that, for many people, positive thinking is an ineffective strategy—and often an obstacle—for successfully coping with the anxieties and pressures of modern life. Norem presents evidence of the benefits of "defensive pessimism," which, according to her, has helped millions to manage anxiety and perform their best work. The question here is how defensive pessimism works. Is it refraining from taking decisive action? Is it frightened by the challenges of daily life? This sound likes to remain within their comfort zone.

Positive thinking is good as a motivational psychological device; the problem arises when an individual believes that merely thinking optimistically will do the work. This is only half the truth. The other half is that the individual himself or herself has to do the planning and the tasks needed for the goal to be accomplished; during this process of working for the crystallization of the goal, a person can and should maintain a positive attitude and remain confident. Thus, effective positive thinking is not just expecting good things to happen but taking action for those things to become real in the physical world.

A psycho-sociological interpretation of mass behavior indicates that most people jump into misleading programs, seeking easy and quick solutions to their problems. Humans are easily brainwashed by schemes and seek to hear statements or facts that validate or reinforce their unconscious wishes. This is because since we were children we have been programmed by the media with unrealistic and false beliefs.

These psychological schemes are so ingrained in our minds and have been rationalized so much as the normal outlook on life that most of the time, we are not even aware of them. Any information that contradicts or challenges these cherished unconscious beliefs is usually automatically discarded or undermined. Many people hold irrational beliefs and are not even conscious of this. The "herd mind" predisposes people to react adversely to any idea that challenges their core beliefs and questions their conformity. This notion of "conformism" has been portrayed by Albert Camus in his novel *The Stranger* and described by Jose Ingenieros in his book *El Hombre Mediocre* (The Mediocre Man).

In a Christian, consumerist, and capitalist society, there is a subtle mass indoctrination that conditions human minds, inflicting a theology of powerlessness and unworthiness. We are brainwashed by suggestions from our parents, grandparents, church leaders, and mainly the mass media. Religious organizations play a great role in this mass indoctrination. In predominantly Catholic countries, we have been told since we were born that we are sinners and unworthy, that only baptism and confirmation can redeem us, and that we need a savior. Nevertheless, after baptism and confirmation we are still sinners; Protestant preachers teach every Sunday that we are unworthy to live if we don't accept their biblical interpretations. Even worse, according to Calvinism, humans are at risk of eternal damnation for both original and personal sins; thus, we cannot do anything to save ourselves. They affirm that because of Adam and Eve's fall, humankind is damned for eternity[9] (*The Belgic Confession of Faith*, 1561). Following the thesis of the German sociologist Max Weber, it can be fairly affirmed that American capitalism has its roots in Calvinism via the Puritans.[10]

All this conditioning makes people subconsciously believe that their existence is unworthy because they are sinners. As a consequence, during their lives, many people will sabotage their happiness and success because they feel undeserving. The problem is that most of the time, people do not realize that these ideas of guilt and unworthiness dwell deep in their subconscious minds.

Inflicting fear and eternal damnation on people is an effective mechanism for control and manipulation. Significantly, one of the major psychological maladies of our society is a sense of guilt and powerlessness. The idea behind this seems to be that since we are unable do anything to reverse the sin committed by Adam and Eve, people are led to conformism; they become herd-minded and dependent on another person (often on a clergyman) for the solution to their problems. In extreme cases, they become so complacent that they want others to think and make decisions for them.

As a reaction to this tendency, in the nineteenth century, American Transcendentalist philosopher Ralph Waldo Emerson proposed the concept of "self-reliance," the need for each individual to avoid becoming herd-minded and conformist. The sense of conformism makes us want to become followers and to believe what leaders in different fields want us to believe. That is why many gurus and religious leaders who boast having the ultimate truth and the power of deliverance from evil are looking for followers who will believe in them and trust them blindly. This is a perilous attitude; we need only remember apocalyptic false religious prophets such as David Koresh, Jim Jones, and Charles Manson, who each believed himself to be the final prophet and led their followers to mass suicide or murder.

Unfortunately, in the spiritual and metaphysical realm, there is nothing easy and no quick fix. An individual who wants to achieve or attain something worthy has to work and invest time and effort to yield results.

Easy, quick-fix programs are similar to the snake oil that past charlatans used to sell in public settings; they claimed to offer a panacea—a remedy for all maladies existent and nonexistent. Regrettably, quick fixes never render permanent results; however, they can work temporarily as placebos as long as a person blindly believes in them. We have to learn once and for all that everything of worth in life demands effort and commitment.

Mitch Horowitz seems to be the scholar who has the best

understanding of the notion of positive thinking and how deeply it has influenced the American way of thinking. In the early 1900s, such ideas were seen by the Christian establishment (Catholic and Protestant) as negative elements deriving from esoteric and occult teachings and considered anti-Christian and dangerous. However, the impact of this philosophy in all areas of American life is undeniable; it is the cornerstone of the modern American lifestyle and way of thinking.

In metaphysical terms, *a need always comes first and then comes the solution.* The New Thought movement and its offshoot, positive thinking, were born to fill the vacuum for a new way of thinking—a new spirituality that transcends the narrow and fanatical teachings of religious organizations. This is why the New Thought movement was appropriately characterized by New Thought writers as "practical American spirituality."

Immediately after the American Civil War, Americans were seeking alternative outlets for their spirituality and inquiries. They wanted more fulfilling religious experiences than those provided by the narrow and dogmatic organizations of the time.

Horowitz, in his excellent investigation regarding the influence of New Thought in American life, asserts that "a sociological study of the 1950s found that most inspirational literature published in America between 1875 and 1955 had some kind of New Thought bent."[11] He further writes:

> In the 1930s, nonreligious figures like Dale Carnegie (*How to Win Friends and Influence People*) and Napoleon Hill (*Think and Grow Rich*) rode the wings of New Thought to worldwide fame. The popularity of mind-power philosophy hit its peak in the Reverend Norman Vincent Peale's 1952 mega-seller, *The Power of Positive Thinking,* which reached into churches and living rooms across America.[12]

However, during the past decade, there has been a reaction against these quick-fix programs coming from various fronts. Professor Anne Harrington, in her book *The Cure Within*, surveys the methods of healing induced by suggestions and placebos in

America. She devotes a whole chapter, over 130 pages, to analyzing the phenomenon of Peale's positive-thinking ideology. Interestingly, after an in-depth investigation, she concludes that self-help programs and the power of positive thinking are merely placebos.[13]

Currently, there is abundant psychological material that suggests that spending a lot of time *thinking* about one's hopes and dreams without *effective action* will lead nowhere. *Positive thinking is only half the process of creation.* Positive thinking by itself could hold people back from reaching their goals. One cannot sit and hope, pray and imagine, make up great affirmations and wait for the desired goal to fall into one's lap or manifest as a miracle. Decisive action needs to be taken toward what one wants expressed in one's life. *Positive thinking and the law of attraction without firm action could just be considered a label for wishful thinking.*

Positive thinking is the power of the mind to deliberately select thoughts, feelings, and emotions aligned to our purposes in order to attract similar thoughts and feelings. It has been said that to achieve one's goal one has to reach the feelings—that is, to be in vibrational alignment with one's desired object. Finally, a person should *act* with assurance that he or she already has what is being wished for. I will elaborate more on this in the chapter titled "The 'As If' Principle and the Power of Assumption."

Mitch Horowitz approaches positive thinking from the inside, as someone who has practiced this philosophy since he was a teenager. Early in his childhood, his family had financial struggles; nevertheless, he subsequently became successful professionally and personally. He states that while he was an adolescent, he "visualized better tomorrows, and became a determined self-improver."[14] And for him, the system worked because he *took action* to materialize his dreams. In this case, positive thinking was a head start, an incentive to achieve what he aimed for. Positive thinking acts as a psychological motivational device; allegorically speaking, it is similar to the North Star, which helps us navigate as we head toward our goal. Horowitz appropriately captures this idea in an article he wrote for *Quest* magazine, a journal of the Theosophical Society in

America. He acknowledges that "positive thinking did not miraculously solve all of our problems. . . . If my thoughts didn't change reality, they helped navigate it. And maybe something more."[15] He also acknowledges the influence of many factors in our lives, and here is the key: "Our thoughts contribute 'something extra' to our life circumstances."[16] Indeed, in metaphysics and occult sciences, *thoughts* are regarded as causative factors.

As indicated in the Introduction of this book, regarding my personal experience, I can testify that *positive thinking and positive action* have worked wonderfully for me; however, one aspect needs to be emphasized: positive thinking will not work when people hold self-defeating patterns in their minds that sabotage their aims in life. Thus, an honest introspection is necessary to determine the kinds of thoughts that dwell in the subconscious mind. Unfortunately, many behavioral researchers and psychologists disregard the importance of the subconscious mind, which is the most powerful element in humans' personalities.[17] In addition, one has to be aware of the influence of socially accepted thoughts, some of which can be detrimental; here resides the necessity to choose and recognize those ideas that are constructive and beneficial and dwell on them.

The well-known inspirational speaker Esther Hicks states that the reason for not getting one's longings in life is because "you are holding yourself in a vibrational holding pattern that does not match the vibration of your desire."[18] The teaching of Abraham, which I describe more fully in a later chapter, is based on the premise that we live in a vibrational universe, where everything is in a state of constant vibration, including one's thoughts, emotions, the walls of one's house, the chair where one sits, or any other visible or invisible object for that matter. This notion is very similar to the Hermetic Principle of Vibration expressed in *The Kybalion*.[19] Since everything in the universe is in a vibratory state, humans are interpreters and modifiers of these vibrations through their physical senses. Hence, according to Abraham, one's desired object is out there; one needs only to get into vibratory alignment with the desired goal or object in order for it to manifest in the physical realm.[20]

At the risk of sounding repetitive, humans are not aware of the inner beliefs that dwell in their subconscious minds, which are the result of lifelong indoctrination. Because of this, the person may project his or her own shortcomings and prejudices onto others. This is in accord with the Law of Correspondence: "As within, so without." Conversely, when an individual puts his desires for success, love, and happiness out to the universe, the universe will respond accordingly. In order for something to be manifested, there must, therefore, be congruence between a person's desires and the contents of that person's subconscious mind.

Thoughts and feelings are real forces of *attraction and rejection*; they are automatic ways of reacting to ideas and beliefs depending on an individual's belief system. That is why *positive thinking* is important, to keep the mind focused on uplifting and constructive thoughts. A belief system, which is a body of thoughts, can play a discriminatory or selective role. Humans make decisions according to their predominant beliefs and interpret their experiences and observations in ways that reinforce those core beliefs. They will automatically discard the ones that are in conflict with their predominant beliefs (whether hidden or open). In other words, whatever does not support their core beliefs is systematically discounted or ignored; events in their lives will unfold according to their predominant beliefs, although most of the time they may be unaware of this.

There are some beliefs so ingrained and rationalized in our minds that they are part of our "normal" outlook on life. Most of the time, these hidden beliefs control our lives and create our external conditions. That is why it is said that a man is literally what "he thinks in his heart." A person's character is the sum of all the person's thoughts and attitudes, whether correct or incorrect. Some people are willing to improve their circumstances but unwilling to honestly explore core beliefs that dwell deep in their subconscious minds. They therefore remain bound to these false beliefs and consequently perpetuate and replicate the same circumstances and situations over and over again. The problem is that the subconscious mind has been programmed with negative information.

In conclusion, self-help and positive thinking rightly conceptualized and properly applied can be useful; the complements to them are *determination and positive action*. Both are part of the whole system of self-improvement and becoming successful. The best service that positive thinking, as a self-help device, can do in those difficult moments of life is serve as a psychological mechanism for inspiration and motivation, providing hope and encouraging endurance, thereby preventing the person from falling into despair and hopelessness.

Hence, self-help and positive thinking can function as mechanisms of enticement or incentive and keep the mind positively focused on the end desired. They can also serve as mental motivation during the process of achievement. Overall, the individual has to be willing to invest time and effort in reaching the goal for which he or she aims, and not simply hope for miracles. Otherwise, positive thinking can easily become wishful thinking or a "cotton-candy theology or a philosophy for dummies."[21]

CHAPTER 4

The Fallacy of
the "Power of Now"

If the blind lead the blind, both will fall into a ditch.
—MATTHEW 15:14 (NIV)

THE GREEK PHILOSOPHER Heraclitus the Obscure, also known as Heraclitus of Ephesus (c. 535–475 BCE) is regarded as the father of the dialectic method.[1] He stated in the fifth century BCE, "You cannot step down twice into the same river. Nothing remains still." Modern science has now demonstrated that everything is in eternal vibration.

The dialectic method and the Hermetic Principle of Vibration teach us that nothing in the whole universe is stagnant, static, or in a state of paralysis; everything is a flow of energy—everything is in a cycle of birth/development/decay. And time is included in this. Time is an abstract concept—an artificial device—used in the physical plane for practical purposes, whereas there is no such thing as *now*—as something that can be considered stagnant. Life is a dynamic process in which reality is a combination of being and nonbeing. Hence, what we call reality is a process of eternal becoming. This has been acknowledged by most philosophers, from Heraclitus to Georg W. Hegel.

New Age writer Eckhart Tolle, who proclaimed himself a "spiritual teacher," popularized the basic teachings of Zen Buddhism in the Occidental world under the concept of the power of Now and proposed techniques for achieving permanent peace of mind, happiness, enlightenment, and a blissful life. He argues that humans should never have any problems or distress as long as they are in the Now; he seems to be saying that being in the Now will make problems solve themselves.

Much of what Tolle proposes is highly speculative; for example, he says that to improve the world, people must live in the present moment, in the Now (absence of time), and that under those conditions all the problems of daily life will disappear and people will be happy. At first it may seem that these ideas might work temporarily because of the enthusiasm and expectation invested by the believer, but in the long run, they are detrimental to one's psychological well-being because one will find that these rosy promises are not practical.

Tolle's book *The Power of Now* falls into the category of self-help programs, as it promises an easy-fix solution to daily life problems. In that sense, it will be treated and analyzed accordingly.

Since it came on the market, the book *The Power of Now* has aroused controversial reactions; some naïve people praise the book, and others more alert to these kinds of scams severely criticize it. The adverse reaction is mainly from mental health practitioners and learned authors. The book doesn't offer new, profound spiritual wisdom at all; what Tolle promotes is the Buddhist/ Hindu technique of mindfulness. He essentially extols fundamental Buddhist teachings.

In the book's introduction, Tolle confesses he used to suffer continual anxiety, panic attacks, and suicidal ideation. During these anxiety attacks, he had an incident that he describes as an "illumination"; he realized he was not the one who was thinking—his mind was. This epiphany led him to make a clear differentiation between the "Self" and the "I."[2]

Tolle says the above experience took him to a state of "indescribable bliss and sacredness" and he "spent almost two years sitting on park benches in a state of the most intense joy."[3] He depicts enlightenment as something very simple, which anybody can reach on the spot. He also claims that Buddhist monks, Christian nuns, therapists, and people with life-threatening illnesses have written letters and e-mails to him describing "a lessening or even a complete disappearance of sufferings and problem-making in people's [lives] as a result of reading *The Power of Now* and putting the teaching into practice in everyday life."[4]

The positive aspect of Tolle's book is that he stresses frequently the fact that the inner self is present in every human being and we need to be connected with It. Granted! The problem is that he oversimplifies the enlightenment process and makes it sound too easy. Incidentally, the subtitle of his book is *A Guide to Spiritual Enlightenment*. Tolle states, "I speak of a profound transformation of human consciousness—not a distant future possibility, but available now—no matter who or where you are." Furthermore, he promises that his readers can, "from enslavement to the mind, enter into this enlightened state of consciousness and sustain it in everyday life."[5]

The above statements contradict the fact that thousands of monks in Buddhist monasteries around the world struggle for many years to attain enlightenment even though they follow rigorous disciplines such as fasting, meditation, contemplation, and demanding daily schedules as part of their efforts. Tolle claims that enlightenment is very simple and easy and that anybody under any circumstances can reach it.

The $64,000 question, then, is since this book was published, how many people have become enlightened by reading it? The Law of Correspondence says that if people follow the same procedure, they will get the same results. Since the process of enlightenment proposed by Tolle is very simple, one can only wonder whether, at this point in time, there are millions of people who have become enlightened after reading *The Power of Now*.

I believe that Tolle had a genuine experience of an altered state of mind as a result of his struggle with obsessive and negative ideations. But this is a *sui generis* (unique) *case specific to his circumstances.* He was tormented with suicidal ideations and self-destructive thoughts that were creating much anguish and anxiety in him. The epiphany was when he realized that his obsessive thoughts were responsible for such mental struggle. That sudden revelation is what he called "enlightenment." Hence, he uses the term "enlightenment" to describe the distinction he made between the mind's thinking and the Self. *This was his "eureka"*—a psychological realization that he was overshadowed and possessed by his mind's obsessive suicidal ideations. This is *not* an authentic or mystical enlightenment like that of sages and genuine spiritual gurus who, after long years of meditation, discipline, and spiritual practices, reach the stage of illumination. Tolle's incident appears similar to the psychological process called "holotropic states of consciousness." Psychiatrists Stanislav Grof and his wife, Christina, conducted extensive research and investigation for many years on all kinds of altered conditions of mind, or "nonordinary states of consciousness," which they call a "holotropic state of mind." They reached the conclusion that consciousness can be altered in many ways. Grof wrote:

> Holotropic states are characterized by a specific transformation of consciousness associated with dramatic perceptual changes in all sensory areas, intense and often unusual emotions, and profound alterations in the thought processes. They are also usually accompanied by a variety of intense psychosomatic manifestations and unconventional forms of behavior.
>
> The content of holotropic states is often spiritual or mystical. We can experience sequences of psychological death and rebirth and a broad spectrum of transpersonal phenomena, such as feelings of union and identification with other people, nature, the universe, and God.[6]

Thus, it can be confidently theorized that Tolle's intense mental anguish triggered an altered state of mind known as "holotropic experience." According to the Grofs, this state can also be reached with techniques such as "chanting, breathing, drumming, rhythmic dancing, fasting, social and sensory isolation, extreme physical pain, and other elements."[7] It can also be experienced through spiritual practices such as profound concentration, meditation, traumatic events in life, and so on.

The above interpretation is further verified by the fact that Tolle's first chapter is devoted to proof that "you are not your

mind." He considers the mind to be the greatest obstacle to enlightenment. But he does not clearly define what he means by "the
mind." Here is our definition: The mind is a tool for the Self; as
any other instrument, it can be used for good or evil. Akin to a
knife, which can be used to cook and serve a delicious meal or to
harm oneself. An undisciplined or untrained mind can over-
shadow the real self, and in some cases the mind can be domi-
nated by subconscious negative patterns. In this case, the "mind"
takes over individual reasoning and does the thinking on its own.
This was the case with Tolle's experience.

Tolle's definition of enlightenment is awareness of oneness
with God, which he calls "Being." In his own words, it is a "natural
state of *felt* oneness with Being. It is a state of connectedness with
something immeasurable and indestructible. Something that, almost paradoxically, is essentially you and yet much greater than
you."[8] He further states, "To regain awareness of Being and to
abide in that state of 'feeling-realization' is enlightenment."[9]

Tolle mentions that he likes Buddha's definition of enlightenment, which is "the end of suffering." Then he corrects Buddha's
statement, indicating that "enlightenment is not only the end of
suffering and of continuous conflict within and without, but also
the end of the dreadful enslavement to incessant thinking."[10]

Tolle states that mainstream culture's belief regarding ordinary people is that enlightenment is a superhuman achievement,
a goal that is impossible to attain. For instance, "The majority of
Buddhists still believe that enlightenment is for the Buddha, not
for them."[11] Buddhist communities could take this statement as
inappropriate; there are millions of monks around the world who
are faithful followers of Buddhist teachings, who practice daily,
rigorous discipline for many years, including fasting, celibacy,
daily meditation, and so on. Now a person who has not lived
under these rigorous conditions is somehow telling them, look what
I got in just a few days out of my struggle with suicidal ideations—
something you cannot attain in decades of rigorous discipline in
isolated monasteries.

Interestingly enough, we find that Tolle's definition of enlightenment is different from the Buddhist concept of Nirvana.

Traditionally in Buddhism, the term *Nirvana* has been understood as a transcendent or blissful state of mind in which there is neither suffering, nor desire, nor sense of personal self; the individual is released from the effects of karma and the cycle of death and re-birth, called *Samsara*. A related Buddhist term is *moksha*, which is a state of perfect happiness and peace, in which there is release from all forms of suffering and attachment. It should be noted that in Buddhism there is no soul, God, or savior.

On the other hand, in Hinduism, the ultimate goal is spiritual emancipation from the sensorial world, which is pursued through different methods of yoga. One of these is meditation and raising the kundalini—life force energy—through the seven spiritual, inner psychic centers, or chakras, to attain illumination or to be absorbed with the Godhead and become one with the Absolute. Hence, in Hinduism, illumination is the absorption into and unification with the One—yoga, which means "oneness."

Tolle considers identification with the mind to be the greatest obstacle to reaching enlightenment. Then he dares to correct French philosopher Rene Descartes's famous statement "I think, therefore I am." Tolle argues that Descartes "equates thinking with Being [God] and identifies with thinking."[12] This is a flagrant misinterpretation; what Descartes stated is that the process of thinking—the ability to think—made a person realize of his capacity for awareness. To quote Tolle:

> The philosopher Descartes believed that he had found the most fundamental truth when he made his famous statement: "I think, therefore I am." He had, in fact, given expression to the most basic error: to equate thinking with Being and identify with thinking."[13]

Tolle's problem is that he is unable to distinguish the mind from the Self. Thinking is the foundation for awareness. If there is no thinking, there is no awareness. Thinking is the faculty that makes us conscious of the Self and of our surroundings. In the physical world, one has to have a foundation on which to stand. That is why science always starts with a postulate or thesis as ground for further development. As Archimedes stated, "Give me a point to stand on, and I will move the earth." Descartes started with a thesis, "I think," to arrive at the conclusion, "I am conscious." This topic will be thoroughly discussed in the last chapter of this book.

As to the main question, who is the real thinker? The answer is the inner self or the "I Am," which is an individualized entity of the universal consciousness. Western and Eastern mystery traditions teach that the only thinker, the only doer, is the higher self. This will also be further discussed in the last chapter. The problem arises when the false ego, or false identity, overshadows the real self, or consciousness, and gets in the middle and acts as the thinker, usually with destructive and negative consequences. When this happens, most people develop obsessive thoughts that haunt them.

Since the mind is the problem, Tolle, to resolve this problem, proposes to get rid of the mind, which he considers the enemy. He states, "The good news is that you can free yourself from your mind. This is the only true liberation."[14] Tolle should be reminded that, according to the discipline of psychology, the mind is considered the part of a person that thinks, reasons, feels, and remembers. Furthermore, if a person gets rid of the part of him- or herself that thinks, feels, and reasons, he or she reduces being human to a state of an inanimate entity without any capacity for self-development and self-expression.

Tolle proposes a separation between the mind and the Self. His definition of ego is a "false self created by unconscious identification of the mind."[15] Thought cannot exist without consciousness. Thanks to the mind, a musician is capable of creating wonderful musical compositions, and a mathematician of appreciating an elegant solution in mathematics, and so on.

The key is to discipline the mind so it can become an ally to the individual rather than become an enemy. The Self uses the mind to think. A problem arises when the "false mind" takes control over the thinking process. That is precisely the case of the person who has obsessive ideas and suicidal ideations, as Tolle experienced himself. In normal circumstances, people usually have control over their minds.

Tolle contradicts himself with the following statement:

You are unconsciously identified with [the mind], so you don't even know that you are its slave. . . . The beginning of freedom is the realization that you are not the possessing entity—the thinker. Knowing this enables you to observe the entity. The moment you start watching the thinker, a higher level of consciousness becomes activated.[16]

Generally, the mind consists of two parts, the self-conscious and the subconscious. To which mind is he referring? In the subconscious mind dwells the self-ego, a self-created entity that can be considered "software" formed by the social environment and education in our upbringing. This sometimes turns into the "false self" or "false identity," becoming predominant in some people and overshadowing the inner self. This false identity is governed mainly by the demands of sensorial life, that is, through gratification of the five physical senses.

Thus, a type of "software" resides in the subconscious mind as a result of societal programming. This software runs the majority of people's lives, dictating their destinies; it is the false ego, the result of all of their past history, coming from the collective cultural mind-set they inherit, the body of ideas, feelings, and emotions that result from being programmed. When this false mind or false ego takes over, it becomes the charioteer and the driver of the human personality.

Another of Tolle's flaws is that he does not clarify specifically what he means by the term "Now;" it seems he equates with the present moment. According to Tolle, "The present moment holds the key to liberation."[17] Thus, "in the Now" means to be aware of the present moment—an indefinite present—a condition in which the past and future become part of "Now;" this appears to be an attempt to stop time altogether, so people can live in an eternal now, which seems like illogical reasoning. The fact of this physical universe is the flow of time. Human capacity to remember past events is proof that there is no such thing as "Now." Furthermore, since time and space are intimately interrelated, the notion of no time implies no space. In physics, space and time are considered to be one entity: space-time. When the element of time is eliminated from the equation of time-space, there is no physical reality. In the material universe, where we live right now, right here, we are bounded by physical laws.

I understand that duration of time in the mind of a person can be very subjective depending on the circumstances. For instance, for a person who is enjoying a delightful vacation and another who is serving time in a prison, the lapse of time would be quite different due to their situation and perception of time. Many artists and inventors do experience a state of "flow" in which they create their work without awareness of the passage of time.

At this point, it is imperative to differentiate solar/spatial and psychic/astral time; the first is set by the solar and planetary movements, while the second is perceived in altered states of mind. Solar/spatial time is determined by the movement of the planet Earth around the sun and can be defined as physical reality bound by the laws of physics, while psychic, or astral, time is unrestricted and is outside the physical realm. Mental or subjective time is an individual's perception of time as a continual unfolding of ideas and events.

Metaphysically speaking, in this physical realm, and according to quantum physics, we live in an everlasting, ongoing flowing of probabilities. The truth is that the only real thing is consciousness; it is our higher self that perceives the physical realm through our physical senses. The fact that a person's corporeal body is occupying space in this world is proof enough that human bodies are "crucified" in the cross of time and space while they are in the material plane.

The absurdity of the power of Now can be demonstrated by the fact that an individual trained in meditation techniques is able to stop the train of thoughts running in that person's mind but cannot stop the flow of spatial time.

The Hindu sacred book *The Bhagavad Gita*, in its first chapter, teaches people to take *action* and not withdraw from worldly duties. In this epic, the hero, Arjuna, finds himself on a battlefield, where he observes his friends, instructors, and relatives on the opposing army's side; he loses courage, falls into despondency, and decides not to fight. Consequently, he requests permission from Krishna (the Hindu Godhead) to retire from the battlefield in favor of a life of meditation. Krishna advises Arjuna that the primary goal of a human being is *action*—action without attachment to the outcome. Krishna further explains that Arjuna as a warrior should fight to set the proper example of *duty* and not be concerned about the outcome of his actions.

The power of Now does not have inherent power unless you use the present moment to plan or create your future. Planning is better than correcting past mistakes; hence, good planning avoids potential pitfalls and future correction of projects that were left unplanned.

The peace that Tolle mentions having achieved after he attained *enlightenment*, when he "spent almost two years sitting on park benches in a state of the most intense joy,"[18] can be explained by the fact that Tolle was not assaulted by destructive and overbearing thoughts anymore. For an ordinary person, "sitting on park benches" for about two years is completely impractical, because at the end of the day one has to feed one's body, accomplish family business, and put food on the table for one's family. One cannot say to the children, "I did not go to work because I was sitting on a park bench enjoying the Now." Likewise, a person cannot say to his landlord, at the end of the month, that he cannot pay the rent because time is an illusion—the month did not pass: "I am in the Now." The expression "Time heals all wounds" indicates the passage of terrestrial time.

Every subject is indeed two subjects—the head and tail of the coin; in this case, the notion of time also implies space. Thus, one cannot talk of time leaving aside the concept of space. Because time and space are head and tail of the same coin, we are bound to both, which are extremely important for the purpose of developing consciousness. For instance, our physical bodies are born, grow, and die. We use a physical body while we are trapped in time and space. Our bodies live in the confines of these categories.

Humans use time for practical purposes. It would be folly to deny that our physical bodies were born, grow, and are in the process of decaying; while we reside in the physical dimension, we are using a physical body, which is trapped in time and space. We can transcend physical limitations and enter another dimension through meditation and altered states of mind, but at the end of the day, we come back to take care of our families and personal business unless we renounce family ties and all our possessions and withdraw to faraway mountains to live a hermit's life. Even as a hermit, one has to feed and clothe one's body.

Unfortunately, since we are humans encased in a corporeal body, we are earthbound creatures who obey physical laws; in this realm, there is no static moment or "Now." The Eternal Now is somewhere else out in the spiritual realm and not in the physical one. If everything were happening now, we should be able to see the dinosaurs, Cro-Magnon man, Jesus, and Buddha all at the same time—right now, right here. All the ancient civilizations—the Incas, Lemuria, and Atlantis, for example—should coexist in this present moment, in the physical realm. We do not see them because they existed in the past.

On the other hand, Tolle's argument can be considered a problem of semantics because in absolute terms, the concept of time is a human invention to designate fractions of moments based on the Earth's rotation on its axis and revolution around the sun. Everything in life is a constant flow, a movement, a current of energy that is continuously rolling. This is not an empty statement; modern science (physics), existential philosophy, metaphysics, and so on consider life as such a flow of energy, in which nothing is static, dormant, or immobile. What we call "reality" is nothing solid, but a flow of probabilities; consciousness fixes these probabilities into actualities. I will discuss this more in a later chapter.

When Zen Buddhism propounds the concept of the "now," its intention is to express the idea of *awareness*, which is the basic element of meditation. Awareness, or being mindful of what is going on in our minds, means watching our streams of thoughts and being alert about events and situations in life. Hence, instead of the term "now," we prefer the term "awareness," which means being aware of the kind of thoughts one is nursing. Reality in general is composed of pockets of instances or minimoments, fractions of time, but all these moments cannot happen at once in the Now, at the same time. They are a progressive and continuous process; similarly, if one sees Niagara Falls, the appearance is that huge amounts of water are pouring over the cradle below, but if we closely analyze the torrents of water, we will see they are made up of millions of drops that together form a body of water.

If the "power of Now" assumption as described by Tolle were true, the planet Earth would be a paradise; most people would live free of any problems. Money would come freely to one's pocket; rent, food, and other expenses would be taken care of by themselves just because people are in the Now. But this is not the case; meaning, there is something missing to this recipe. Regarding this kind of faulty thinking, the great Qabalist of the last century, Paul F. Case, stressed the importance of action regardless of a person's spiritual level. He wrote:

> Persons who talk about having nothing but constructive thoughts are making meaningless noises. You can't build a house unless you cut trees, or quarry stones, or take clay and mold it into bricks. You can't paint a picture unless you take the color out of the tubes. The statue never appears until the sculptor cuts away the stone which hides the figure he has imaged.[19]

All the promises of the power of Now fail because they are constructed on faulty assumptions; they are half-truths that appeal to the public because they offer a quick solution to people's problems. This is why snake oil salesmen have done very well in the market. People love to hear or read what they want, wittingly or unwittingly. There is nothing that cannot be commercialized as a panacea of easy solutions to all of life's problems. The underlying idea seems that by being in the Now, one can make all of life's problems disappear. On the contrary, one can get rid of worries temporarily, but the problems will continue until they are resolved.

Theoretical physicist Fred Alan Wolf postulates that we live in parallel universes and that the closest one to us is the physical one, where our bodies are encased. We use this body/brain to manipulate physical reality. Spiritual traditions teach that, through meditation or altered states of mind, we can transcend the physical dimension and enter another, which, for lack of a better word, we can call the metaphysical dimension.

We can transcend the limitations of physical constraints through altered states of mind such as concentration, meditation, and other spiritual practices; in which case, time becomes an eternal present. This is confirmed by the great Swiss psychiatrist Carl Gustav Jung. He suggests that "the psyche at times functions outside of the spatio-temporal law of causality."[20] He further mentions that "the life of the psyche requires no space and no time."[21]

Hence, people who claim there is no past and no future are either completely deluded or may be living in another reality and not in the physical one. Nevertheless, physical reality does have a counterpart, which is the psychic realm.

Evidence that there is no static now comes from the fact that physical, mental, and spiritual change and growth indicate an on-going process—time elapses during every point of the change. This illustrates that physical time is a dynamic process in the physical realm. Time in the physical realm is a linear progression with fixed starting and ending points. In his wisdom, Solomon stunningly declared, "There is a time for everything, and a season for every activity *under the heavens*: a time to be born and a time to die, a time to plant and a time to uproot . . ." (Eccl 3:1–3, NIV; italics added).

Life and everything in this universe are in a dynamic process of vibration. Even dense forms of matter such as rocks and metal exist at very low rates of vibration. The flowing of life is a dynamic process and cannot be stopped. Nothing remains motionless.

According to Tolle, there is neither yesterday nor tomorrow, only Now; if a person is in the Now, he or she cannot be in the past or in the future. What about space, where the *physical body* is? Yesterday I was in Chicago, and today (now) I am in New Jersey. The ensuing question is, if there is no past or tomorrow, why are people aging, and why are trees growing and dying, seasons pass-ing, and so on? Undoubtedly, time has passed since Tolle was born; he cannot claim that he is still a baby. Tolle is confusing the Now with awareness of the present moment. Meditation, concentration, and psychic experiences cannot be equated to stopping time; rather, they take the mind out of reality to a state where there is no time and space.

The only thing that is permanent is consciousness at all levels of awareness. A man who celebrates his twentieth birthday is celebrating the addition of one year to his age in relation to the previous year. In the process, changes have happened to his body; his reasoning faculties have been transformed into those of an adult. Time has elapsed since he was one year old; his body has changed; he has accumulated life experience and has become more mature and wise than he was as a one-year-old. Mentally, he can claim that he is in the Now, but the reality is that he is a completely different individual than he once was.

Another theoretical concept that needs to be clarified is the question, how do we define reality? Undoubtedly, my reality is different from that of other people. My reality is based on my level of awareness, my belief system, the type of education I received, and environmental factors where I reside. Thus, my personal reality is unique. The problem arises when we assume that other people should see and perceive external causation (reality) exactly as we do. Everybody has his or her own personal reality, which is colored mainly by the factors mentioned above. Tolle's reality was tinged heavily by his obsessive negative ideas.

Furthermore, we should recognize that the reality we experience is constrained by our biological limitations. The specific social and natural environment, in other words, the *umwelt*, determines what we imagine reality is like for a being with different physical senses. For instance, the social opportunities of a youngster born in a poor country lead that kid to have a different perspective about life than a child born in an industrialized country. In summary, we can say the nature of reality is based on the level of awareness and "how our umwelt shapes and constrains what we know as reality."[22] This has been verified by renowned neuroscientist David Eagleman in his book *The Brain: The Story of You* (2015).

It is important to clarify that I am not arguing against the concept of Now as awareness or mindfulness; what I am calling attention to is that there is no such thing as fixed time or a static moment. The concept of Now cannot be sold as a panacea of easy solutions to all of life's problems. Tolle promises his readers eternal peace of mind and enlightenment, a life without any struggles or problems. Again, this is the idea sold to many who bought and read Tolle's books and to his followers; supposedly by this time they are enlightened with the power of Now.

An individual can get rid of obsessive ideas with meditation, relaxation, and spiritual practices, but daily life problems will continue until they are solved. People do not realize that to live free of challenges in life implies boredom and stagnation; such utopic conditions are not good for those who want to develop their human potential.

Buddha's teaching of mindfulness was directed mainly to his disciples and to monks, who made a commitment to devote their whole lives to seeking *satori*, or enlightenment. These people are prepared to spend most of their time meditating in monasteries or secluded places. They survive with the food and clothing given from their surrounding communities; they do not get bags of royalty money from making innocent people believe they can do something that requires rigorous and longtime discipline of the mind and body. In order to achieve satori, monks have to relinquish all social and family responsibilities, live in isolated places such as monasteries, and engage in strict meditation and spiritual disciplines.

In the Occidental hemisphere, ordinary people at the end of the day have to pay bills, feed their families, and pay taxes; a person cannot say to his creditors or to the IRS that time has not passed. Life is far more complex than Tolle seems to suggest.

Following the teachings of Zen Buddhism, Tolle recommends that one "be fully and completely in the *present*," and as a result, "no problem, no suffering" will prevail in the person. He advises, "In the Now, in the absence of time, all your problems dissolve. Suffering needs time; it cannot survive in the Now."[23] Granted!

For how long? One can be out of time for a certain period, but then one has to come back to reality and confront the problems that one has been trying to avoid or escape.

Zen Buddhism advocates the middle path and the concept of "Now" as a way to express the idea of *awareness and mindfulness*. It seems that Tolle envisions a physical world that is still and quiet, which is a paradox. Tolle wants people to stop time and make it immobile. Nothing is still, not solid matter and not the electrons that are moving around the nuclei of their atoms at high velocities. People's bodies are never still; they are constantly moving. Thousands of cells are constantly dying, and thousands of others are constantly born. People's stomachs digest food, blood circulates through their veins, and so on. A person's body is not the same as it was yesterday, since old cells have died and new cells have been born.

Tolle says, "The primary cause of unhappiness is never the situation but your thoughts about it." This was the basic premise of cognitive behavioral therapy, which was very popular in America in the 1960s.

From the above deliberation, it is fair to conclude that there is no such thing as a static now as Tolle conceived, but only an unfolding and becoming reality. In psychological terms, psychologist and motivational speaker Dr. Lee Pulos describes the fluid nature of reality in human activities with the following statement: "The future creates the present against the background of the past."[24] Indeed, an envisioned future creates the present moment as the desired goal a person wants to achieve and impels the person to take action. Modern studies on neuropsychology and self-discipline have demonstrated the fact that present behavior is dictated by images of reaching a desired aim.[25]

The common flaw found in the writings of Tolle and many self-help authors is their dismissal of the power of the subconscious mind altogether. That is one of the reasons they miss the point. The universal subconscious is the basis of reality; without it, nothing can exist. It is the medium through which everything we know as reality becomes actualized. This subject will be discussed in detail in the final chapters of this book.

Tolle's *The Power of Now* has so many incongruences that analyzing all of them would require another complete volume. The question here is how this book full of inconsistencies has sold over two million copies (a fact mentioned on the back cover of Tolle's book). Recently, I came across a remarkable self-help book written by psychic Patricia L. Mischell and published in 1985, titled *Beyond Positive Thinking: Mind Power Techniques for Discovering How Extraordinary You Really Are*; this work is much better in all aspects than Tolle's book, but it has not had the luck of having been read by Oprah Winfrey, and thus did not become a bestseller.

Independent author Von Braschler, who is an authority on subtle human energy bodies and astral travel, penned a very interesting book titled *Seven Secrets of Time Travel: Mystic Voyages of the Energy Body*, wherein he applies a metaphysical and scientific approach to the concept of time; quoting P. D. Ouspensky, Russian esoteric writer and disciple of mystic George I. Gurdjieff, he said, "We can use meditation to reach heightened consciousness and awareness and escape the limited dimensions of our physical world."[26] However, Braschler acknowledges the reality of the physical world; he says, "Nothing we do physically will allow us to escape the laws of physics and our fixed place in space and time."[27] Furthermore, Braschler's book provides specific exercises to transcend the limitations of physical reality and "to explore and experience nonordinary reality beyond our limited physical perception."[28] I greatly recommend this book.

So we come to the author L. Ron Gardner, who claims to be "an accomplished mystic who regularly abides in a state of blissful atonement with the spirit." He also says he has practiced almost all forms of meditation for forty years, including Transcendental Meditation, Self-Realization Fellowship meditation, Buddhist *Vipassana* meditation, and Zen meditation. He believes he has the experience and mystical credentials to openly challenge Tolle, i.e., the expertise necessary to "deconstruct Tolle's esoteric teachings." His radical assessment is that "Tolle is simply a histrionic ranter full of empty rhetoric."[29]

Gardner's book title is explicit about this: *Beyond the Power of*

Now: A Guide to, and Beyond, Eckhart Tolle's Teachings. The express purpose of Gardner's book is to refute Tolle's ideas as expressed in *The Power of Now.* I came across Gardner's book after finishing the draft of this essay. This appears to be an act of synchronicity; it complements the ideas I outlined previously.

Gardner's work is well written and displays higher scholarship on the subject. Similar to Tolle, Gardner is a self-proclaimed "mystic-philosopher and spiritual teacher."[30] Gardner provides some clarification regarding the many misleading or incomplete statements in Tolle's book and gives his interpretation of the enlightenment process. As Tolle tends to overgeneralize certain ideas, Gardner points out that much of Tolle's worldview is wishful thinking that envisions a utopia. Gardner further indicates that the aim of his own book is "to explain and extol the *true* power of Now and castigate Tolle for failing to identify and describe it."[31]

Gardner's work is well structured and organized; he classifies his criticism into three fundamental subjects: "1) Tolle's attack on the human mind, 2) Tolle's understanding of the power of Now, and 3) his 'new earth' prophecy."[32] Regarding the first item, contrary to Tolle's consideration that the mind is a "powerless abomination," Gardner considers the mind to be creative, with a capacity to choose freely. He also asks the question, *What exactly is this power of Now?* This criticism is similar to my position that Tolle never defines what he understands as "Now." Gardner's viewpoint is that "the *true* power of Now is the Holy Spirit, which is the same divine light-energy as the Hindu *Shakti* and the Buddhist *Sambhogakaya*[33] (italics in original). This statement is intriguing and needs further examination. The third item is concerned with a different book by Tolle, titled *A New Earth: Awakening to Your Life's Purpose.* That work is not part of the present discussion.

Gardner's theological concept is Trinitarian: the Father, the Son, and the Holy Spirit; he states that Tolle fails to consider the Holy Ghost, or Spirit, the true power of Now, in the enlightenment process, so Gardner classifies "Tolle as a two-dimensional, rather than a three-dimensional, mystic."[34]

Gardner rebuts virtually every single point that Tolle makes and also presents a list of Tolle's faults. He criticizes the following of Tolle's points: "1) emotions can be trusted more than thought; 2) time is a mind-created illusion; 3) psychological time is insanity; 4) the present moment is the Now; 5) the 'inner' body is the direct link to the Now; 6) your cells stop aging when you live in the Now; 7) women are spiritually more evolved than men; and 8) animals such as ducks and cats are Zen masters."[35]

Gardner also adds that "Tolle's teachings are replete with erroneous ideas."[36] Since Tolle's book is written in a style of questions and answers, Gardner paraphrases chapter and subchapter titles of Tolle's book and presents his own responses to Tolle's questions. This is a convenient way to compare the answers of both authors to the same questions. Gardner further claims that his book is structured as a study guide to *The Power of Now*.

Gardner is not free of error; in his analysis of *The Power of Now*, he combines Buddhist, Hindu, and Christian teachings. For instance, he asserts that the *true* power of Now is the Holy Spirit, which is the same divine light energy as the Hindu *Shakti* and the Buddhist *Sambhogakaya*. This is not really a description of Now; what Gardner is trying to describe is the universal life force that permeates the whole universe and is expressed in humans as the kundalini energy; in psychological terms it is the psycho-spiritual force lying at the base of the spinal cord in humans. This energy has nothing to do with the concept of Now. Furthermore, Gardner asserts that his purpose in writing his book is not only to debunk Tolle but, more important, to provide explicit instructions on how to connect to and channel the true power of Now, light energy. Again, he is talking about *energy* and not about the Now. He later identifies the kundalini as *Shakti*, which is the feminine vital life force. Different practices of yoga and proper meditation have the power to awaken this energy and arouse it to trigger enlightenment.

Unlike Tolle, who does not explain or describe how the power of Now works, Gardner equates Now with the *Hindu Shakti and the Christian Holy Spirit*. In Hinduism, Shakti is the personification of the divine feminine creative power, which is sometimes referred to as "the Great Divine Mother." Hindu spiritual tradition regards the kundalini as a sleeping serpent waiting to be awakened. In modern esoteric psychology, the kundalini has been called an unconscious, instinctive, or libidinal force.

It is important to stress that according to Tolle, the power of Now is similar to the "power of your presence."[37] However, Gardner attempts to find a common factor among three different religions that equates to the power of Now.

Gardner introduces exotic concepts from different religious traditions that have nothing to do with the concept of Now; out of nowhere, he associates the Holy Spirit with Tolle's concept of Now. According to Christian dogma, the triune God is manifested as Father, Son, and Holy Spirit. It should be mentioned that in metaphysical schools, the Holy Spirit is considered the feminine aspect of God.

Gardner at several points attempts to correlate Buddhist/ Hindu teachings with Christianity. He repeatedly mentions his experience of being touched by the Holy Spirit. Interestingly enough, Tolle does not consider the kundalini to be the Holy Spirit, nor does he mention the Hindu goddess Shakti.

In spite of all these criticisms, paradoxically, Gardner at the end states that he agrees with Tolle's core teachings but does not agree with the details.

My position is the opposite of both Tolle's and Gardner's. I deny the notion of Now, which Tolle understands as the present moment and Gardner conceives as Shakti or the Holy Ghost. The concept of Now has nothing to do with the psychic energy called kundalini, and there is no Now as a static, petrified, immobile, and fixed thing; everything is in a state of vibratory flow, and time is eternal movement. Both Tolle and Gardner base their viewpoints heavily on Oriental philosophies and religions. My argument in discussing this issue is based on Western philosophy, as exemplified by Hermetic Qabalah. I consider the only real thing to be our perception of the Now as something flowing or as time passing. I will further elaborate on this in the final chapters.

At the onset of any creation, whether physical, mental, or otherwise, the first step is to set an *intention*; one cannot leave the mind blank and expect something to happen. The intention sets a direction for the action. As simple as it may sound, this is the crux of the matter. We live in a purposeful universe; the so-called power of Now does not any have inherent power, because it lacks intention and consequently has no direction.

Thus, the magic of tomorrow starts with a firm intention. Setting definitive intentions (minigoals) amounts to prepaving upcoming events. Thus, adopting the premise that the power of Now is the power to create in the present moment, we can conclude that the magic of tomorrow is to manifest our goals. Failing to set goals or intentions equals leaving our lives and destiny to the mercy of the unknown. *Intentions* are desires that are means of influencing the future. This is not a stretch of the mind. This has been recognized by authors and researchers such as Wayne Dyer in *The Power of Intention*, Lynne McTaggart in *The Intention Experiment*, and Jeanne Achterberg in *Intentional Healing: Consciousness and Connection for Health and Well-Being*, among other scholars in the fields of psychology and personal development. They put forward the thesis that intentions can be potent means for healing and paving the future.

In summary, as long as we exist in the physical plane, we are constrained by time and space. The future is full of possibilities yet to come, and precisely in those possibilities resides the power of making the right decision and taking the right action to make things happen as we want. People have the option to declare the future reality of their mental patterns to be whatever they want it to be. These mental patterns, with persistence and work, can be solidified into actualities. As Paul F. Case says, "*What you hold in consciousness, it becomes!*" Through our minds, we are using a powerful agent called by different names: life force, Fohat, Ruach Elohim (the Spirit of God), and so forth.

Finally, the modern discipline known as autogenic training, which is a technique that involves deep relaxation and autosuggestion similar to biofeedback, demonstrates that mental rehearsal and imagination of desired outcomes influence the type of future we create. Perhaps one of the better examples of its use is by champion athletes, who use autogenic programming to enhance their performance. Autogenic training involves relaxation and autosuggestion with the intent to create images of the future (imagination); this most likely will influence present behavior. That is, the goal image visualized for the future draws or leads human action toward achievement of the aim visualized. Right planning, which is the opposite of dwelling in the Now, avoids potential pitfalls and future repair projects caused by lack of planning.

This supports the idea that the future creates the present. Once the desired goal is formulated as a clear-cut image and accepted by the subconscious mind, the subconscious mind will do its best to bring about the goal. Our various images of our future—what we expect to happen or what we are afraid will happen—have the same probability of occurring. These images also subtly influence our current decisions and actions. The disadvantage of *no creation* is that it deliberately withholds our creative power and puts us at the mercy of other people's creation or at the mercy of the collective's random creation.

The future is a virtual reality that is coming forward, according to the goals set beforehand. Thus, the power of Now is to consciously create in the present; it is the occasion of giving form to the stream of life that flows through our consciousness. Hence, any intention to stop the flow of life force is a fallacy. People should take a proactive attitude toward their lives. This means the present moment should be the stage for creating one's future.

The fallacy of the concept of Now can be further challenged by the fluid and ongoing nature of reality expressed by the Hebrew names of God. The Hebrew sages expressed this idea in the Divine names Ehyeh and Yahweh, both of which mean the flow of a conscious energy.

Biblical scholars and Jewish theologians concur with the above interpretation. For instance, theologian Rabbi Arthur Green identifies the sacred name Ehyeh with tomorrow.[38] He affirms that the biblical assertion "I am who I am" (Exodus 3:14, NIV) means "I am becoming." In this way, he indicates that "I am" is consciousness expressed as possibilities and that what we call "reality" is in the process of eternal unfolding. It is the all-encompassing energy pervading the whole universe; this energy is now called the zero point field by scientists. From these deliberations, we can conclude that the concept of Now is a relative and hollow term; the only now is the eternal unfolding of possibilities becoming actuality.

Rabbi Green concludes: "Ehyeh: I am tomorrow."[39] With this assertion, he suggests that God, expressed as pure consciousness, is in the process of eternal unfolding. The "All-that-Is," the all-encompassing energy that pervades the whole universe, is in eternal forthcoming reality; the only reality is the universal life force manifested as light or consciousness. I will elaborate further on this fascinating subject in pages ahead.

The present is evolving into the future right now, right here—nobody can stop it. Attempting to stop it is similar to trying to stop Niagara Falls with our hands. Everything in the universe is a flow of energy; physical reality is a fluidic energy in nature. That is why it has been said that future plans and projects create the present of human activities.

The truth of the matter is that nothing that exists is static or immobile; planet Earth rotates on its own axis at 1,015 miles per hour; at the same time, it is revolving around the sun at a speed of 67,000 miles per hour. Moreover, the whole solar system is orbiting the center of the galaxy at about 514,000 miles per hour.[40] At the microscopic level, electrons and protons are eternally moving. However, everything seems quiet and peaceful.

It is interesting to find commentaries on Amazon.com from readers who highly praise *The Power of Now* as a path to enlightenment or as a panacea that changed their lives. It seems those assessments had momentum when the book became a *New York Times* bestseller and most likely because of the endorsement provided by Oprah Winfrey on her TV program. Ordinary people have a tendency to depend on opinions of those who are in influential positions in the mass media. On the other hand, there also are critical readers who find the book to be nonsense literature, a rehash of Buddhist teachings, and the like. There is an interesting commentary by a reader of Tolle that deserves to be quoted; it gives the real perspective of an ordinary mother who struggles with daily problems and feels despondent because Tolle's admonitions seem to not work at all in her case. She wrote:

> I keep waiting for the day when someone writes a version of Buddhism for the working mom. I think that person should herself be a mother with at least one ADHD child. She should be clinically depressed and have a couch potato for a husband. If she manages to help the child grow into someone with a good marriage and a real profession, I'll buy all of her books. Unfortunately, what we keep getting is philosophies created by self-satisfied, introverted, childless hermits like Tolle. There is nothing wrong with an introverted, childless, hermit being self-satisfied. What is wrong is suggesting that his way of being represents *the* path to enlightenment for everyone. I would say that all he has found in Buddhism is a treatment for his (self-acknowledged) form of depression and suicidal thoughts. I am glad he is well and happy and [wish] him the best . . . but I won't buy any more of his books because they are just Buddhism repackaged and linked to an attitude I am not fond of.[41]

Furthermore, an interesting book review written by author Andrea Sachs and published in *TIME* magazine entitled "Channeling Ram Dass" makes the following assertion about *The Power of Now*:

> What is Tolle telling readers that they seem so eager to hear? His Zen-like message, reminiscent of that of hippie guru Ram Dass, is that happiness is achieved by living in the present: "In the Now, in the absence of time, all your problems dissolve." But the book, awash in spiritual mumbo jumbo ("The good news is that you can free yourself from your mind"), will be unhelpful for those looking for practical advice.[42]

Finally, it should be mentioned that Eastern (Buddhism, Hinduism, Sufism) and Western (Christian, Hebrew and Hermetic

Qabalah) traditions stress the meditative method as means to reach a peaceful state of mind and get mystical insights. In fact, the most effective way to have access to the inner self is through meditative and contemplative practices. Thus, rather than advocate the power of Now, it would be better to promote the *power of meditation*.

CHAPTER 5

The "As If" Principle and the Power of Assumption

*Act with assurance, proceed calmly as if Omnipotence
is at your disposal and eternity before you.*
—ANONYMOUS

I T IS STAGGERING to find that gems of ageless wisdom have been
transmitted through maxims, proverbs, and sayings from time
immemorial. For instance, the above epigraph is a wonderful inspiration for conducting our lives with self-reliance and optimism.
It provides assurance on the favorable outcome of right and positive actions. Here is another similar old occult maxim: "Trust God's
disposal of events, knowing that all the power that ever was or will
be is under your will." These are nice and insightful proverbs, but
one has to initiate the process of creation without attachment to
the outcome. Another old maxim states, "Man proposes, and God
disposes." Those who understand the real meaning of these quotations will be able to reap the fruits of their awareness.

The underlying message of the above precepts is that something
beyond human rational explanation resides in the "X" factor that
makes things happen; this has been called the "luck factor" and
other names. This "X" factor is the power of the unseen that can be
explained by what psychologist Richard Wiseman called the "as if"
principle and Neville Goddard named the power of assumption.
Although neither of those propositions was new, they were not fully
spelled out or clearly explained before.

Famed Qabalist Paul Foster Case had already indicated that in order to perform the "Great Work (the perfection of the human personality), one has to act *as if* we were doing something of our own volition"[1] (emphasis added). The notion here is that "something" beyond humans is doing the job through us. Jesus Christ expressed this idea in the following sentence: "Very truly I tell you, the Son can do nothing by himself; he can do only what he sees his Father doing, because whatever the Father does the Son also does" (John 5:19, NIV). To acknowledge this truth is a sine qua non for achieving the Magnum Opus, or the Great Work.

In contemporary times, psychologist Richard Wiseman has devoted decades of research and investigation to human behavioral science and advances the thesis of the "as if" principle"[2] to change human behavior for positive results.

The "as if" principle is based on the assertion made by American philosopher William James, who wrote, *"If you want a quality, act as if you already have it."* With this statement, James implicitly suggested that our actions influence our thoughts and feelings. This viewpoint complements the traditional one-sided belief that thoughts and feeling determine our actions; however, the opposite is also true; the modification of habitual human behavior changes thoughts and feelings as well. Thus, according to this thesis, it is possible to alter our thoughts and emotions by changing our behavior. It can be said that there is a symbiotic or reciprocal relationship between thoughts and actions as they influence one another.

William James's assertion was the golden thread for Wiseman's extensive sociological and psychological investigation. Conventional psychology is based solely on the premise that thinking affects behavior; Wiseman's hypothesis was to validate the fact that action modifies thinking. Then, Wiseman concludes that the modification of habitual behavior also changes the person's frame of mind.

According to the "as if" principle, an individual who is feeling sad should act as if he is happy; if he is angry, should act as if he is calm; if he is feeling lonely, he should act as if surrounded by friends; if he feels insecure, he should act confident, and so forth. And per Wiseman, mainstream academia is taking this proposition seriously;

he asserts that "New experiments into the As If principle are now being regularly reported at scientific conferences and published in academic journals."[3]

Although the credit is given to James about the notion of "as if," it was latent in the essays of his predecessor, Ralph Waldo Emerson. Moreover, this notion has been known implicitly in esoteric and occult literature for several hundred years. It can be found dating back to the 1800s in writings by French magician Éliphas Lévi. After Lévi, Paul F. Case also wrote about the "as if" notion in his books and correspondence lessons about the Tarot and Qabalah.

New Thought writer Neville Goddard postulates a similar idea under the designation of the power of assumption, which is the title of the third chapter of his book the *Power of Awareness*. His basic postulate is "Man's chief delusion is his conviction that there are *causes other than his own state of consciousness*"[4] (emphasis in original). Moreover, Goddard's thesis is not limited to changing a person's frame of mind, but extends to a complete modification of the human personality. In addition, people can achieve their dreams and goals, create their desired social reality, have radiant health, and so forth.

One of the contributions of Goddard to esoteric psychology is the understanding of how the mind works in its creative process, which is the concept of positive expectation and assumption. He advises that the best way to impress the subconscious with the desired outcome is to *assume* that one has already realized one's wish in the present moment, and to act accordingly. To think or ponder on the obstacles before the crystallization of an aimed goal is to hinder the expression of it, because the subconscious mind will accept the sense of difficulties and obstacles and will proceed to manifest them accordingly. Goddard also stresses the idea that it is important to pretend that the object desired is already in one's possession. This would be a powerful suggestion to the subconscious mind to manifest the desired goal. So, as per Goddard, anticipating or assuming *the feeling* is a big step toward the expression of one's wish—one consciously helps the wish become crystallized.[5]

Interestingly enough, the notion of "assuming" is nothing new either, as Goddard himself acknowledges when he quotes Shakespeare, stating, "Assume a virtue if you have it not" (*Hamlet*, Act 3, Scene 4). Furthermore, this theory is based on the innate power that lies within human beings. Moreover, the secret of assuming is to dwell on the idea that the desired wish is already manifested in the present moment. As Goddard categorically affirms, "You can create an ideal of the person you want to be and *assume that you are already that person*"[6] (emphasis in original). He further advises to have faith in the desire assumption until it becomes manifested. He considers the "assumption" theory to be the "Crown of Mysteries" and exhorts his readers to "learn the art of assumption, for only in this way can you create your own happiness."[7]

Thus, the power of assumption is a technique for mental creation, and its scope of application is universal, while the "as if" method is circumscribed to the modification of states of mind based on the changing of behavior. Power of assumption is more general and is directed not only to changing our thinking but essentially to the formation of our personal reality and achievement of our dreams and desires based on the inherent power of the inner self. Furthermore, the power of assumption can be applied to physical and mental healing, to financial prosperity, harmonious relationships, and so on; the list is endless. It is an especially effective component of imaginative techniques—to see in the mind's eye the desired object *as if* it is already achieved. In this sense, the "as if" principle can be subsumed in the power of assumption.

In my opinion, both the "as if" principle and the power of assumption are psychological devices that enhance autosuggestion. This assessment is endorsed by Napoleon Hill's definition of autosuggestion. He writes, "Autosuggestion is a term which applies to all suggestions and all self-administered stimuli which reach one's mind through the five senses."[8] The key words here are "all self-administered stimuli."

The power of assumption, nowadays, is used as an effective method of imaginative techniques. Again, the key is to see the mental picture being as real as possible, viewing it "as if" one already possesses it in the present moment, *not* in the future. Since there is confusion about the terms "visualization" and "imagination," I will make a short digression to clarify these terms. Visualization is forming the mental image of something that may or may not already have existence. It usually requires previous knowledge of the object in question and thus involves mental examination of an image from all possible angles as though it already exists; for example, one can visualize one's house or car exactly as it will appear. Imagination is the power to create something that one wants to possess, such as a new car, a new house, prosperity in business, and so on. Imagination does not necessarily require previous knowledge of the object in question. Unlike visualization, imagination is not concerned with the intricacies of details. In short, to imagine is to create something and to visualize is to reconstruct something that exists in the physical world.

Returning to our interesting theme, how is it that actions influence the mind? The answer resides in the role of the subconscious mind, a role that is usually neglected by many psychologists and behavioral scientists. P. F. Case indicated that human behavior provides a powerful suggestion to the subconscious mind. For instance, if one wants perfect health but does not eat healthy food, breathe properly, exercise, practice good hygiene, get appropriate rest, and so on, one instills negative suggestions to the subconscious mind. Remember, that subconscious has deductive reasoning; it takes conclusions from the premises given—in this case, from the actions or behavior.[9] Hence, there has to be congruency between our desires and our behavior. The most contradictory message one can give to the subconscious mind is to aspire for perfect health but to be engaged in unhealthy behavior that denies wellness.

These deliberations seem to be consistent with what quantum physics now affirms, which is that the basis of reality is an ongoing stream of probabilities: meaning that reality is in an eternal process of becoming, in which man's thinking (thought-forms) and actions have a definitive influence on a specific outcome. Hence, if we see our goals in life *as if* they are already manifested, the outcome will follow.

In metaphysical terms, the concept of "assumption" is an

attempt to materialize life force energy in the desired purpose. Clinical psychologist Lee Pulos popularized the saying "The future creates the present against the backdrop of the past," a notion that supports the above concept. Pulos's proposition is innovative and provides a psychological basis for the creation of our future reality. His thesis is the opposite of the conventional opinion that holds that "the past creates the present," which leads to the thinking, "I am a product or victim of my past."[10]

Pulos's proposition is based on the ideas of theoretical physicist Fred Alan Wolf, who articulates, "Everything in our reality works on the theory of a double-wave action—the outgoing energy and the returning echo wave. Every person in the world is casting out hundreds of waves of possibility with every thought, goal, dream or plan of action."[11] For instance, a desire such as "This summer I am going to Cusco-Peru to see the Machu-Picchu ruins" expresses a longing, which is a "quantum wave of energy that travels from the here and now to the there and then of one's future. It then returns as a double-wave, or echo wave, from the future one put out to one's here and now."[12]

Thus, reality is malleable, and consciousness is the builder of that reality. Setting a specific *intention* is a powerful way to influence the future. Thoughts, feelings, and intentions are the means that can pave the road for future success or failure.

William James has indicated, "The greatest discovery of my generation is that a human being can alter his life by altering his attitudes of mind." As stated before, everything has its complement or counterpart. In this case, the dichotomy is *thoughts–actions*; there is a symbiotic relationship between these two. Thoughts influence behavior or initiate action, and in turn, action has an influence on the mind-set of an individual. So both are complements to each other.

According to Wiseman, since James formulated the "as if" principle, hundreds of experiments have been performed to verify the validity of his thesis, and surprisingly, they found this principle to be sound and have a practical application to people's lives. Wiseman strongly believes that this theory can "help people feel happier, avoid anxiety and worry, fall in love and live happily ever after, stay slim, increase their willpower and confidence, and even slow the effects of aging."[13] If this is the case, this practice could counteract the negative effects produced by the fake self-help and pseudo-positive-thinking methods, which can lead to depression, procrastination, and anxiety.

Indeed, self-help coaches and false positive-thinking gurus can inflict detrimental effects on unaware people; they make people believe that they lack power of their own to change themselves as well as to confront problematic situations in their lives. These self-help coaches and fake gurus promote their books, programs, or seminars under the disguised idea that they will be helpful to those who feel powerless in their own lives. As can be seen, this notion is the opposite of the power of assumption.

Although the power of assumption is not well known by that name in metaphysical, New Thought, and esoteric circles, it is nevertheless a technique that has been used as an effective means to manifest desires and goals in life since the turn of the twentieth century, with the rise of the New Thought movement. Since that time, the power of assumption has been an important part of the New Age metaphysical modalities of healing, as well as other self-help practices, such as visualization and imaginative techniques.

To explain the power of behavior on individuals' thoughts and emotions, Wiseman mentions Zimbardo's classic Stanford Prison Experiment, a landmark psychological study of the human response to specific situations—in this case, to the circumstances of a fictitious prison environment. The participants in this experiment were all volunteers. They were put in circumstances similar to real roles, but in captivity. Although the people randomly assigned to the roles of guards and prisoners were aware of the fictional circumstances, they nevertheless acted as if they were in a real situation. After the experiment was over, participants confessed they'd never thought they would have behaved the way they did. In some instances, the "guards" were authoritarian and abusive, and the "inmates" were submissive and passive. The study is proof of the way social roles can change our behaviors.

Wiseman presents this study as conclusive evidence of "the power of acting under the "as if" principle,[14] However, he misses the real reason for the behavior the participants displayed in the experiment. Wiseman says, "People's sense of unique identity comes from their name, clothing, and appearance. In the prison study, all of these were removed, causing people to lose their own sense of identity and replace it with the role they had been assigned."[15] This may be true to some degree, but it does not give a satisfactory explanation to the whole scenario—the inner motivations for such behavior. He neglects the influence of the mass media and social environment. I confidently posit that participants' behaviors expressed in the roles they were assigned were latent in the volunteers' subconscious minds as they had already been conditioned by the media and society. In other words, the volunteers responded according to the roles learned and instilled in their subconscious by negative news on TV, in movies, and in video games, to which, unfortunately, children are exposed during most of their free time. Thus, when these people were assigned specific roles to play, they acted instinctively, carrying out learned behaviors. Thus, in some way, they were already predisposed to act as they did. This calls attention to the detrimental influence of the negative and violent content of the mass media.

In summary, the "as if" principle and the power of assumption are effective psychological components to the concept of self-help. They can play a motivational factor in achieving our life projects. They provide self-confidence and assurance to keep the mind on the positive side. Hence, they are important elements for creation of the "luck factor."

PART TWO

Self-Help and Self-Healing

CHAPTER 6

Self-Help and Therapeutic Suggestions

All placebos are concealed suggestions.
—ALBERT AMAO SORIA

ANOTHER PREVALENT METHOD of self-help is the so-called complementary and alternative medicine (CAM), which comprises all types of healing without medicine: mental/mind, faith, and Christian Science, as well as other healing methods. These therapies allegedly have the underlying purpose to help a sick person. However, in my opinion, they are merely different placebo modalities. I will elaborate on this subject hereafter.

In modern times, healing without medicine in America can be traced to the European influence of the nineteenth century. French neurologists Hippolyte Bernheim (1840–1919) and Jean-Martin Charcot (1825–1893) were the first who could reproduce the symptoms and stages of hysteria while a person was under hypnosis and then proceed to change those symptoms or make them disappear using suggestion.

At the same time, the Nancy School of hypnosis, led by Bernheim, proved that people have different levels of suggestibility and are prone to being hypnotized accordingly. Thus, *suggestion*, discovered to be the key for changing people's behavior and maladies, became a fundamental mechanism for healing. Indeed, the power of suggestion is a substantiation of the placebo effect.

In ancient times, the medicine man, the shaman, the magician, the witch, or the "old wise man" was seen as a powerful doctor or person who could solve not only personal problems but also physical ailments. The reputation of these people as *healers* was a significant component of the suggestion instilled in the ill person. The rituals, ceremonies, and remedies prescribed by these healers were powerful placebos to stimulate and activate the imagination and emotions of the sick person toward wellness.

The above can be explained by the fact that scientific medicine and technology of the time were incipient; the healing business was confined to shamans, medicine men, priests, or religious leaders. People then believed that all diseases were a result of the sins committed by the ill person, or due to the anger of the gods; therefore, sacrifices, rituals, and special healing ceremonies were performed to placate the gods' and goddesses' anger. It should also be remembered that before modern medicine was developed, healing practices were associated with *magic and witchcraft.*

As medical science and technology developed, healings that had been regarded as supernatural or as miracles became verifiable and scientifically demonstrable in the present. Explaining this phenomenon was precisely the aim of my book *Healing Without Medicine: From Pioneers to Modern Practice.* There, I demonstrate that the cures that occurred in shrines, old cathedrals, evangelical crusades, tent revivals, healing camps, faith healings, and so forth, which were considered "miracles," or events beyond scientific explanation, were actually cures due to either placebo, spontaneous remission, or self-healing. Nevertheless, people of the past credited such cures to saints, healers, hypnotists, priests, shamans, and the like because they did not know better.

Another point that I examine in *Healing Without Medicine* is the power of thought to heal people. Furthermore, I explain the underlying principle behind so-called mind, spiritual, and faith healing, and put in plain words why this kind of treatment works where conventional medicine fails. The book surveys the most prominent leaders of the New Thought movement, who used mental and spiritual means to regain their health from supposedly "incurable" diseases. I elucidate why some people do not respond to any kind of treatment, with or without medicine.[1] Finally, I concluded that:

All healing without medicine is SELF-HEALING; humans have an inner capacity for self-healing.

Conclusive evidence of collective suggestion is seen in the cases called the "royal touch" or "king touch." The kings of England and France in the Middle Ages performed "healing miracles" by laying their hands on the sick. The question is, did these kings have any inherent faculty to perform these cures? The answer is, absolutely not. People were healed due to autosuggestion and collective suggestion. Moreover, the fact that the king usually performed the healing ceremony in the presence of a Catholic priest heightened the suggestion. Furthermore, some kings claimed that they were appointed by God to be king; in addition, there was a common belief that kings had some divine power to heal their people. As a result, reportedly, thousands of people were cured by these kings. Regarding this topic, we have a firsthand eyewitness who reported the following:

> Wiseman, a noted surgeon of several centuries past, has written of the royal touch: "I myself have been an eyewitness of many thousands of cures performed by his majesty's touch alone, without the assistance of medicine or surgery."[2]

In modern times, journalist Norman Cousins in his book *The Anatomy of an Illness* observes something interesting: "Respectable names in the history of medicine, like Paracelsus, Holmes, and Osler, have suggested that the history of medication is far more the history of the placebo effect than of intrinsically valuable and relevant drugs."[3]

Along these lines, university English teacher and writer Lolette Kuby, after "experiencing profound self-healing"[4] from breast cancer, penned a book entitled *Faith and the Placebo Effect: An Argument for Self-Healing*, in which she presents essential premises for self-healing. Kuby is correct when she asserts the following: "Most physicians would agree that 'prior to the advent of scientific medicine near the turn of the century, most remedies administered by physicians had little or no curative power.'"[5]

The above quotations raise the ensuing question: How is it people in the past were cured when medical science and scientific technology were in an embryonic state and just emerging out of superstition and magic? To properly answer this question, we need to consider that mainstream medical science of that time did not know about the effect of placebos. In the case of Phineas P. Quimby, considered the discoverer of mind healing, the medicine prescribed by his doctor was calomel (a mercury-based medicine), which was actually killing Quimby rather than healing him. Moreover, the power of the placebo effect was unheard-of then.

Norman Cousins is an outstanding example of how the placebo effect works; he regained his health from a crippling condition that doctors of the time considered irreversible, with laughter and massive doses of ascorbic acid (vitamin C). There is an element that needs to be considered: beliefs. Cousins acknowledges that his faith in the ascorbic acid would do the job, with the following confession:

> I was absolutely convinced, at the time I was deep in my illness, that intravenous doses of ascorbic acid could be beneficial—and they were. It is quite possible that this treatment—like everything else I did—was a demonstration of the placebo effect.[6]

Placebos work in a manner similar to that of hypnosis and self-hypnosis. The conscious mind has to be in a state of relaxation and receptivity in order for the subconscious to be reached; the idea is to bypass the analytical and judgmental conscious mind to reach the subconscious and instill a suggestion or an image of health into it. Since the subconscious mind does not understand words or distinguish between what is real and what is false, it will take a clear-cut image presented to it as a factual thing.

It seems that the majority of human beings conduct their lives as if they are hypnotized by their own set of personal beliefs and predominant habitual mind-sets. In addition, socially accepted beliefs and the external social environment can become means of influence for good or for evil.

Medical doctor Lissa Rankin presents many cases of spontaneous healing and placebo effects in her book *Mind Over Medicine: Scientific Proof That You Can Heal Yourself.* Rankin states that the book is the result of her blogging on the Internet after finding that she could heal herself. She received inspiration and healing suggestions from people in response to her blogging activity.

In her blog, she tells many stories of people who have cured themselves through spontaneous healing or inexplicable remissions. In the introduction of her book, Rankin provides excellent examples of suggestion and the placebo effect. For instance, she mentions cases such as a woman whose cancer shrank away to nothing after the doctor made the woman believe she had received radiation therapy even though the radiation machine was not working properly. Another case is of a man who, instead of having surgery for his "incurably" blocked coronary arteries, chose a healthy diet, exercise, yoga, meditation, and supportive group therapy sessions and regained his health. A woman who broke her neck pursued faith healing instead of seeking medical intervention and recovered completely "without any medical treatment," and so forth.[7]

The fundamental premise Rankin propounds is that a person has the power to heal by changing how his or her mind thinks and feels;[8] this is reminiscent of the teachings of Quimby and the pioneers of the New Thought movement. Quimby in the 1860s advanced the thesis that people have the power to heal themselves by changing their frame of mind.

Rankin does not mention the teachings of the New Thought movement or the proponents of mind healing; instead, she embraces all the CAM that has been categorized by scientific investigation as mere *placebos.* Her book can be considered personal evidence of the power of the mind to heal.

The mind-body connection has been referred to by many authors and medical doctors to explain inexplicable remissions; however, an important complement to that equation is missing:

the subconscious mind. The subconscious mind is an agent of healing; in fact, nobody can be healed without its intervention. The subconscious mind is the builder of our bodies, transforms the food we eat into new cells, replaces the outworn cells with new ones, keeps our hearts beating, and so forth. It performs all these tasks without the participation of the conscious Self. The subconscious mind keeps humans' bodies healthy or causes illness in response to suggestions received from the conscious Self and the social environment.

Recapitulating the above, although there is a symbiotic relationship between the mind and the body, we should be mindful that there is no body that heals itself even though that is how things appear. The subconscious mind is the invisible agent, a higher and more powerful driver than the conscious mind; this agent is also known as the subjective mind. Another extremely important thing to consider is the metaphysical law that states that *the subconscious mind is amenable to suggestion*. And suggestion is merely a placebo.

A firm *belief* or *faith* is a powerful self-suggestion; these are the key words that explain the mystery of healing and many puzzling cures in religious settings. Placebos reach their highest degree of effectiveness when they are backed up by a strong faith; this expedient readily activates the healing powers of the subconscious mind.

Émile Coué, who studied at the Nancy School of hypnosis, well understood the healing powers of the subconscious mind, as did New Thought minister Joseph Murphy. Both stressed the importance of the subconscious in the process of healing and proposed that people can cure themselves using autosuggestion.

Thus, the genuine role of a healer is to instill positive suggestions in the subconscious of the ill person; in that way, the healer brings the patient from a *place of fear* to a *place of empowerment*. In other words, the healer assists the patient in his or her own healing. This is possible because the human body has an immense capacity to regain its balance (health). Thus, it can be said, the placebo effect is conclusive evidence that the subconscious mind is the healer of the body. Dr. Rick Ingrasci states the same idea in a different way: "*The placebo effect offers dramatic proof that all healing is essentially self-healing.*"[9]

The problem is that the majority of ordinary people have relinquished their power of self-determination, that is, control over their well-being and health. They live at the mercy of other people's mental influence, such as conventional wisdom, mass communication, and social media, which are powerful instruments of mind manipulation.

Now comes into play the most important metaphysical concept—the *Law of Attraction*—propounded by the New Thought movement since the 1800s and lately popularized by the nonphysical teachers identified as Abraham. (More about this is discussed in a later chapter.) The main postulate is that thoughts are the framework, and emotions/feelings are the points of attraction.

If the above is true, why is it that people don't always get what they want? This is a very important question that we will attempt to answer. The concept of *attraction* also implies its counterpart, that is, the notion of *rejection* (or resistance); this notion is usually neglected in the equation. I have already elaborated on this subject in the chapter entitled "New Thought and the Law of Attraction" in the book *Healing Without Medicine*. There, I hold the position that *humans attract or reject according to their "state of being" rather than according to what they want to achieve or prevent.* For the sake of clarification, the state of being is different from the Self or the "I Am." The "state of being" can be defined as the point of vibration that consists of the summation of a person's core beliefs plus his or her habitual state of thinking and feeling.

Ordinarily, humans are usually not aware of the inner and occult beliefs that dwell deep in the subconscious mind, which most of the time contradict his goals and dreams in life. For instance, a person with a tendency to be judgmental, critical, and cynical most likely will also nurse feelings of insecurity, inadequacy, and unworthiness, and because of the latter, he will project his feelings onto others. This is in accord with the Law of Correspondence: "As within, so without." Therefore, a person will experience reality according to one's state of being rather than according to one's desires. As indicated above, the state of being is the point of attraction or rejection.

It is worth reiterating that thoughts and feelings, which are parts of a belief system, are also real forces of *attraction and rejection*; they are automatic ways of reacting to certain situations. A belief system can play a discriminatory or selective role. Humans make decisions according to their predominant beliefs and interpret their experiences and observations in ways that reinforce their core beliefs. They will automatically discard things that are in conflict with their predominant beliefs (whether hidden or open). In other words, whatever does not support their "core beliefs" is systematically excluded or disregarded. Thus, events in their lives will unfold according to their predominant beliefs, although most of the time, they are not aware of this.

There are some beliefs so ingrained and rationalized in our minds that they have become part of our "normal" outlook on life. These hidden beliefs control our lives and create our external conditions most of the time. A person's character is the sum of all his or her thoughts and inner beliefs, whether correct or incorrect. Some people want to improve their circumstances but are unwilling to honestly explore their core beliefs that dwell deep in their subconscious minds. They therefore remain bound to these false beliefs and consequently perpetuate and replicate the same circumstances and situations over and over again.

When it comes to chronic disease and healing, we must look beyond conventional medicine; we must first look within ourselves. Family relationships, eating habits, healthy lifestyles, and stress factors really matter, and an environment free of anxiety and worry is extremely important in keeping a healthy body and a sound mind.

In a medical setting, self-suggestion starts with confidence in the reputation of the hospital, in the physician, and in medical treatment. A doctor with medical credentials from Ivy League universities will raise an individual's expectations to a high level of suggestibility, to the point that the patient will believe that whatever the doctor does, the outcome will be good.

The placebo effect is better understood in psychological and metaphysical terms. The effectiveness of the placebo resides in the capacity to make the patient believe that something is being done toward the patient's healing. Indeed, a placebo is a suggestion that bypasses the conscious mind and instills a suggestion in the subconscious mind; once the subconscious mind accepts the suggestion, the healing process will occur as long as the subconscious of the patient does not harbor beliefs that contradict the healing suggestions. In conclusion, it can be said that all *placebos are hidden suggestions*; they change the expectation of the subject from a mind-set of illness to one of becoming well. Therein resides the whole matter.

If the individual does not believe in the practitioner or in the treatment, the placebo will not work, and healing will not occur. The reason that different therapies work for different people is because one of them will "strike a chord" in a particular patient and activate the patient's subconscious mind. Ultimately, the patient heals him- or herself with the help of a placebo, which acts as psychological motivation.

My definition of "placebo," among the thousands already formulated, is that *a placebo is a psychological phenomenon, a concealed suggestion that is conveyed to the patient through means such as pharmacologically innocuous substances, complementary and alternative therapies, New Thought modalities (positive-thinking and self-help modalities), and so forth, with the aim of making the patient believe that something was done to alleviate his or her ailment.* That is, the key is changing the mind-set of an individual from a state of illness to a state of wellness, whether by using fake medicine, false medical procedures, CAM, self-help, positive thinking, or other means. Once the belief is impressed on the subconscious mind of the individual, healing will occur.

It cannot be stressed enough that the dominant force that dictates people's destiny is their belief systems and expectations. As stated earlier, a person's belief system keeps the person hypnotized and determines one's personality traits and destiny. Hence, it can be said with confidence that a belief system is the control panel—or the command system—of our lives. Unfortunately, in most people, the belief system consists of a person's limiting and self-sabotaging mechanisms, which must be changed to uplifting and constructive beliefs.

Furthermore, our personal definitions, the framing or the meaning we give to the events of our life experiences, have a powerful suggestive influence on our subconscious. In one sense, every person makes one's own law and is the author of the constitution (belief system) of one's personal world.

The truth of the matter is that we have been affected by the power of suggestion since we were born, whether or not we are aware of it. This is also part of what is called "anonymous authority" because it runs our lives from the deepest region of the unknown (the subconscious mind). New Thought writer William Walker Atkinson well understood this aspect when he wrote: "The child is governed almost altogether by the feelings and emotions, and from the effect of impressions and suggestions received from those around it."[10] Indeed, scientific studies in child psychology confirm the notion that the character and personality of an individual are already fashioned by the age of seven and maybe earlier than that.

Again, suggestions or "mental perceptions become a part of who we are regardless of our awareness of them. Everything in our lives began with suggestions of some kind,"[11] said hypnotist Del Hunter Morrill. He correctly expresses the role of suggestion in the lives and fates of humans in the following terms:

> Those suggestions affect how we think, how we respond, and how we act. They create our belief systems, our cultural mores, our philosophies and habits. We carry suggestions over from our past existences, from our genetic heritage, from our ancestors and culture, from our parents and other family members, from friends and enemies, and from what we have read and seen and experienced. We carry suggestions from our environment and from all of the various institutions to which we have directly or indirectly related.[12]

Thus, it can be said that the lives of common people are usually dictated by the influence of indirect suggestions, which are the predominant ideas of socially accepted beliefs, which are part of the collective mass consciousness. It cannot be denied that people are somehow conditioned by the type of society in which they live. Yet at the same time, every person lives in two worlds: one is the external, real world, and the other the person's own private world. Personal happiness or misery is the direct consequence of the congruence of one's private world with the external world.

A retired family physician, Harriet Hall, wrote interesting articles about the impact of some religious organizations on the health of their members. She analyzes Scientology, Jehovah's Witnesses, Christian Science, the Followers of Christ (a Pentecostal sect based in Oregon), and others. In a 2014 magazine article, she discloses that a "recent news article reported that 86% of holy water samples tested in Austria contained fecal matter (holy shit!)."[13] This incident brings to mind the case of Bernadette Soubirous (Saint Bernadette), who claimed she saw an image that people later named the Virgin of Lourdes; she found water from a spring near the grotto where she saw the image. The water supposedly had healing properties, and people started drinking it. "A commission from the town of Lourdes examined the quality of the water and found that it was highly contaminated and did not have any curative attributes."[14] The query here is, how could some people have reported being healed with this contaminated water? This is what we will try to answer later in this book.

Hall further states that "Christian Science adults and children have died of treatable illnesses, leading to more than 50 prosecutions for manslaughter or murder. . . . Several studies have shown that Christian Scientists have a shorter than average life expectancy."[15] The author also mentions cases of the Pentecostal Church based in Oregon, where infants died from untreated medical conditions, and their parents were convicted of criminal mistreatment. In this case, I posit that healing by mental means could be effective when a person has reached the full age of reason, is receptive to the treatment, and is able to take responsibility. Prayers and mental treatment work mainly when they are applied to oneself as a means of autosuggestion.

Professor Anne Harrington, after a thorough investigation of religion and the placebo effect in the healing arena, concluded, "Religion, it has been suggested, is a system that, to a believer, can produce a supercharged placebo effect—and *now we have the scientific evidence to prove it*"[16] (italics added). Precisely for that reason, some Protestant religious leaders have taken and continue to take advantage of their followers' credulity, making them believe that they (the religious leaders) are the healers or the conduits for the divine Spirit to heal. Most of the time, people regain their health due to collective suggestion; those who have heard or learned that someone was cured become more prone or mentally conditioned to be healed.

It is interesting to note that at the beginning of the twentieth century, when Christian Science was emerging as a powerful religious movement around the world, one of the greatest pioneers of the New Thought movement, William Walker Atkinson, published the books *Suggestions and Autosuggestion* (1909) and *Mind-Power: The Secret of Mental Magic* (1912), in which he explains the mechanism of mental healing through means of suggestion and autosuggestion.

Atkinson was well ahead of his time; in 1909, when the term "placebo effect" had never been heard, he was already aware of that notion and called it "Masked Suggestion." He defined this as "suggestion wearing the veil of some outward form or belief—operating to cure people of disease."[17] He further indicated that throughout human history, there have been numerous incidents of the employment of placebos (Masked Suggestion).[18] He provided an excellent example to demonstrate how suggestion works as a placebo and heals people who believe in it. He wrote:

> There is a well-known case related of a "Sacred Bone" which obtained great repute in the Middle-Ages from its wonderful power to heal diseases. This bone had been brought from the Holy Land by two soldiers of the crusades, and was supposed to be a portion of the skeleton of some great character of the New Testament. It was only upon the death of one of these soldiers, years after, that the truth became known. On his death-bed the soldier confessed that he and his companion, becoming drunk on the journey, had

lost the real relic which they were transporting from the Holy Land. Fearing to return home without it, they substituted the bone of a sheep which they found in a field. Much to their surprise this sheep-bone operated as the means of wonderful cures, and they agreed to keep the matter silent. In this case, as in many [others] of a similar nature, the faith and belief of the people, acting along the lines of Suggestion, operated as a dynamic power for producing physiological changes and operations, which resulted in the restoration of health to many a suffering mortal. After the disclosure of the nature of the relic, the cures ceased at once, and many of those who had been healed became sick again.[19]

Wonder of wonders, in 1909, Atkinson was also cognizant of the influence of negative suggestions that can lead to illness, which in modern terms are called the "nocebo effect." He mentioned cases of negative suggestions:

A house surgeon in a French hospital experimented with one hundred patients, giving them sugared water. Then, with a great show of fear, he pretended that he had made a mistake and given them an emetic instead of the proper medicine. Dr. Tuke says: "The result may easily be anticipated by those who can estimate the influence of the imagination. No fewer than eighty—four-fifths—were unmistakably sick."[20]

He further presents another situation:

We have had the personal assurance of a reputable practitioner of medicine, that he once attended a case in which the patient believed that she had taken a dose of strychnine by mistake. When the physician arrived, the patient was showing all the symptoms of poisoning from strychnine (she had previously witnessed the death of a dog from a similar poison) and only recovered after the usual antidotes and treatments had been administered—as it was she was weak for a long time afterward, notwithstanding the fact that after the doctor had left, the bottle of poison was found untouched, the woman having taken some harmless mixture.[21]

In order to demonstrate modern cases of the placebo effect, collective suggestion, and self-healing, it is worth studying the Christian Science movement as a case study; this group perfectly fits the requirements for such investigation for the following reasons: (A) The origin of this sect was specifically a healing enterprise; initially, Mary Baker Eddy taught mental healing as a means of earning some money based on the teachings of Quimby, due to her impoverished situation.[22] (B) Quimby believed that he had discovered how Jesus healed people. (C) Eddy followed that idea and used Jesus's teachings and the Bible to rationalize her healing business. (D) Eddy's small group of students and followers nominated Eddy as their religious leader; then, the organization became a religion. Finally, (E) Christian Science is a modern religious organization that keeps statistical information, research, and studies available for further scrutiny.

CHAPTER 7

Christian Science and Collective Suggestion

S OCIAL AND COLLECTIVE suggestion is an extremely powerful psychological instrument for manipulating the minds of people for good or evil. For example, consider the compelling stimulus of mass suggestion exerted by political leaders such as Hitler, Stalin, and Mussolini, among many others. It is staggering to watch videos of Hitler's parades, where people appear mesmerized by his speeches. Similar situations happen with religious leaders with charismatic personalities and excellent oratory skills. They are effective manipulators in evangelic crusades, camp meetings, and temples with massive attendance; they have the capacity to mesmerize the multitudes; in this way, they set the mood for tremendous manipulative indoctrination. These kinds of massive meetings have the specific purpose of converting and proselytizing people.

Medical doctor Franz Anton Mesmer (1734–1815), using methods similar to what now can be called therapeutic touch or Reiki, performed cures with great success in Austria, Germany, and France. Sick people flocked to him, and he was able to heal them by the hundreds. Many among both rich and poor testified to being cured by Mesmer's therapeutic system, in some cases, of long-term chronic illnesses.[1]

In the middle of the eighteenth century, Mesmeric healing was introduced to America by a French doctor, Charles Poyen, who came to New England to give public demonstrations on Mesmerism. Phineas P. Quimby initially learned from him and applied this technique in his early stages of healing; later on, he developed his own theory and came up with ideas such as "Illness is in the mind of the sick person," and "Man creates his own illness in his mind; change the beliefs and you will cure the illness."

As the story goes, Mary Baker Eddy came to Quimby asking for healing and learned from him the new method of healing without medicine, named mental, or mind, healing. The basic tenet is that wrong ideas held in a person's mind create all kinds of maladies. Later on, Eddy twisted this principle and created a method of healing based on *denial*—there is no illness, no sin, no suffering, no death; sickness is not real, it is merely an "erroneous belief."

Eddy founded the Christian Science (CS) Church, one of several American religious organizations that spread very quickly around the world, in the latter part of the 1800s and the first half of the 1900s, due to collective suggestion. According to biographer Caroline Fraser, "Between 1906 and 1926, the number of Christian Science churches in the United States increased from 635 to 1,913, and the membership of the Church more than tripled, from 65,717 to 202,098."[2] These are estimates—Mary Baker Eddy prohibited the release of any information regarding Christian Science membership numbers and churches; thus, there is no way to have accurate information. However, during the last decade, according to Dr. Harriet Hall, who has been studying this case for some time, "the number of U.S. churches has fallen from 1,800 to 900, and by one estimate they have fewer than 50,000 members in the entire world."[3]

Eddy authored the textbook *Science and Health with Key to the Scriptures,* which has been a bestseller for decades because it was a textbook and all members of the church were required to have a copy. Some members bought copies for their families believing that the book had some kind of "incantation" for healing that would benefit their families and close relatives. The Women's National

Book Association selected Eddy's textbook as one of the "Seventy-Five Books by Women Whose Words Have Changed the World."[4] In 1995, Eddy was inducted into the National Women's Hall of Fame.[5] Paradoxically, most of the new generations of Christian Scientists will radically disagree with these honors, as I will examine hereafter.

Most of the new generation of CS has experienced the negative consequences of the deceitful doctrine of CS for their families. They have seen parents, siblings, and children dying for lack of medical care. They are the ones who are raising their voices through memoirs and books expressing their struggles living in CS households. They have been called CS "survivors." Incidentally, in recent years an organization has appeared named "the Ex-Christian Scientist," which provides information, resources, and support for those who are departing from the Christian Science Sect. A great deal of information and many testimonies can be found on its official website.[6]

For instance, an ex-CS member, Caroline Fraser, who was formerly on the editorial staff of *The New Yorker*, penned an exhaustive book named *God's Perfect Child: Living and Dying in the Christian Science Church* (1999). Although this work is self-contradictory, as I will discuss in pages ahead, nevertheless she unveiled the false pretensions of Eddy as a divinely inspired religious leader. Fraser grew up in a CS environment, she had access to Christian Science's documents, and she interviewed prominent leaders of CS and ex-members of this organization. Thus, her sources can be considered firsthand. Since she was raised as a Christian Scientist, her narrative is a close account of the manipulations and mechanisms of the CS organization. Fraser argues against and debunks many of Eddy's false and grandiose claims.[7]

There is another extremely interesting book that sheds further light about how CS adults die for lack of medical treatment. The author, former CS member Lucia Greenhouse, penned the work *fathermothergod: My Journey Out of Christian Science* in 2011. Greenhouse's family were affluent members of this sect for many years, and she and her siblings grew up in a strict CS environment. The tragic situation occurred when her mother became very sick and Greenhouse's father did not allow any medical treatment; as a consequence her mother passed away. This book is a memoir and direct experience of a person who has lived in a CS environment. The irony is that Greenhouse's maternal grandfather was a medical doctor, her maternal grandmother a registered nurse, and her maternal great-uncle a plastic surgeon.

Moreover, Barbara Wilson, also an ex-member of CS, has published another remarkable story about her struggle growing up in a CS household. The name of the book is *Blue Windows: A Christian Science Childhood*. Here we have a case of a person struggling with mental illness. The question arises as to whether a "denial therapy" such as the CS method can heal mental health issues. According to the description on the book cover, Barbara Wilson was "taught by her Christian Scientist family that there was no sickness or evil, and that by maintaining this belief she would be protected. But such beliefs were challenged when Wilson's own mother died of breast cancer after deciding not to seek medical attention." Somehow Wilson was able to survive a childhood surrounded by mental illness, disease, and death.

CS's practitioners call their mental technique of therapy a "scientific method of healing," although it basically consists of praying and affirmations. A healing based on denial does not go along with science at all. However, Eddy attempted to elevate her method of healing to the level of a science, and her followers still believe that their religion is scientific. Incidentally, Eddy named her organization the "Church of Christ, Scientist"; however, this sect is neither Christian nor scientific. To be called Christian, it has to follow the teachings of Jesus Christ, but this organization does the opposite. Jesus never denied the reality of evil or sin. He never denied illnesses; instead he cured them and did it gratis.

An American medical doctor named John M. Tutt (1879–1966)[8] converted to Christian Science to become a CS practitioner,[9] and portrayed Eddy as follows:

> When Mary Baker Eddy, through divine revelation and pure reason, discovered Christian Science, she also recognized the inescapable demand for proofs of its practicality. . . . In this she but

followed the example of Jesus, who proved in his healing and saving works the Science of his Christly mission and ministry.[10]

Dr. Tutt was a medical doctor before he converted to CS. Reportedly, he "was healed of severe mental and physical problems"[11] by CS treatment. Subsequently he left the practice of medicine and became an active member of the CS organization. In 1912 he was ordained as a Christian Science practitioner.[12]

The question here is, how did a medical doctor become a mental/faith healer? This can be explained as follows: In the early 1900s mainstream medicine was still in an embryonic stage of development. It is not an exaggeration to speculate that medical doctors of the time had little success curing their patients; that was one of the reasons why people sought alternative ways of treatment such as homeopathy, shamanic/herbal curing, mental and faith healing, and other methods. This also suggests that in most cases people regained their health mainly due to what is now called placebo effect, spontaneous remission, mind/mental curing, or suggestion. Precisely, one of the purposes of my book, *Healing Without Medicine: From Pioneers to Modern Practice,* is to scientifically demonstrate how millions of people were healed without medicine but by the methods just mentioned. The healing of Mary Baker Eddy and Dr. Tutt also falls into those categories—mind/faith healing.

It should finally be mentioned that Dr. Tutt might have been very successful in curing people as a CS practitioner due to the fact that his medical credentials gave him a powerful aura to instill suggestion and placebo on his patients. Again, members of Christian Science believe that Eddy discovered a divine science, a "final revelation" from God, and claim that the CS textbook *Science and Health* was divinely inspired. One can only wonder why a book "divinely inspired" contains so many inconsistencies and revisions. Incidentally, according to Caroline Fraser, Eddy was a "compulsive revisionist of her own writings—issuing 432 editions of her textbook, *Science and Health,* and revising it until the month before she died—she was also an unapologetic revisionist of her own history."[13]

Indeed, this textbook underwent so many corrections since its initial publication in 1875 that later editions were completely different from the original one. In the later editions, even the title of the book, which was initially *Science and Health*, was changed to *Science and Health with Key to the Scriptures*. The additional words, *"with Key to the Scriptures,"* suggest that this textbook gives the secret to understanding the Bible. For Martin Gardner, an American mathematician, scientist, and writer, that presumption is not true. He also found numerous incidents of plagiarism in the CS textbook.[14]

A little historical background would do well for understanding the origins of CS. On February 1, 1866, two weeks after Eddy's mentor, Quimby, passed away, she fell on an icy street and reportedly injured her back. Quimby was not alive to heal her; however, she had a spontaneous remission a few days later and claimed that she had had a spiritual revelation. Indeed, Christian Scientists consider this, "the fall in Lynn," to be the birth of their religion. Decades later Eddy wrote that, on the third day after the fall, she had been helped—meaning that she regained her health—by reading a certain Bible passage. This intimates that she had a spontaneous remission. However, her pretensions went too far when she claimed that she had come to fulfill the scriptures and asserted that "healing, as I teach it, has not been practiced since the days of Christ."[15] Quimby was the first who said that he had discovered how Jesus Christ cured people without medicine and freely gave his teachings to anyone.

Subsequent to her healing, as a means of earning some income, since she was jobless and penniless, Eddy started giving classes on mind-healing techniques that she had learned from Quimby. As this initiative was very successful, she started ordaining and licensing "practitioners," so they could practice the healing technique on other people. From the beginning, she viewed this opportunity as a great business enterprise. Here lies one of the big differences between her and Quimby: instead of practicing healing by herself as her mentor Quimby did, she started ordaining practitioners in a manner similar to giving a franchise for use of this mind-healing method.

The advertisement below, which appeared in the *Banner of Light*, July 4, 1868, from Mary Baker Eddy, then Mary B. Glover, demonstrates what was stated above. This is two years after Quimby's death. [16]

DR. ROUNDY AND WIFE,

CLAIRVOYANT, Magnetic and Electric Physi-cians, have recently furnished a house onQuincy avenue, in QUINCY, MASS., where they are still Healing the Sick with good success. Board and treatment reasonable. Address, QUINCY, MASS.   6w*—June 6.

ANY PERSON desiring to learn how to heal thesick can receive of the undersigned instructionthat will enable them to commence healing on a principle of science with a success far beyondany of the present modes. No medicine, elec-tricity, physiology or hygiene required for un-paralleled success in the most difficult cases. Nopay is required unless this skill is obtained. Ad-dress, MRS. MARY B. GLOVER, Ames-bury, Mass.,Box 61.   tf†—June 20.

MRS. MARY LEWIS, by sending their autograph,or lock of hair, will give psychometrical de-lineations of character, answer questions, &c.Terms $1.00 and red stamp. Address, MARY LEWIS, Morri-son, Whiteside Co., Ill   June 20.—20w*

The technique of combining religion with healing is a sure avenue for manipulation. Faith and belief make the recipient highly suggestible. Eddy and her practitioners claimed to have cured thousands of people of all kinds of maladies; some of those illnesses had been diagnosed as "incurable diseases" by the conventional medicine of the time. Currently, members of this organization strongly believe that those cures without medicine took place and credit Eddy's technique for those healings. However, I contend that Eddy and the CS practitioners unknowingly used suggestion and placebos in their healing treatment. In fact, the whole issue of mind /spiritual/faith healing boils down to these two simple words: "suggestion" and "placebo"; this has been fully demonstrated in *Healing Without Medicine*.

Performing healings in the name of a divine power or deity or making people believe that a healer has been entrusted by some divine entity with healing powers is the most effective way to influence the believer. Some Protestant ministers claiming these prerogatives or privileges take advantage of their church members. One example that comes to mind is Benny Hinn, who claims to perform miracle healings in the name of the Holy Spirit or God; however, investigation into these claims has found no cases of people actually being healed by Benny Hinn.[17] Incidentally, James Randi, the American conjurer known as "the Amazing Randi," has discussed the results of his comprehensive study of evangelical faith healers and found all of them to be fake healers. For those readers interested in delving into the core of this issue, Randi's book *The Faith Healers* is recommended. This work unmercifully unmasks and denounces all the evangelical preachers that claim to be spiritual healers.

Ordinary people are being made sick by negative suggestions (nocebo effect), and others are being made well by positive suggestions (placebo effect). During our whole lives, we are subject to these influences. Thus, it can be said, our lives are influenced by suggestions to some degree or another. Along these lines, in the Occidental world, Christian religion (Catholic and Protestant) has instilled suggestions and feelings of unworthiness and guilt in people's minds from early childhood. According to church fathers and most Protestant leaders, humans are sinners from birth. In fact, one of the conditions to be accepted in any Protestant church is a requirement to confess that one is a sinner and worthless and that Jesus Christ came into the world for one's salvation. All this conditioning since early childhood instills in people's subconscious the idea that their existence is unworthy. Thus, during their lives, many people will sabotage their happiness and success because they feel undeserving. The worst thing is that most of the time, people do not realize that these ideas of guilt and unworthiness are harbored deep in their subconscious minds.

The power of mass suggestion is extremely influential on suggestible people; this is known in psychology as "collective hysteria," applicable to groups of people that under shared circumstances experience the same emotions. This can be observed in sporting events, political campaigns, patriotic events, evangelical crusades, and the like. In these situations, when the political leader, religious leader, or gang leader excites strong public sentiment, people will do things that they normally would not do.

Lolette Kuby well understood the role of the mass media in suggesting illnesses to people. In her book *Faith and the Placebo Effect*, in a chapter titled "Propaganda for Illness," she correctly encapsulates this idea as follows:

> The mass hypnosis induced by continuous repetition of illness propaganda would be less dangerous if fear and anxiety were all promoted: More invidious is its message that sickness is somehow desirable. Programs such as *ER* . . . convince Americans that illness is inevitable and deliver the appalling idea that sickness makes life interesting.[18]

As CS grew, the function of ordaining practitioners was delegated to CS churches. The organization quickly expanded to become an international congregation, with churches in all the states of the Union and abroad. Eddy went from being an impoverished woman to becoming rich practically overnight. The CS mother church located in Boston is a testimony to the impetus of this development.

For the sake of clarification, a CS practitioner is a person who has been indoctrinated in Eddy's teachings and dogmatically believes in this doctrine of denial of illness, that sickness is only a wrong belief. Such a person invests some money to become an authorized practitioner and has to pay dues to be in the official list of practitioners. New CS healers usually operate under the tutelage of a seasoned practitioner. The allegiance to Eddy and to the church rules and regulations is absolutely strict, under the penalty of excommunication. The CS church has a directory of its authorized practitioners. Reportedly, in the past, many of these people became practitioners as a means of obtaining some extra income

and then became fairly prosperous.[19] As per Eddy's own admission:

> In the early history of Christian Science, among my thousands
> of students few were wealthy. Now, Christian Scientists are not
> indigent; and their comfortable fortunes are acquired by healing
> mankind morally, physically, spiritually.[20]

The following can be considered a typical example of collective suggestion and autosuggestion. When CS was in the peak of
its popularity and splendor, thousands of people reported being
healed by the Christian Science technique; some of these occurrences were verified by medical doctors. In the final section of the
latest version of the CS textbook *Science of Health with Key to the
Scriptures*, Eddy included a whole chapter named "Fruitage,"
which contains one hundred pages of carefully chosen testimonials from people cured of all kinds of illness, mainly by reading
the CS textbook. Eddy stated that she chose only "a few letters
from *The Christian Science Journal* and *the Christian Science Sentinel*"[21] (official periodicals of the CS church). The irony is that
she does not give any credit to the CS practitioners who were
instrumental in most of these cures. This shows her megalomani-
acal character (obsession with exercising power). It is interesting
to note that Eddy carefully chose the testimonials in which people mentioned that reading the CS textbook led to their being
cured. One may wonder which CS textbook they referred to, because there are several textbooks, each one different from the
previous edition. Of course, the testimonial letters do not contain
the full names of the individuals giving the testimony or the
dates they were written.

According to Caroline Fraser, by 1989, CS periodicals reported
"some 53,900 testimonies" of spiritual cures.[22] The sad note is that
most of these cures were not spiritual at all. The healings were the
result of self-healing: spontaneous remission, suggestion, and the
placebo effect. Unfortunately, CS does not keep records of how
many adults died under the care of its practitioners; even worse,

CS does not keep records of the horrific stories of child deaths due to parental neglect in failing to seek medical treatment.

Here we find a very interesting story about how authentic spiritual healing takes place. This case is similar to that of Malinda Cramer, cofounder of the Divine Science Church, which practiced "the Presence of God." Lolette Kuby, after regaining her wellness from breast cancer, had two mystical revelations, which she called "a vision of Jesus."[23] This experience would be identified by C. G. Jung as a typical case of "numinosity." ("Numinous" is defined as having the power or presence of a Divinity, arousing spiritual or religious emotions.) Kuby is honest enough to acknowledge the following:

> Jesus did not heal me, and his appearance did not induce me to take him as savior. Quite the opposite: He proved to me that I was my own savior.
> God did not heal me. He said nothing about cancer and nothing about health. . . . He said only, "I Am here. I Am God."[24]

Kuby's above description of her self-healing is an eloquent explanation of Eddy's own healing; it also elucidates most of the cures performed by her organization.

CHAPTER 8

Exploring a Scientific Rationale of Self-Deception

I "laughed" my way out of a crippling disease
that doctors believed to be irreversible.
—NORMAN COUSINS[1]

How did these apparent "miracle healings" take place? How was Norman Cousins cured without medicine, from a supposedly incurable disease? Here, I am going to provide further psychological and scientific evidence to confirm the thesis "All cases of healing without medicine are self-healing."

Robert L. Park, atheist professor of physics at the University of Maryland, had a near-fatal accident: While he was walking on a trail, an oak tree, about three feet in diameter, fell on him and inflicted many potentially deadly injuries. Two Catholic priests who were walking on the same trail witnessed the incident; they administered the last rites of the church, thinking he would not survive. After his recovery from his injuries, he wrote the book mentioned before, *Superstition: Belief in the Age of Science.* Why did this huge tree fall on him? We don't know for sure, though a religious person might say it happened because he is an atheist. That is a debatable conjecture. In any event, in this book, he makes an interesting observation that explains the process of self-healing. He wrote:

We recover from most of the injuries and illnesses that afflict us without either prayers or medicine. Like all animals, we have built-in repair mechanisms: broken bones knit, blood clots stop bleeding, damaged nerves regenerate, the immune system mobilizes to destroy invading microorganisms, and so on. Modern medicine can often intervene to assist nature in the healing process, perhaps by administering an antibiotic to fight an infection that threatens to overwhelm the immune system. But if the patient then recovers, how do we know the medicine was responsible?[2]

When people say that they regained their health under the care of a CS practitioner, I believe they are sincere. However, I am also convinced that these healings were the result of one of the following processes: spontaneous remission, suggestion, or autosuggestion, similar to the placebo effect. In other words, these people healed themselves. Some incidents were due to collective suggestion, indirect suggestion, and psychological pressure by the CS practitioners. On the other hand, one should note that most of these people regained their health because they had psychosomatic illnesses. Other healings resulted from spontaneous remissions. Bear in mind that the human body is a "miracle health machine" that has tremendous capacity to heal itself. This is evidenced by the CS claim that thousands were healed just by reading the CS textbook. How this could happen? The answer has been already indicated above, several times. I call the attention of the reader to the case quoted earlier from William W. Atkinson, in which he offered the example of the sheep bone brought from the Holy Land by two soldiers of the crusades, which cured thousands of people in the Middle Ages. One should also remember the well-known cases of "king's touch" or "royal touch." All these arguments provide convincing evidence that these kinds of healing are due to suggestion and autosuggestion.

The basic doctrine of CS has been formulated by Eddy as follows: "Christian Science exterminates the drugs, and *rests on Mind alone as the curative Principle*, acknowledging that the divine Mind has all power"[3] (italics added). She further claims that pain, suffering, and disease are unreal; therefore, practitioners recommend that their members avoid doctors or any kind of medication.[4] Precisely for this, CS has been sued for child medical neglect in many circumstances.[5] CS does not admit to these trag-edies; they hold that CS members are responsible for their own problems because they were not in the right state of mind. Eddy frequently uses the term "aggressive mental suggestion" to mean the influence of people's negative thoughts over the well-being of another. She disregards the fact that life is composed of myriad factors outside a person's control and that tragedies and illnesses cannot be explained solely as the result of others people's negative influence.

The actual role of the CS practitioner is similar to that of an ordinary counselor who gets monetary compensation for his or her services. The practitioner usually performs consultations, ei-ther over the phone or in the practitioner's office, and in some cases goes to the home of the ill person. The practitioner listens to the troubles of the patient and, accordingly, conveys to the patient the idea that the illness is unreal, says the practitioner will pray for the patient, and gives the patient some affirmations extracted from the Bible and the CS textbook. This is like giving mental anesthetics to someone so he or she can endure life. The troubled person has to repeat the affirmations as a mantra in order to get well. This is similar to the technique later proposed by Émile Coué known as conscious autosuggestion. Thus, CS treatment can be characterized as talking therapy and conscious autosuggestion. The truth is, the sick person autosuggests him- or herself with the affirmations given by the CS practitioners. From this, one can in-fer that Eddy and the CS practitioners unknowingly or knowingly use suggestions—a mental placebo—in their treatment.

Dr. John M. Tutt, who regards Eddy as having been divinely inspired, gives us the key to understanding the CS method of heal-ing; he has been an experienced CS practitioner for many years and is an authority on this matter. Tutt describes the role of a CS practi-tioner as follows:

> The third aspect of public practice is that of persuasion. The prac-titioner is a persuader. His healing ministry is convincing proof of the power of the Christ to reform the repentant, taking away the sins of worldliness and opening the portals of spiritual life. He is

most persuasive in the spiritual thought he thinks and in the consequent spiritual life he leads.[6]

It is astonishing to find that a medical doctor such as Tutt equates healing with taking away the sins of the sick person and defines a CS practitioner as "persuader"; with these words, he acknowledges that the CS practitioner is a person who insinuates suggestions and "affirmations." According to Thesaurus.com, some synonyms for persuasion are "seduction, blandishment, brainwashing, enticement, exhortation, conversion, etc."[7] These words describe exactly how the CS practitioner works. It is not healing by divine intervention but by means of suggestion. One can only wonder how a medical doctor such as Dr. Tutt became a CS practitioner; was he unsuccessful at curing people with medicine and medical technology? Or did he realize that placebo and suggestion are more effective methods of curing than are conventional methods?

Anybody who acts as a healer motivates the sick person to regain his or her wellness by means of suggestion, no matter what kind of technique the healer uses. The power of suggestion in healing the body and the mind is undeniable and cannot be stressed enough. In addition, another key term that explains these occurrences is the "placebo effect," which is now familiar to the medical field.

It should be borne in mind that during the time of Quimby and Eddy, the terms "suggestion," "autosuggestion," and "subconscious mind" were almost unknown in America, since psychology as a science was in its infancy. However, the concept of "belief" has been known as a powerful psychological mechanism since ancient times. Incidentally, the medieval physician Paracelsus (1493–1541) accurately encapsulated this:

> Whether the object of your faith be real or false, you will nevertheless obtain the same effects.... Faith produces miracles; and whether it is a true or a false faith, it will always produce the same wonders.[8]

For those reasons, Martin Gardner regards "Mary Baker Eddy's Christian Science to be neither healing nor revelatory but, rather, a farrago of wild imaginings."[9] According to Gardner, Eddy suffered from "delusions of grandeur" and "delusions of persecution."[10] She suffered from extreme paranoia and fears and believed that her enemies were killing her mentally, by a method she called "malicious animal magnetism" (MAM) and "aggressive mental suggestion." She referred to MAM as "mental assassination."[11]

I have noted elsewhere the mechanism by which CS works, its method of proselytization, and its powerful brainwashing machine. Christian Science has created an efficient network of support and reinforcement. First, it provides the patient with "healing affirmations" extracted from the Bible or *Science and Health*. These affirmations must be repeated as mantras all day long. Second, it has a powerful, organized support system through a network of practitioners who are available at all times. In the event that patients feel any symptoms of relapse, they are instructed to call the practitioner immediately to receive a "healing affirmation" suitable to their health condition. Third, the patient is asked to attend Sunday services and Wednesday testimonial meetings at a local Christian Science church. The Wednesday meetings are devoted explicitly to sharing "healing testimonies" from members of the church who were cured with this method. These gatherings are powerful suggestions that heighten the confidence of the patient; they constitute potent verbal suggestions that enhance the healing process; they can be defined as an effective form of waking hypnosis. If a person does not participate in or resonate with the mental environment of this "festivity of gratitude," he or she will likely feel inadequate. In some cases, the mental pressure of the group environment will eventually lead newcomers to stand up and articulate fake testimonies in order to be part of the community.

Some believe that the affirmations extracted from the Christian Science textbook or the Bible could work as mental narcotics to help a patient endure illness and life's difficulties. One of the rules of CS is that, if a patient finds him- or herself in a difficult situation, he or she is supposed to contact the practitioner immediately by telephone or other means. The practitioner "straightens out" the thinking of the individual with affirmations, which act as "mental medicine." The patient pays fees to the practitioner for these consultations.

During its initial years, Christian Science grew rapidly, thanks to a momentum of immense collective suggestion, of which the movement's leaders took advantage. They organized the newcomers into classes, delivered lectures, assigned practitioners to patients, and gave instructions on how to treat one another with affirmations and prayers. Knowingly or unknowingly, the practitioners were training their patients in the methods of autosuggestion without having a clear concept of the principles of mental healing. Nevertheless, the practitioners used them effectively.

Although the method of healing propounded by Christian Science is absolutely illogical, thousands of people regain their health because of autosuggestion and self-healing, which was heightened by mass suggestion (collective placebo effect). I call these kinds of incidents *derivative benefit*, a form of indirect healing resulting from a collective suggestion produced by witnessing others' affirmations of being cured. Since the death of Eddy in 1910 and the consequent decline of fervor, the *egregore* (collective psychic energy) of this institution has been weakened; thus, current reports of mind healing by Christian Science practitioners have dropped tremendously.

The final stroke is given by Kuby, who experienced a dramatic self-healing. Seeking to find a rational explanation to her healing, she had the following "internal dialogue," which deserves to be quoted:

> Who healed me? *You healed yourself.* How can I heal myself? I have no such power. *Yes, you have the power.* How is it possible that I have such power? I am not God. *You are not God, but God is you*[12] (italics in original.)

The only objection I have here is with the last three words quoted above, which seem a grammatical error. I don't think that Kuby meant to say that "God is you"; instead, she might have intended to say that "God is with you" or "God is within you."

Caroline Fraser's book *God's Perfect Child* is a good work to consult; however, there are several fundamental contradictions in her assessment of the Eddy's legacy concerning the New Thought movement, positive thinking, self-help programs, and the modern modalities of healing without medicine. In the preface of her book as well in its last pages, she expresses her opinion that the New Thought movement, positive-thinking, and self-help programs are direct offshoots of Christian Science.[13] She goes on to assert that the works of Norman Vincent Peale, Bernie Siegel, and Napoleon Hill, as well as the classic work *A Course in Miracles*, were heavily influenced by Eddy.[14]

The above view is commonly held to be true by all educated Christian Scientists; for that reason, it needs to be clarified once and for all. The New Thought movement, since its beginning, followed the teachings of Quimby through its first pioneers, Reverend Warren F. Evans and Julius and Annette Dresser, and later by their son, Horatio Dresser, a prolific writer in the New Thought movement and philosophy. The first three aforementioned not only opposed the absurd teachings of Eddy but also practiced mental healing as taught by Quimby. Incidentally, Julius and Annette Dresser met Eddy when she came to the hotel, in an almost semiparalytic condition seeking healing from "Dr." Quimby, who had an office at the International Hotel in Portland, Maine. Eddy had to be assisted by others to climb to the second floor, where Quimby's office was located.

The interesting thing is that Fraser mentions Julius Dresser, indicating that he was "Quimby's patient who had known Mary before she became Mrs. Eddy; she had turned to him for aid [healing] after Quimby's death."[15] This is evidence that Dresser was already practicing mental healing before Eddy; she requested mind healing from Dresser after she fell on the icy street and developed something similar to a health condition, before she was healed by Quimby. The fall took place on February 1, 1866.

The most surprising thing is that Fraser completely omits mention of Reverend Warren Felt Evans (1817–1889), who was a pivotal pioneer of the New Thought movement. As indicated before, Evans was initially a Methodist minister, who then became a

Swedenborgian minister. Evans came to see Quimby in 1863 at his office in Portland, Maine, seeking healing; once he was healed, and with Quimby's authorization, he opened a mental-healing office in the same year. Having had a solid Swedenborgian education, he was able to provide a theoretical basis and explanation for mental and spiritual healings.

It is extremely important to keep in mind that Eddy published her initial textbook, *Science and Health,* in 1875; however, Reverend Evans had already published three books on mind healing: *Mental Cure* in 1869, *Mental Medicine* in 1872, and *Soul and Body* in 1875.

In passing I should mention the mystic Emanuel Swedenborg (1688–1772), who was a Swedish theologian and philosopher and tremendously influenced Evans as well as Ralph Waldo Emerson. In addition, the English judge Thomas Troward (1847–1916), considered the father of mental science, was also very influential on the pioneers of the American New Thought movement. Thus, it can be asserted that American metaphysics and the New Thought movement have their basis in the mystical teachings coming from Swedenborg and Judge Troward.

Fraser's above assessment that the New Thought, positive-thinking, and self-help movements derive from Christian Science does not even come close to the truth. Unfortunately, it seems Fraser still has some remnants of CS indoctrination to which she was subjected while she was a member of that organization, since early childhood. This contradiction is demonstrated by the fact that Fraser initially vehemently attacks and debunks CS doctrine and its founder, Eddy, and then praises CS as having influence on American metaphysics.

The Fraser incongruities are evidenced by her own motivation for writing her a book. She states:

> This book is dedicated to . . . demonstrate that the Church has, throughout its history, been dedicated to an idea that can kill people, facts that demonstrate that the Church has had an unfortunate influence on the legislative and statutory level, seriously eroding the rights of children to equal protection under the law.[16]

For the purpose of clarification, when Fraser mentions "Church," she is referring to the CS church. Likewise, when she uses the word "scientists," she is referring to members of this cult (Christian Scientists). This is the typical language of the organization.

Fraser herself indicates that the philosophy of Eddy owed very much to Quimby, Emerson, and New England transcendentalism; she further stresses that Eddy's theology was Quimby's. This assessment can be verified in the following quotation from her book:

> Quimby inspired Eddy's vocabulary—not just individual words and phrases, "divine Mind," "malicious animal magnetism," "Christian Science"—but an entire language of ideas that would frame her inchoate desires, frustrations, and fears. But where Quimby gave her a vocabulary, Ralph Waldo Emerson framed the world in which she found herself, and the strange, distorted echoes of Emerson resound in everything she ever wrote."[17]

Fraser further asserts, "*Science and Health* and her other writings are shot through with [Transcendentalist] notions and language; in many ways, her [Eddy's] work is an unconscious misreading of Emerson."[18]

Consequently, from Fraser's own assessment it can be inferred that Christian Science stemmed from the philosophies of the Transcendentalists, Emerson, and Quimby. If this is the case, the role of Eddy was that of an intermediary of the theology and doctrine of the above-mentioned personalities. Thus, the credit should be given to them. Eddy was not even a correct intermediary; she twisted all the teachings that came from them. As far as I know, none of these authors considered life to be an illusion, illness to have no reality, or death and suffering to have no existence.

Fraser further confirms my contention when she states, "The theological logic of Christian Science, in particular, derives from Emerson and the Transcendentalists."[19] As per Fraser's own words, "Quimby's association of his healing method with that of Jesus and his equation of 'Christ' with 'Science' were all adopted, for her own purposes, by Eddy."[20] How then did Fraser reach the conclusion that the New Thought movement, positive-thinking, and self-help programs are offshoots of Christian Science? Definitely, this is a slip of the tongue or a mystery, coming from a person holding a PhD from Harvard University. Perhaps, since she grew up in the CS organization, the CS education could still have residual influence on her, resulting in a biased view.

Furthermore, Fraser indicates that "New Thought gave rise to a number of organizations."[21] She also affirms that Myrtle Fillmore was the founder of the Unity Church of Christianity. Actually, Charles Fillmore was the founder of Unity Church with the assistance of his wife, Myrtle. Charles Fillmore was a prolific writer of the New Thought movement. The reason Fraser fails to mention Charles Fillmore is a mystery. In passing, although Unity Church emphasizes spiritual healing through prayer, it does not reject medical treatment.

Fraser does not mention the role of Judge Thomas Troward, whose influence on the New Thought pioneers was tremendous. Moreover, she disregards the New Thought pioneer William Walker Atkinson, who wrote extensively about New Thought philosophy.

It is extremely important to stress the following issue: Fraser is a former CS member and a Harvard PhD; for those reasons it is difficult to accept her inconsistencies and contradictions. She adamantly attacks Eddy and her Christian Science in all aspects but then considers Eddy the "mastermind" who originated all these modern ways of healing, such as positive thinking, the self-help movement, motivational theories, and even all modern alternative modalities of healing.

In the preface of Fraser's book, she lists a set of books that according to her are direct offshoots of Eddy, such as Napoleon Hill's *Think & Grow Rich*; Norman Vincent Peale's *The Power of Positive Thinking*; Werner Erhard's *est*; Joyce Brothers's *How to Get Whatever You Want Out of Life*; ideas from Deepak Chopra's *Ayurveda* about becoming "ageless" and "timeless"; Bernie Siegel's *Love, Medicine & Miracles*; Marianne Williamson's *A Course in Miracles*; Louise Hay's *You Can Heal Your Life*; and Andrew Weil's *Spontaneous Healing*. As per Fraser, "They all came out under Mary Baker Eddy's overcoat."[22] Fraser omits completely what she herself indicates in later pages in her book: the inspiration and legacy of Quimby, Reverend Evans, Emerson, William James, the Transcendentalists, Judge Troward, Atkinson, Georg Hegel, Oriental (Vedanta) philosophy, and many others that profoundly influenced the authors just mentioned.

In the last part of her book, Fraser reiterates the above assertions and goes into more detail. She debunks Caroline Myss, whom she considers a self-proclaimed "medical intuitive,"[23] as well as Dolores Krieger's therapeutic touch, which she compares with Mesmer's healing techniques. She criticizes the works of Dr. Larry Dossey and Dr. Deepak Chopra, indicating that they are "pseudoscience and disguised the fact there is little support for their theories offering carefully chosen testimonials."[24] Again, Fraser goes on to indicate that "*A Course in Miracles* is directly influenced by CS."[25] She states, "No one who has read *A Course in Miracles* can fail to notice its conceptual and rhetorical similarities to *Science and Health*."[26] According to Fraser, CS influenced Elizabeth Clare Prophet's church, the Pentecostal Word of Faith, the televangelist Benny Hinn, and several others.

Fraser also mentions L. Ron Hubbard, founder of Scientology, indicating that he followed "Eddy's footsteps. Deeply intolerant of criticism, he isolated himself with certain handpicked followers and exhibited paranoid fears of unconscious mental attack. . . . Like Eddy, he had a tendency toward grandiosity."[27] Indeed, Eddy showed all those characteristics.

Finally, there are two outrageous sentences in Fraser's book that need to be addressed. One is Fraser's assertion that many Christian Science churches have been accepted "into the fellowship of Christianity."[28] This is an extreme statement; as far as I know, Christian fundamentalists consider CS a cult and out of mainstream Christianity, as they don't really follow Jesus's teaching. Fraser's second assertion is that "Madame Blavatsky's theosophy was influenced by Eddy's *Science and Health*."[29] It is well known that Helena Blavatsky's scholarship on Eastern and Western religions surpasses Eddy's by far. Blavatsky (1831–1891) wrote based on Hermetic and esoteric philosophy, which at that time was not accepted by conventional Christian society. Furthermore, Blavatsky's books deal with Tibetan Buddhism, Indian Vedic sacred scriptures, and Western esoteric and occult matters that Eddy did not know anything about. Eddy scorned and despised this kind of literature, because she was a Christian fundamentalist. Finally, Blavatsky talks about Ascended Masters (trans-Himalayan occult teachers—the Mahatmas) who helped her in developing her philosophical doctrine. Blavatsky's goal was the study of comparative religion, which she pursued in an effort to form a synthesis of science, religion, and philosophy. She considered the universe to be essentially a unity and believed that consciousness, life, and substance are fundamentally one. How could Blavatsky have been influenced by Eddy's writings when the two systems are virtually opposites?

It has been already mentioned that the whole CS doctrine rests on the fact of denial—denial of reality, denial of sin, denial of illness, denial of death and suffering, even denial of hygiene. Thus, CS doctrine should be called "denial therapy." In addition, Eddy strongly stressed her teachings based on the dichotomy of "divine mind" and "mortal mind." She consistently taught that there was no evil; however, she lived most of her adult life fearful of even the thoughts of other people, which she called "aggressive mental suggestions." Eddy did not read the Bible properly to understand the oneness of life. This is precisely one of the faults of many Christian preachers; they only quote parts of the Bible that are of interest to them and neglect basic teachings of Jewish sages. For instance, they do not mention God saying: "I form the light, and create darkness: I make peace, and create evil: I the LORD do all these things" (Isaiah 45:7, KJV).

Eddy ruled her CS church with an iron hand; she enforced the reading of only two books: the Bible and her textbook, *Science and Health*. Eddy's fundamental tenet consists of the following statement: Humankind is the image and likeness of God; thus, since God is perfect, so is humankind. In this perfection there is not illness, death, sin, and so on. "You are a perfect child." I understand that the inner self or higher self in each individual is perfect, but not the personality. That is why we are in this valley of sorrow and tears working at perfecting our personalities through tests and trials. Was Eddy indeed perfect? It is up to the reader to judge.

Jesus Christ never expected people to be perfect. Here we have an example, when the scribes and the Pharisees brought to him a woman who was caught in adultery: they asked Jesus if they should stone her; Jesus answered, "He that is without sin among you, let him first cast a stone" (John 8:7, KJV). Jesus acknowledged that humans are indeed imperfect, and that fact cannot be denied.

According to Martin Gardner, Eddy's central precept was that reality, illness, and death are illusions. However, she was afraid of persecution by heretics in her church and attributed her nervous disorders and extraordinary fears to them. She believed that enemies were killing her through MAM, "malicious animal magnetism." Furthermore, Eddy had a lifelong morphine addiction and used the drug to deaden her back pain. She was fearful most of the time, filled with obsessive ideas, irascible, and suspicious of everybody. She was a relentless liar; she persistently denied that she ever met Quimby, claiming that her doctrines came as a direct transmission from God. [30]

Robert Peel, who was a longtime member of Christian Science and the author of a three-volume biography of Eddy, regarding the first editions of Science and Health, has this to say: "Sentences are chaotic, punctuation erratic, quotations inexact, meanings obscure. . . . Grammar and organization are so crude that a single paragraph can go on for over half a dozen pages, and run-on sentences, dangling participles, and overwrought language abound." [31]

Author Martin Gardner has indicated about Eddy's writings that "her early scribblings, before her works were carefully edited and polished by others, were almost as crude as the 1875 edition of Science and Health." [32] Gardner further affirms that Eddy copied shamelessly, often word for word, from John Ruskin, Thomas Carlyle, Charles Kingsley, Swiss critic Henri Amiel, and others. [33] There is also a strong possibility that Eddy may have had access to Reverend Evans's books, as both were initially patients of Quimby. Gardner quotes paragraphs by these authors and makes a parallel with Eddy's statements.

Eddy's biographers Willa Cather and Georgine Milmine, in their book *The Life of Mary Baker G. Eddy and the History of Christian Science* (1909), demonstrate that Eddy took some ideas from Quimby's manuscripts without giving any credit to her mentor.

Perhaps because Eddy consistently affirmed that there is no death, there were insistent rumors, when she passed away, that her fanatic followers might have installed a telephone in her grave, "for Mrs. Eddy's use should she rise from the death."[34]

CHAPTER 9

Religion and Placebo Healing

The placebo effect is the good news of our time.
It says, "You have been cured by nothing but yourself."
—LOLETTE KUBY[1]

IN THE PAST, healing without medicine, in the Occidental world, was restricted to the Church priesthood. Any type of healing without medicine outside the scope of the Catholic Church and conventional medicine of the time was considered sorcery or witchcraft. The unspoken instruction was that the clergy and ecclesiastical institutions were entitled to perform "healings," which supposedly was a mandate coming from Jesus, who said to spread the Gospel around the world and who cured people gratis. This tradition continued until the enlightenment of the eighteenth century. At that time, two Catholic priests, Father Johann Joseph Gassner (1727–1779) and Father Maximilian Hell (1720–1792), using different approaches performed cures outside the religious aura of the church.

Father Gassner, one of the famous exorcists of the eighteenth century, used exorcism as a means to restore people's health. The underlying idea was that sickness was the result of invasion by negative forces or possession by devils. He exorcised, with great success, patients in the presence of Catholic and Protestant church authorities, physicians, noblemen of all ranks, members of the bourgeoisie, and skeptics as well as believers. His every word and gesture and those of his patients were recorded by a notary public, and the official records were signed by the distinguished eyewitnesses.[2] Father Gassner had great success curing patients by "driving out demons" from sick individuals. The interesting thing is, when he was unable to cure people by this method, he used to send them to see a medical doctor. In that manner, he avoided criticism from both the Church and the medical community.

At the same time, Hungarian astronomer and priest Maximilian Hell was also successfully healing people suffering from various ailments by using iron magnets (magnet therapy). Hell was the one who introduced his friend Franz Anton Mesmer to magnet therapy and encouraged the young medical doctor (Mesmer) to use magnets in his medical practices. In my book *Healing Without Medicine: From Pioneers to Modern Practice*, I describe Mesmer's progression from his theory of "mineral magnetism," to "animal magnetism," and finally to "personal magnetism."

Like medieval physician Paracelsus, Mesmer believed in the existence of a universal life force composed of fluid energy. This energy flowing from the stars, concentrated in magnets, was called "mineral magnetism" and, concentrated in living creatures, was known as "animal magnetism." Furthermore, Mesmer believed that bodily fluids possessed polarity and that misalignment of these negatively and positively charged poles could result in illness. Thus, the application of magnets was done to realign the fluid energy in the body.

Mesmer eventually discontinued the use of iron magnets entirely to embrace the idea of "personal magnetism," which is the belief that the physician himself was a magnet and able to channel the invisible "magnetic fluid" that pervades the universe into the body of the sick person, bringing the patient into the balance necessary for a cure. By the year 1775, Mesmer was having great success curing people from all walks of life. His method of healing was simply looking into the eyes of the patient, touching the affected area, and doing passes around the body of the ill person.

When Mesmer learned that Gassner was also having success curing people using exorcism, Mesmer claimed that Gassner's cures resulted from the rearrangement of animal magnetism and not from the removal of demons from the sick person. Mesmer further stated that the priest Gassner was undoubtedly an honest man, but that he was curing his patients through animal magnetism without being aware of it.[3]

Gassner is remembered in history as the last celebrated exorcist of his time, having performed cures still within the aura of the Catholic Church. On the other hand, Mesmer, with the success of his magnetic treatments and animal magnetism theory, established a new method of healing without medicine that retained no ties with religion at all.

The modern trend of spiritual healing is currently practiced by many religious organizations, including Christian Science, the Pentecostal Church, the Faith Tabernacle Church, and many smaller congregations who practice faith healing. The members of these sects reject all medical treatment in favor of spiritual and mental treatment carried out by different methods, such as praying, exorcisms, anointing with oils, and so on. The effectiveness of these practices relies on the faith of the believer. Dr. Harriet Hall states that "Scientology discourages any use of medication. Pain and other symptoms are treated by a method called 'Assist.'"[4] The Scientology handbook does not describe exactly what the procedure of the *assist* method is, except that it indicates that the treatment invokes the assistance of the spirit. Below is the description given in the Scientology website:

> In Scientology an *assist* is an action undertaken to help a person confront physical difficulties. If a child has fallen and hurt himself, an assist can help him overcome the trauma. If a person has a toothache or has had a tooth pulled, an assist can help relieve the pain. When people are ill, assists can ease the discomfort and speed recovery. Even broken bones respond to assists. These and many other conditions can be improved by application of procedures classified under this heading of "Assists."[5]

On the other hand, members of Jehovah's Witnesses refuse blood transfusions. From personal experience, I should mention that two of my maternal aunts in Peru died because they preferred death to disobeying the Jehovah's Witnesses mandates.

It appears that humans' psychological tendency is to use narratives or myths to make sense of or rationalize events in their lives. This is also the case in the healing arena; that is why people obtain healing with diverse kinds of therapies. As the saying goes, "Different strokes for different folks." In other words, different placebos work for different people. Any approach or procedure of healing will work as long as it generates hopes and expectations. A physician, minister, or psychologist, faith in a saint, shaman, or evangelical preacher; an innocuous injection; an inspirational book; or even a fake surgical procedure can generate a placebo effect in many people.

The expectation expressed in positive belief produces tangible results most of the time. The most remarkable incidents take place in religious environments such as churches, cathedrals, or sites considered sacred places, such as the Virgin of Lourdes grotto; these settings enhance the faith and imagination of the believer to their highest degree.

It is clear that a powerful healing force can be activated by an inspirational religious message, regardless of its legitimacy. Steven Starker describes an "inspirational message" as follows: "It lifts the spirit, engenders and supports hope, and keeps people striving toward their goals. It also fends off feelings of helplessness, hopelessness, despair, and depression."[6]

As opposed to a placebo, there is also a nocebo, which can be defined as a detrimental suggestion that negatively affects an individual. A practical example will clarify this idea: some suggestible people can be made sick by others when they are repeatedly subjected to negative comments about their health and physical appearance. Sometimes, comments such as saying a person looks terrible or is too skinny and pale can become powerful suggestions that lead a suggestive person to become depressed. That is why it is important to be careful about expressing our judgments and opinions to others.

In the case of Eddy, it is well known that during her whole life, she relied on homeopathic medication although her personal "dogma" was the "Mind as the only curative Principle."[7] As per her own admission, "I indulge in homeopathic doses of *Natrum muriaticum* (common salt)."[8] In her textbook *Science and Health*, she mentions the following case, which proves my thesis that she was using placebos to cure people, although she may not have been aware of it. She writes:

> A case of dropsy, given up by the [medical] faculty, fell into my hands. It was a terrible case. Tapping had been employed, and yet, as she lay in her bed, the patient looked like a barrel. I prescribed the fourth attenuation of *Argentum nitratum* [common salt] with occasional doses of a high attenuation of *Sulphuris*. She improved perceptibly. . . . It then occurred to me to give her **unmedicated pellets** and watch the result. . . . She went on in this way, taking the **unmedicated pellets**—and receiving occasional visits from me—but employing no other means, and she was cured.[9] (bold added)

Author Martin Gardner also noticed that Eddy used placebos to heal people. In his book *The Healing Revelations of Mary Baker Eddy*, he quotes the following from Eddy:

> The highest attenuation we ever attained was to leave the drug out of the question, using only the sugar of milk; and with this original dose we cured an inveterate case of dropsy. After these experiments, you cannot be surprised that we resigned the imaginary medicine altogether, and honestly employed Mind as the only curative Principle.[10]

Homeopathic medicine regards symptoms of illness as normal responses of the body as it attempts to regain health. The idea is that if a substance causes a symptom in a healthy person, giving the person a very small amount of the same substance may cure the illness. This is like giving the body "a push"—a suggestion to produce healing. In theory, a homeopathic dose reportedly enhances the body's normal healing and self-regulatory processes. A homeopathic health practitioner uses pills or liquid mixtures containing only a small amount of an active ingredient for treatment of disease. Many homeopathic remedies are so diluted that no molecules of the original substance remain. For medication purposes, they are similar to a coated sugar pill, analogous to placebos.

Eddy was well aware of faith healing; for that reason, she demanded absolute belief in her CS textbook and obedience to her rules from her disciples, under the risk of being expelled from the organization. However, she denied that her system was faith healing. The following quotation from *Science and Health* is a typical example of the placebo effect:

Homeopathy furnishes the evidence to the senses, that symptoms, which might be produced by a certain drug, are removed by using the same drug which might cause the symptoms. This confirms my theory that *faith in the drug is the sole factor in the cure.* The effect, which mortal mind produces through one belief, it removes through an opposite belief, but it uses the same medicine in both cases.[11] (emphasis added)

She reduces the cause of illness to "beliefs." In the case of the placebo effect, the change of belief is caused solely by the patient's psychological expectation and desire to get better. Thus, homeopathic treatment is also a placebo. This assertion is supported by the fact that studies by the pharmaceutical industry found that some old drugs had to be abandoned because they were no more effective than placebos.

The fact that the subconscious mind is the healer of the body is verified in the case of the placebo effect. A placebo, which is an innocuous substance, does not act on the disease but on the subconscious mind of the individual. The only healer is the subconscious mind. A placebo tricks the subconscious mind into the belief that something has been done and can sometimes result in miraculous healings, such as curing various kinds of cancer or other incurable diseases or making long-standing tumors disappear. A placebo, which can be a sugar pill, an injection, a medical procedure, or any other type of therapy, doesn't directly influence the illness being treated.

Placebos are closely connected to expectations. A placebo makes the person believe in something along the lines of what he or she expects to happen. If the person believes that he or she is getting a strong medicine, the placebo will convey the message to the subconscious, causing healing. The effect occurs because the patient believes in the substance, in the treatment, or in the doctor. The patient's subconscious mind somehow causes physical changes in the body.

Some believe that many illnesses improve over time even without treatment. Such is the case in spontaneous remission; in this case, the body's inner capacity activates the healing process, which is called spontaneous healing. In other circumstances, a cure can be achieved by changing the patient's state of mind from fear and worry to hope and faith.

CHAPTER 10

Faith Healing and Mass Suggestion

There is a miraculous healing power in your subconscious.
—JOSEPH MURPHY[1]

AN INTERESTING ARTICLE entitled "Becoming a Faith Healer: An Insider's Look at the Business of Revealed Religion" gives an account of unethical practices of some Protestant ministers. The article was written by Dustin White, who was trained from the time he was very young to become a faith healer in a local Pentecostal church in Minot, ND. He was chosen by the minister of the church because the spirit was working on the young boy to perform the job of faith healer.

White narrates that his minister confided in him that "it was sometimes necessary to *fake* miracles in order to help inspire faith in others. This deception, I was told, should 'not be seen as lying' because it was bringing people to faith."[2] This statement seems really unethical; how could a minister of a church, who supposedly is preaching the word of God, say such things? This is indeed is very shameful behavior. I wonder whether the minister has any kind of remorse for manipulating the faith of his congregation when he goes to bed at night or prays to God."

The most interesting part of this excellent article describing Dustin White's experience as faith healer is the accurate description of the method used to heighten the receptivity of churchgoers to create the perfect condition for healing. He writes:

It was also important to know how to create an environment that lent to creating emotional ecstasy. An effective tool to this end was music, which we used to create the "right state of mind." Through the use of music, we were able to create the impression that God had entered into fellowship with the congregation. Combining this with the "heartfelt" words of a charismatic minister, the potential to create an ecstatic uproar in the church was almost guaranteed. I later discovered that it was also a surefire way to get the congregants to open up their wallets.[3]

The key words here are the creation of the "ecstatic moment" or the "right state of mind," which is a heightened state of mind, of receptivity in the believer to instill a suggestion so that the healing will be done. This heightened state of mind can also be created in evangelical crusades or faith-healing meetings, through mass excitement that strikes a spiritual chord in the believer.

White also mentions how his minister trained him to do fake exorcisms on both people and their homes, as people believe that demonic influences create many illnesses and dysfunctions in families and businesses; however, this topic is outside the scope of this book.

The extreme reliance on or belief in unethical ministers can also lead to parents neglecting the medical care of their children, with serious detrimental consequences. This is because some religious ministers or CS practitioners favor faith healing rather than allowing the parents to seek medical treatment for their children. For instance, in recent years, several incidents of children dying because of their parents' resistance to seeking proper medical treatment for them, due to their radical religious beliefs, have become public. The stories are usually similar: A child becomes sick; the parents reject conventional medical treatment and instead turn to faith healing or prayers. Sometimes, the child dies as a consequence of this. I say sometimes, because in other cases, the child may regain health due to spontaneous remission or self-healing.

Well-known author Cameron Stauth wrote an interesting book in 2013 entitled *In the Name of God: The True Story of the*

Fight to Save Children from Faith-Healing Homicide. He gives a horrific account of faith-healing abuses within a Christian fundamentalist church named the Followers of Christ, based in Clackamas County, Oregon. Incidentally, this church had support on the national level from the Church of Christ, Scientist (Christian Science).

The state of Oregon used to have laws that protected religious groups who practiced faith healing from prosecution for medically preventable deaths. Children were dying from medically treatable maladies. A man from within the radical sect The Followers of Christ, who had lost his own child to these health practices, anonymously served as Stauth's informant and provided valuable information to the police for investigation into child medical neglect cases.

As a consequence of the above, concerned parents created an organization named Children's Healthcare Is a Legal Duty (CHILD), Inc., in 1983, with the specific purpose to "protect children from harmful religious and cultural practices, especially religion-based medical neglect."

Former CS members Rita and Douglas Swan, after the death of their son, Matthew, were actively involved in creating this institution. While the Swans were CS members of the Christian Science Church, they were advised by CS practitioners not to seek medical treatment for the child, claiming that they (CS practitioners) were able to heal Matthew. Finally, when a practitioner gave permission to take the child to a hospital, it was too late to save Matthew. This is only a single example; those who are interested in this subject should visit the website "Victims of Religion-Based Medical Neglect," sponsored by CHILD.[4] On this website there are several stories of parents who lost their children to faith healing. One can only wonder about the hundreds of incidents of child death that are not reported publicly.

At this point it is extremely important to establish the fundamental difference between Phineas Quimby and Mary Baker Eddy. The former never denied illness or the fact that people can regain their health under the care of a physician. Quimby's method was explanatory suggestion and modifying the patient's own feelings and beliefs. In contrast, Eddy went to the extreme of denying the existence of disease, death, and evil, claiming they are an illusion, a lie, an error.[5] Eddy herself clarified the essential distinction between her system of thought and Quimby's as follows: "What is the cardinal point of the difference in my metaphysical system? This: that *by knowing the unreality of disease, sin, and death*, you understand the allness of God. This difference wholly separates my system from all others"[6] (italics added).

Christian Science healings have been successful mainly because there have been cures due to collective suggestion and others resulting from autosuggestion and spontaneous remission. CS practitioners prepared the mind of the patient with verbal suggestions to receive the necessary mental impressions. The patient was advised by the practitioner to hold a mental attitude of denial of the existence of any disease; the sick person was told to accept this assertion as a condition for recovery. The patient was not allowed to formulate any objection to the method of treatment; instead, he or she was asked to blindly believe in the CS textbook. In a manner similar to a hypnotic session, the patient was asked to enter a passive and receptive state of mind to listen to the practitioner's instructions. The practitioner usually made statements about the unreality of the illness; these were repeated over and over until the suggestions sank into the subconscious mind of the patient. At the end of the session, some suggestible patients found some relief, and others felt that they had recuperated. If the healing session was successful, the practitioner was credited with the healing; if it failed, the patient was blamed because he or she did not hold fast enough to the idea of denying the illness.

Thus, CS uses a compelling method of indoctrination on its members and patients, insisting that they believe in its absurd system as a prerequisite for being healed; this can be considered a kind of waking hypnosis. In addition, the effectiveness of Christian Science in the early years was due, in good part, to generating expectations among naïve people and producing a kind of mass suggestion. Over the years, some churches, such as New Jersey's Plainfield Christian Science Church, Independent, have separated from the mother church, the First Church of Christ, Scientist, in Boston, because of the dictatorial and dogmatic rules imposed by the mother church's leaders. Nowadays, the reduction in the number of churches and membership in this organization is evident. One serious disadvantage of Christian Science is that the church forbids its patients from employing medical care or using any kind of medicine. This is a dangerous recommendation that can put a sick person at a serious disadvantage, as in the case of Lucia Greenhouse's mother, who passed away for lack of medical attention, mentioned in Chapter 7.

Although Eddy instructed Christian Science members to avoid doctors and medicine and taught the unreality of disease, sin, death, and suffering,[7] she was frequently attended to by medical doctors, particularly in the last years of her life. This was in direct contradiction to the tenets of her religion. In fact, Eddy acknowledged the use of drugs, saying, "I experimented by taking some large doses of morphine, to see if Christian Science could not obviate its effects, and I say with tearful thanks, 'The drug had no effect upon me whatever.'"[8] Should we understand this last sentence to mean she might have needed higher doses to feel the effects?

It would be folly to deny the power of drugs and medicine in generating changes in the physical body; they are compositions that have the capacity to alter or release chemical properties in the body that can increase the efficacy of mental healing. Modern New Thought practitioners do not discourage patients from using appropriate medicine. The problem arises when there is an excessive dependence on chemicals that can damage other parts of the body, doing more harm than good. On the other hand, average people are deeply convinced of the power of medicine, and in some cases, their recuperation could be due to placebo effects. We cannot deny the tremendous scientific advances made in the medical field in diagnosing and treating severe health problems or accidents with severe corporeal injuries. In the cases of organic illnesses and physical atrophies, mental healing should be considered complementary to medical treatment.

In a social atmosphere of incredulity and doubt, a patient cured by mental means has little chance of permanent success. Every doubt existing in the minds of those surrounding that person is conveyed telepathically to his or her subconscious and operates as a powerful adverse suggestion. Thus, reinforcement and support are extremely important for the healing process to be successfully concluded. Interestingly, in two instances, Jesus Christ warned the blind people he cured not to say anything to anybody about their healing, precisely because he knew that the skepticism and negative environment they would encounter would be detrimental to the consummation of the healing.[9]

In addition, it seems Jesus Christ was aware that the sick person heals him- or herself. He said, "Thy faith has healed you," "According to your beliefs, it will done to you," and so on. At this point, everything in life boils down to the key word "belief." Making the sick person believe that something has been done toward healing is precisely the underlying factor in the placebo effect.

R. Barker Bausell, a retired University of Maryland professor and research director of the National Institutes of Health, after a thorough investigation about the effectiveness of complementary and alternative medicine, concluded that "CAM therapies are nothing more than cleverly packed placebos."[10] Furthermore, another scientist in the medical field, Edzard Ernst, MD, PhD, and his team researched CAM for twenty years and arrived at the same conclusion as Bausell. Ernst asserts that even some conventional medical procedures are placebos.[11]

Thus, it can be said with confidence that all healing performed by the founder of CS and its practitioners was due not to divine intervention or the CS textbook but to suggestion, autosuggestion, and placebo. One of these three psychological devices triggered the inner mechanism for the body to regain its wellness. People healed themselves, as Eddy stated, through their beliefs. Thus, my personal conclusion about the CS healing method is that it offers conclusive evidence of the power of *suggestion to cure.*

On prepaid TV evangelical Sunday services, one can hear testimonies of hundreds of people claiming to have been healed of all sorts of illnesses, such as breast cancer, twisted ankles, broken bones, tumors, and so on. I do not deny that such healings took place; what I challenge is the idea that the healing was performed by the evangelical preacher. Any paraphernalia (the Bible, the cross, or any relic) are only placebos. The truth of the matter is that all healing without medicine is done by the people themselves. Furthermore, the prayers broadcast via the mass media can also act as actual placebos or suggestions.

Jesus Christ himself stated that the people's faith and belief cured them. The biblical Gospels are full of quotations that validate what I am trying to convey. When Jesus was asked to perform a healing, he asked questions such as the following: "Do you believe that I am able to do this?" "Yes, Lord," they replied. Then he touched their eyes, and said, "*According to your faith let it be done to you.*" "And their sight was restored" (Matthew 9:28–30, NIV). On another occasion, he said, "*What you have believed will be done for you!*" (Matthew 8:13, NIV, emphasis added). This suggests that Jesus's requirement for healing was faith.

The truth of the matter is that there is an inner power inside everyone, of which all need to be aware. "Behold, the kingdom of God is within you" (Luke 17:21, NIV). Jesus Christ taught that the father who is within him is the same father who is within all people (John 14:9–11; 17:21, NIV). The message is that people need to regain their inner power, increase their feelings of self-worth, and improve their emotional states. Jesus also said, "Whatever you ask for in prayer, believe that you have received it, and it will be yours" (Mark 11:24, NIV).

Should the reader need further information, my book *Healing Without Medicine: From Pioneers to Modern Practice* is available at local public libraries; if further proof is needed, the reader can procure the book by Lissa Rankin, MD, *Mind Over Medicine: Scientific Proof You Can Heal Yourself*, or the book *The Faith Healers* by the Amazing Randi (James Randi) and see for him- or herself how many "public healers" and evangelical preachers deceive naïve and gullible people.[12]

Ordinary people usually credit someone else or something else when they are healed. It may be true that someone else guided them or facilitated the placebo, but it was they who allowed

themselves to do it, and it was their subconscious mind that actually did the work. As I already indicated, "All healing without
medicine is self-healing."

Finally, one can only wonder how one person can get so much
fame and credit as a spiritual leader with a system of healing based
on denial therapy, placebo effect, and mass suggestion. That is an
open question.

PART THREE

The Oneness of Life

CHAPTER 11

The Mental Universe

*The ALL is Mind; the Universe is mental, which means that
the Underlying Reality of the Universe is Mind.*
—THE KYBALION[1]

MONISTIC IDEALISM IS a philosophical system that emphasizes the preeminence of one mind (consciousness) as the
primary reality. It regards consciousness as the ground for what
we call physical reality. Everything, including all matter, exists
within and is part of consciousness. From this point of view, matter is an epiphenomenon of consciousness, rather than the reverse.
Physicist Amit Goswami in his book *The Self-Aware Universe:
How Consciousness Creates the Material World* has written a great
deal on this topic.

The entire universe is in a perpetual state of vibration, expansion, and evolution. Thus we are surrounded by infinite vibratory
energy, which some religions and metaphysical schools call by
different names, including Ruach Elohim, Spirit, Fohat, life
power, zero point energy, and so on. It is important to consider
the metaphysical principle that the life power is an expression of
the universal consciousness.

An internationally well-known American/Greek evolutionary
biologist and futurist scientist, Elisabet Sahtouris, has written an
interesting scientific article entitled "A Scientist's Thoughts about
Redefining our Concept of God," where she discusses the unity of

life. She summarizes the thesis and argument I have been developing in this work as follows:

> Our human task now is to wake up and recognize ourselves as parts or aspects of God-as-Nature and behave accordingly. All are One, all harm harms each of us, all blessings bless each of us. What a guideline for choice! The ancients knew it and taught it. But God, through us, is trying out the most dangerous game of all—the game of truly forgetting our nature. A great risk, but it had to be done to try all possibilities![2]

It should be also understood that nothing becomes real in the physical world without the intermediation of the self-conscious mind. Humans were fashioned with a brain that acts as transformer of this life power (electromagnetic energy), which permeates the universe. Consciousness eternally unfolds to express itself in myriad forms in physical reality. The subject and the object are aspects of the same reality. In a figurative way, the Divine Source, in order to express itself, takes its substance and arranges it into innumerable forms, to which humans give names. However, this substance (or mental stuff) is not static or immobile but a "flowing reality." This "flowing reality" is captured or seized by the human conscious mind, which transforms it into a specific type of manifestation.

According to this idea, everything in physical reality should be regarded as the manifestation of this universal cosmic energy. Everything in the universe is made of electromagnetic energy that is vibrating at different rates—the chair where one sits, the book one holds, the clothing one wears, the walls of one's house, the car one drives, and so on; all are made of the same substance.

Albert Einstein demonstrated the immateriality of this world with his famous equation $E=mc^2$. All matter is energy in a vibrational condition—everything in the universe is pure energy at different rates of vibration. Metaphysical schools hold that our thoughts and emotions are the same energy as any physical matter. Furthermore, physicist Max Planck and others have confirmed that we live in a world where everything visible and invisible to our naked eyes is a vibration of energy.

Quantum physics is the study of tiny units radiating waves, forces whose nonphysical movement creates physical reality; it involves the investigation of the ultimate nature of physical reality. Expressed in a different way, it is the study of the behavior of sub atomic particles—the physics of possibilities or choices. It posits that there are no such things as solids or dead matter; everything is in a continuous vibratory state and there is energy even at zero point, or ground state. The brain turns these possibilities into actualities. When something is observed, quanta come together to form subatomic particles, then atoms, then molecules, until finally manifesting in the physical realm in accordance with the thought-form of the observer.

Furthermore, quantum mechanics considers that *atoms are made from spinning, immaterial energy vortices*; consequently, the physical universe is indeed immaterial.[3] According to this theory, *external circumstances are susceptible to being changed by the observer*. Based on this postulate, Wayne Dyer states, "If you change the way you look at things, the things you look at change." That is, everything resides in the individual's attitude; each person experiences a unique reality, different from that of any other individual.

The difference between what we consider solid on one hand, such as matter (diamonds, rocks, etc.) and not solid, on the other hand, such as thoughts and emotions, is only a difference in rates of vibration. Winner of the Nobel Prize in 1918, physicist and contemporary of Albert Einstein, Max Planck eloquently explained the idea that everything in the world is governed by a universal mind (consciousness). Planck explained his concept of the nature of reality as follows:

> As a man who has devoted his whole life to the most clear-headed science, to the study of matter, I can tell you as a result of my research of atoms this much: There is no matter as such. All matter originates and exists only by virtue of a force which brings the particles of an atom to vibration and holds this minute solar system of the atom together. We must assume behind this force the existence of a conscious and intelligent mind. *This mind is the matrix of all matter.*" (emphasis added)

It should be noted that Planck states that "mind is the matrix of all matter." In other words, it can be said that consciousness is the root of all creation.

To the ontological question of who is the thinker, the answer is given by the major world religions; according to the sacred Hindu book the Bhagavad Gita, the Supreme Being Krishna is the only thinker and doer. In the Western mystery tradition exemplified by the Qabalah, God, who dwells in every human being, is the only thinker and doer. This is confirmed by Jesus Christ when he said, "the Father that dwelleth in me, he doeth the works" (John 14:10, KJV).

It is extremely interesting to note that different scholars and authors offer the same message about the life power from different standpoints. Madame Blavatsky (Theosophist), Paul Foster Case (Qabalist), Carl G. Jung (psychiatrist), Joseph Murphy (New Thought minister), and Neville Goddard (New Thought writer and thinker) all taught that the universal consciousness is the origin as well as the substance of the entire universe; their teachings are complementary and support one another.

The only reality is the universal consciousness; everything is made out of it. *The Book of Tokens* is an inspirational poetic meditation on the twenty-two-letter Hebrew alphabet, received by Paul F. Case through his inner self. *The Book of Tokens* states, "For the sake of creation the One Life that I am seemeth [sic] to divide itself, becoming two."[4] Case further clarifies that "This division is called the superior nature and the inferior nature"[5] (underline in original). The superior nature corresponds to the conscious mind and the inferior to the subconscious; however, that distinction of inferior and superior is only for explanatory purposes, as both are exactly equal in importance. Esoteric psychology considers the self-conscious to be the objective, or male, part, and the subconscious is the subjective, or female, aspect. The subconscious is the womb of creation, the mother, known in Qabalah[6] as Binah and in Hindu philosophy as Prakriti.

I propose that humans have inalienable metaphysical rights to accomplish their spiritual development or spiritual awakening. These can be enumerated as follows:

1. the power of self-determination (free will),
2. the right to one's own beliefs, and
3. the will to create one's reality and social environment.

These metaphysical principles are humans' innate and immutable rights for the unfolding of human consciousness. Self-determination is possible only when there is free will; in turn, free will is based on one's level of awareness. A free choice can be made only when someone is fully aware of it. If there is no awareness, there is no free will. Awareness (charged with emotions) attracts the stream of the electromagnetic energy (or quanta).

Then, it is to the quality of thoughts that one must turn to explain *your own universe* (YOU). Author Peter Baksa states, "The theories and scientific research in this particular area of quantum physics lay the ground work for attempting to explain how our thoughts commingle with everything else, and cause matter to manifest in our lives."[7]

It is interesting to mention that in the middle of the nineteenth century, British philosopher, biologist, and sociologist Herbert Spencer (1820–1903) spoke in scientific terms of the existence of the universal life power, which in modern scientific terms is called the zero point field (or zero point energy). Talking about the ultimate reality, Spencer ends his second volume of his book *Principles of Sociology* (1896) with the following words:

> One truth must grow ever clearer—the truth that there is an Inscrutable Existence everywhere manifested, to which he [the man of science] can neither find nor conceive either beginning or end. Amid the mysteries which become the more mysterious the more they are thought about, there will remain the one absolute certainty, that he is ever in presence of an Infinite and Eternal Energy, from which all things proceed."[8]

This statement concurs with the Hermetic Principle of Mentalism. That is to say, the universe is mental, or made of "mind stuff." In addition, Spencer's conceptions about evolution and rhythm are in agreement with Hermetic teachings regarding the principle of rhythm, as will be explained later.

Both Oriental and Occidental philosophies are in agreement that the universe is mental; in other words, everything existent in the whole universe is consciousness or pure spirit, which is manifested in myriad forms in the visible and invisible world. Consciousness is the *one* power, which is intelligent and functional. Humans capture this one force, or electromagnetic energy, via their etheric bodies and express it as thought-forms through their brains. Thought-forms pumped with feelings/emotions tend to become actualities in the physical realm when they are firmly held in the conscious mind.

In addition to the Hermetic Qabalah and Hindu Vedanta, science—notably quantum physics—agrees that ultimate reality is an ongoing unfolding of universal consciousness. Furthermore, philosophers including Kant and Hegel, psychologists C. G. Jung and Viktor Frankl, and scientists Einstein and Planck have all said that humans' purpose in life is to unfold their consciousness.

Occidental civilization and science are both greatly indebted to Greek philosophers Pythagoras, Socrates, and Plato, for they are the ones who established the fundamentals of what is now known as Western philosophy—the science of the mind—which includes the scientific epistemological principles for the future development of science and philosophy. For the purpose of this work, "cognitive epistemology" is regarded as the quest for scientific knowledge based on solid, logical reasoning; in other words, it is the study of how humans apprehend knowledge by rational thinking and intuition.

Socrates was the first person in the Occidental hemisphere to use the logical argument as a way to acquire knowledge; his approach was to assume that he did not know anything, and his purpose in life was to inquire of people who supposedly did know and argue with them to reach a logical conclusion. Descartes, on the other hand, established what is known as *methodic doubt*. He adopted a skeptical attitude regarding the reliability of the information reported by his five physical senses. Furthermore, he put the knowledge of his time to rigorous tests.

At the turn of the twentieth century, a small book entitled *The Kybalion* was published by an anonymous source. The author used the pen name The Three Initiates.[9] Reportedly, the book is a compilation of the teachings of the Egyptian god Thoth, who is the counterpart of the Greek god Hermes. However, nobody knows what the word *"Kybalion"* means. In all esoteric and occult lore, there is no single document that mentions the existence of this book. Regarding the authorship, there are credible reasons to believe that William Walker Atkinson wrote that tractate. Writers such as Philip Deslippe and Mitch Horowitz have presented conclusive evidence to validate Atkinson as the author of the work.[10]

The beauty of *The Kybalion* is that it comprises the essence of the wisdom of ancient Egypt and Greece, which is condensed in seven axioms. The first of them is the principle of mentalism, which embodies the notion that "all is mind," that the universe is mental. In the Bible, this principle is expressed in the following way: "For in Him we live and move and have our being" (Acts 17:28, NIV). This implies that we live inside, not outside, our creator, because God holds his creation in his mind. As per the Hermetic principle, we are in the mind of God; that is why this principle is called mentalism. This was validated by Max Planck, winner of the Nobel Prize in physics, who held the viewpoint that the matrix of reality is mind, or consciousness.

According to this principle, the external reality we perceive through our physical senses is a manifestation of the universal mental stuff. This mental stuff can be considered "the universal, infinite, and living mind." Qabalistic philosophy says that everything is created out of the *mind stuff*, including trees, insects, mountains, houses, our physical and invisible bodies, and so on. These assertions are confirmed by quantum physics, which holds that the universe is immaterial. Finally, the Emerald Tablet, an ancient piece attributed to Hermes Trismegistus, postulates that everything proceeds from the One and returns to the same One.

Dialectical philosophy considers everything to be in a continuous state of transformation and change. Hinduism states that the world in which we live is a world of illusion and falsehood, that physical manifestation is created by an invisible eternal power that exists beyond the material world, which neither the mind nor the senses are capable of grasping.

Now modern physicists are openly affirming that the universe is mental. For instance, professor emeritus of physics at the University of Virginia, Stanley Sobottka, has posted online "A Course in Consciousness," in which he gives preeminence to consciousness rather than to matter. After long elucidations on scientific, philosophical, and religious considerations, he concludes with a premise and a conclusion as follows:

> The premise: Consciousness is all there is. Another word for Consciousness is the impersonal, yet intimate, I.
>
>   Conclusion: "[. . .] The entire manifestation is an expression of Love.[11]

Furthermore, Richard Conn Henry, professor at the Henry A. Rowland Department of Physics and Astronomy at Johns Hopkins University, Maryland, concludes his scientific paper "The Mental Universe" by indicating that *the universe is immaterial—mental and spiritual.*"[12] In the same paper, Professor Henry quotes British astrophysicist Sir James Jeans, who wrote the book *The Mysterious Universe*, first published in 1930 by the Cambridge University Press. The following is the interesting observation made by Sir Jeans:

> The stream of knowledge is heading towards a non-mechanical reality; the universe begins to look more like a *great thought than like a great machine.* Mind no longer appears to be an accidental intruder into real of matter. . . . We ought rather hail it as the *creator and governor of the real of matter*[13] (emphasis added.)

The beauty of all of this is to know that humans' brains are designed to create—that is, to mold and shape—the fabric of the universal mental stuff with our thoughts and desires. It has been said that without the focus of attention, a quantum would be only a "quantum potential." Quantum physics confirms this by recognizing that something comes into actuality when it is observed and processed by our conscious minds. The universal life force that exists now has eternally existed; it manifests in myriad forms in response to human thought.

In my book *Beyond Conventional Wisdom*, I wrote that "science is in agreement with the metaphysical principle of vibration. Everything in the universe is the expression of different rates of vibration. The Qabalistic tradition says that the mind stuff is pure consciousness, which is in the ultimate analysis, light. Therefore, we live in an ocean of vibration, and the substance of the universe is light or mind stuff. Modern scientists have begun acknowledging as true that everything is pure consciousness."[14]

Nevertheless, it seems there is disagreement in the approach to explaining the nature of ultimate reality. And this is due to the fact that the psychic disposition or idiosyncrasy and way of living in the West are quite different from those of the Occidental world. For these reasons, it seems that the most appropriate spiritual discipline for those who live in the Western hemisphere is the Qabalah. This statement has been endorsed by the late esoteric author Dion Fortune, who indicated that the most suitable spiritual path for the lifestyle of Occidental humankind is the Hermetic Qabalah, which she called the "Yoga of the Occident."[15]

A digression is needed here to explain the difference between the Hermetic Qabalah and the Jewish Kabbalah. The Jewish Kabbalah is essentially the Hebrew mysticism that started with prophet Ezekiel. The Jewish Kabbalah includes the Hebrew Scriptures, the Torah, the Sefer Yetzirah (Book of Formation), the Sefer ha Bahir (Book of Brilliance), the Zohar (Book of Splendor), and the Talmud.

Meanwhile the Hermetic Qabalah is a later phenomenon that was originated in the Italian Renaissance. It arose with the Christian Qabalah initiated by Count Giovanni Pico della Mirandola (1463–1494); he was an Italian scholar and philosopher who at the age of twenty-three published the remarkable work *Oration on the Dignity of Man* (1486).[16] It is unfortunate that he died at the very young age of thirty-one. Mirandola was familiar with most knowledge of the time. In his seventy-two Qabalistic *Conclusions,* he wrote, "No science can better convince us of the divinity of Jesus Christ than magic and the Kabbalah."[17]

The modern Hermetic Qabalah basically comes from the fusion of the best teachings of Hebrew esoteric tradition, Neoplatonism, Gnosticism, and Christianity. It embraces the teachings of the Jewish Kabbalah; in addition it incorporates disciplines such as astrology, Tarot, alchemy, and Hermetic philosophy (a collection of texts attributed to Hermes Trismegistus). These disciplines are rejected by the Hebrew Kabbalah, but Hermetic Qabalah is a syncretic system that embraces all the above sources. I am using the word "Kabbalah" to refer to the Jewish tradition and "Qabalah" to refer to the Hermetic tradition. Having made that clarification, we can proceed with our deliberations.

Western philosophy has developed based on rational thinking and scientific experience. People in the West tend to be more practical and directed toward mastering the material world, while those in the East rely heavily on meditative and mystical experiences. Eastern culture is basically devoted to meditation and ascetic life. In addition, according to the teachings of the Western Mystery Tradition (Hermetic Qabalah), humans are supposed to conquer the physical plane rather from escape from it.

The teachings of Hinduism and its offshoot, Buddhism, are fundamentally directed toward training the minds of devotees and disciples, who seriously commit to a lifetime of renunciation, austerity, community work, and ascetic life. This kind of discipline is more suitable to the Oriental mind-set, which is socially and traditionally conditioned to a life of austerity. In the Occident, the modern lifestyle is very different from that of Eastern people. People in the West are more engaged with social activities, family, work obligations, and responsibilities. Western philosophy is devoted to expanding consciousness.

Thus, the two approaches are opposite conceptions for achieving realization. While one pursues the annihilation of the "ego and the Self," the other seeks dominion over the physical realm and over oneself to reach the divine. In Western philosophy the expansion of awareness is of primary importance for gaining mastery over the sensorial realm and the physical world.

Buddhism categorically denies the Self. Buddha affirms that there is no Self or ego. It is only an unsolvable puzzle used in Zen Buddhism to provoke enlightenment. According to Buddhism, "there is no way to know oneself as there is no self to know."[18] Concerning the existence of the ego, Jungian psychologist Edward Edinger decisively affirms that the ego "is the bedrock foundation of every individual's existence; we can't deny that the ego exists, because it is the seat of consciousness. Anything else can be denied."[19]

CHAPTER 12

The Will to Create

*You were born with an innate knowledge that you
create your own reality.*[1] (italics in original)
—ESTHER AND JERRY HICKS

HUMANS' EXPANSION OF consciousness is done through their
creative power. That statement is a sine qua non. Lack of innovative creation means no evolution and, in turn, implies stillness and stagnation. Metaphysical teaching holds that everyone is
consciously or unconsciously creating his or her life's experiences
through his or her thoughts and feelings/emotions. It can be confidently stated, based on sound scientific and metaphysical evidence,
that we are active creators of our personal reality, experiences, and
environment, since we have use of reason.

Humans possess the most powerful device under their belt,
which is the *power of creation in the present moment.* Do not let the
present moment slip away by trying to stop it as the proponent of
the power of Now advocates. It is in this present moment that people prepave their future. Thus, the power of Now is to create. Otherwise, creation happens by default; this means that one's reality
and circumstances will be the creations of other people. The mind,
wittingly or unwittingly, is always creating, based on the focus of
attention to externals, such as the influence of the mass media or
suggestions received from other people, movies, or TV, or the beliefs stored in the subconscious mind. This type of creation is called
"by default"; that is, the individual is not aware of it or mindful

about it. Conscious creation involves setting intentions and goals, along with specific plans to reach those goals. Thus, the present moment—the right now—should be the platform for creation and should not be considered a static moment.

Now, the time honored ontological question[2]: Why do we exist? What is the purpose of human existence? To answer this question, we have to consider first that we live in an intentionally driven world. *The purpose of human existence is to expand consciousness,* and this can be achieved only when we exercise our *creative power.* Humans create their own reality, social environment, and circumstances in life, knowingly or unknowingly. This statement is a sine qua non. Stated in a slightly different way, the purpose of human existence is the *will to create* for the expansion of human consciousness. Humans' task is to conquer the physical plane rather than escape from it. Unaware of their innate power, most humans wander planet Earth aimless and confused.

The above sentences are not a far-fetched theory; ancient mystical thought has been propounding this idea for many years. Humans are the rulers of their own creation; they dictate the laws and regulations for their kingdoms (or own creations), and they live according to those standards. However, many do not take command of their mental power, and they become enslaved to their chaotic imagery or end up at the mercy of external circumstances and other people's mental creations. Thoughts are causative; then, the crucial point is to be in control of our own thoughts rather than to feel victims of them.

It is important to keep in mind that humans are the only creatures on earth with the highly evolved capacity of creative faculties. Certain animals may have some capacity for rudimentary creation and thinking, and others may have means of communicating among their species, but what differentiates humans from all living creatures is our capacity to direct the life power through our minds and creative faculties.

The universal consciousness (or life power) created time and space for the sake of manifesting in physical reality through every sentient being. This life power develops better channels (humans) to better manipulate the physical reality. It needs higher terrestrial expressions for the purpose of its own creation. Actually, the only creator is the higher self through human beings. That is why the life power needs suitable means for expression.

This life power unfolds itself into infinite possibilities of self-expression. Metaphysics, scientific disciplines, major religions, psychology, and quantum physics all agree that ultimate reality is an ongoing invisible energy force or field of infinite probabilities. So when humans become aware of their role as a generative beings, they become better and more efficient codesigners with the Creator. The truth of the matter is that, whether or not we are aware of this role, everybody is constantly creating, either wittingly or unwittingly, through the focus of their attention.

Hence, *the point of power is to create in the Now.* That is the only chance one has to seize the flow of the life force—right now, right here. The subconscious mind is continually generating or creating, whether or not one is aware of this. In order to be a conscious designer, one has to focus one's mind on things one wants to manifest in life. It can be said that to be human is to deliberately shape our own personal reality and social environment.

Incidentally, C. G. Jung asserted "that man is indispensable for the completion of creation; that, in fact, he himself is the second creator of the world." He further said, "Human consciousness created objective existence and meaning, and man found his indispensable place in the great process of being."[3]

Prior to any creation, a person sets a goal or direction for the life power to be focused. As simple as this may sound, it is the crux of the matter when it comes to understanding the process of any creation, whether physical or mental. Since the beginning of the universe, no new element has been added to nature. Everything is composed of the same matter, which continually vibrates and changes forms. This is verified by the first law of thermodynamics (conservation of energy) in physics: "Matter can neither be created nor destroyed, only changed in form." The Bible confirms the above statement. Before God created the universe, "the earth was formless and empty" (Genesis 1:2, KJV); then God created the multitude of physical forms that currently exist on the earth. The primal matter existed before creation as mental stuff, but these materials had not yet been compressed and congealed by God's thought.

The process of creation can be verified even in nature. Astrida Orle Tantillo, professor of Germanic studies at the University of Illinois in Chicago, wrote an interesting book entitled *The Will to Create: Goethe's Philosophy of Nature* (University of Pittsburgh Press, 2002). In it, she argues that the common theme throughout Goethe's work is his desire to demonstrate nature's "will to create." This is true if we consider that the whole universe, including humankind and everything else, is a component of ONE thing that is in constant evolution, or more accurately, in creation. There is a force that gives impulse to creation; evolution results from nature's own creativity and striving to unfold. Everything regarded as reality, physical and nonphysical, is pure consciousness manifested in myriad forms. Man's destiny is to develop consciousness through his power of awareness and creative imagination.

Furthermore, the Bible says that "God created man in His own image, in the image of God created him; male and female he created them" (Genesis 1:27, KJV). This should be understood as saying that every human being is endowed with creative power, although some may not be aware of it. Stated in a different way, humans replicate God's creative faculties on the planet Earth, on a minor scale. It can also be said with certainty that humans are "little gods"—sons and daughters of the *Father*, who dwells in humans. If God is the creator of the whole universe, humans are the creators of their "personal universes," or "your own universe" (YOU). We are at different levels of spiritual awakening or awareness, and each person has to work on that accordingly.

Again, the universal law is that humans are continually creating with their thoughts, feelings, and desires; they are giving form to the life power that flows through them. The external reality that we observe is a mingling of creations by millions of people. The leaders of a society and those who have strong will and determination set the tone for creation in each specific society or social group, as they impose their pattern of ideas and beliefs through the mass communication available.

Paraphrasing Jesus, one can say, "The Father, who dwells in me, creates through me." As the creation of the universe continues expanding and unfolding, humanity's role is to mindfully cocreate with God. There is no external deity but the "I Am," known under multiple names such as Father, Ruach Elohim, Prana, Pneuma, Spiritus, zero point field, and so forth.

The truth is that nothing in the world is solid or unchangeable. Quantum mechanics says that when something is not observed by consciousness, the life force is a state of probabilities. That is, when consciousness, through attention, selects and locks the fluidic energy into a specific thought-form, emotions attract these thought-forms to manifest in the physical plane. However, this attraction occurs only when someone is in emotional resonance with the desired object; otherwise, the attraction does not happen. That is, consciousness can be aware of a thought-form, but if it does not have any emotional investment in that thought-form, there will be no manifestation.

Incidentally, the conscious mind does not do the creating; its power is limited to selecting, choosing, and suggesting. It is the subconscious mind that engages in the creative process in conformity with the selection of consciousness.

Some people unaware of their creative power have relinquished it and inadvertently allow "others" to create their reality for them. These others include the mass media, role models, bourgeois education, and so forth, which can be subsumed under the concept of "conventional wisdom." Conventional wisdom is a powerful means of indirectly implanting subservient beliefs, behavior patterns, and mental subjugation to the dominant socioeconomic classes. Under these circumstances, humans are not fully free to create their reality and experiences; instead, they passively accept things imposed by social media, churches, political organizations, and so on.

Nowadays, metaphysical organizations, psychology, and science, notably quantum physics, agree that ultimate reality is an ongoing unfolding of consciousness, which is manifested by the human capacity to create. No creation means no evolution, which implies stagnation and stillness. This is why the concept of the power of Now as proposed by Tolle is inappropriate. The beginning of every deliberate creation is "intention"; one cannot leave the mind blank and expect something to happen. Human creation starts with an intention or desire; if there is no intention, there is no volition. Thus, volition (energy) follows intention. Intention is a focused thought that sets a goal or direction toward where the action will be directed. As simple as it may sound, this is the crux of the matter.

Here, one of the most important metaphysical concepts, the Law of Attraction, propounded by the New Thought writer William Walker Atkinson in the early 1900s[4] and lately popularized by "Abraham," a group of nonphysical masters who channel through Esther Hicks, comes into play. "Abraham" holds the viewpoint that everything emanates from one source called Source Energy and their intention is to help humankind to remember that we are "extensions of Source Energy."[5] They affirm that humans are creators of their own experience.[6] Furthermore, Chapter 3 of the book *Ask and It Is Given* is explicitly devoted to explaining how humans create their own reality.

The metaphysical process of creation can be explained as follows: *Thoughts are energy in vibration and energy follows thoughts.* The focus of attention locks the life force in thought-forms, and emotions/feelings attract it to manifestation.

By the end of the nineteenth century, American author Thomson J. Hudson formulated his famous hypothesis about psychic phenomena. It has far-reaching importance in the field of psychology and sheds light on how the mind operates in normal circumstances. Before that, psychology had struggled to a find a single coherent theory to explain the manifestations of psychic phenomena as well as the relationship between the conscious and the subconscious minds. Hudson's psychological hypothesis was outlined in my book *Healing Without Medicine* as follows:

1. A human being has two minds: the *objective mind* (self-conscious) and the *subjective mind* (subconscious). Each one is endowed with separate and distinct powers; each one is capable, under certain conditions, of independent action.

2. The subjective mind is constantly amenable to control by suggestion.
3. The subjective mind is incapable of inductive reasoning.[7]

I would add the following as a corollary to the above hypothesis: it appears that the *subconscious has a mind of its own* because it has a capacity for deductive reasoning and acts, most of the time independently of the conscious mind, based on its own inferences. Regarding this subject, I came across a whole chapter Jung wrote back in 1937, entitled "The Autonomy of the Unconscious," which supports the above statement.[8] In general, the subconscious makes inferences from the data submitted to it through attention from the self-conscious mind. Regarding this topic, I further indicate, in my book mentioned above, the following:

> The self-conscious mind is the part that plans, thinks, and takes initiative, but the agent that will carry out these plans and bring them into fruition is the subconscious mind. Therefore, the role of the self-conscious mind is limited to reasoning, initiating, and setting goals. It can discriminate and decide what kind of information to focus upon; it also has the power to reprogram the software of the subconscious mind. Once the "program" is submitted to the subconscious, it becomes automatic or second nature.[9]

Consequently, the role of the self-conscious mind is to conceive an idea (thought) and impress that thought via an image with emotion to the subconscious. The subconscious, in turn, brings into fruition the images submitted to it. All things of the visible and invisible worlds emanate from the universal subconscious mind. The capacity for deliberate creation comes through the power to imagine our personal world. The subconscious is the seat of feelings and emotions.

The subconscious accepts the *interpretation* a person gives to his or her daily life as true; it has no power of discrimination. For instance, a person who has ideas of self-punishment instilled in the subconscious will respond to specific events accordingly. Instead of taking the challenges that life presents as something from which he or she can learn and grow mentally and spiritually, the person will view them as life punishing or the world being against him or her, creating a vicious circle. These interpretations of life experiences are recorded in the personal subconscious and constitute the data or archive from which the subconscious elaborates, by a process of deduction, further conclusions and creates future circumstances that match what is in the person's subconscious mind. Thus, all creation occurs in the domain of the subconscious. The subconscious is not concerned with whether our beliefs are rational or irrational. It always accepts everything submitted by the conscious mind as true.

Regarding affirmations, the most effective ones start with the magical words "I Am" and are expressed in present tense with the feeling that they already have crystallized. Affirmations formulated in future tense acknowledge the lack of something, when the idea is to dwell in the assurance that the supply for whatever one wants is out there at the present time. Napoleon Hill expressed an interesting proposition: "Whatever the mind can conceive and believe, it can achieve." To this, one can add, feel something as true, and the subconscious will do the rest for the desire to be fulfilled.

Neville Goddard's contribution to explaining the process of mental creation is the incorporation of the concept of feelings. Goddard exclaims in his YouTube videos that "feeling is the secret." Indeed, one's desires endorsed with strong emotion have an indelible influence on the subconscious mind. Thus, a suggestion is readily admitted by the subconscious when there is an emotional component to it, which in this case is an authentic feeling for the desired outcome.

Goddard recommends getting into the state desired by simulating *the feeling,* or, as Esther Hicks indicates, getting into vibrational harmony with the desired object. Once one captures the feeling associated with the person one wants to be or the object one wants to have, he or she should release it to the universe and dwell on the assurance that it will be so.

Interestingly, awareness of the trend of our thoughts gives us the capacity to choose those thoughts that are helpful to us and reject the negative ones; in this way, we give direction to the focus of our conscious mind.

The brain is an epiphenomenon of consciousness. Humans use the thinking process as a part of awareness; thoughts cannot exist without consciousness. The problem is that some individuals do not think consciously; for this reason, it has been said that 2 percent of people really think, 3 percent think they think, and 95 percent allow others to think for them.[10]

The dialectical law named the Coexistence of Opposites and the Hermetic Principle of Polarity declare that "everything has its counterpart," which is also its complement. For instance, all things manifested in the physical realm have two sides. Thus, by simple logic, physical reality has to have its equivalent, which is the invisible world from which the physical world springs. Concerning this, Paul F. Case states, in his correspondence lessons, "There are not two antagonistic powers, one making for life, the other for death. There is only a single power which has twofold manifestation."[11]

In order to create our desired reality, we must focus our thoughts in order to influence the quanta—the zero point field—and then attune ourselves to the vibrational harmony of our desires. This process gives form to the formless substance around us—the quanta—from which all things are made and take shape in accordance with thought-forms. When the vibration of a thought-form comes into vibrational harmony with this formless creation, it expresses this thought-form in the physical world as a physical manifestation.

The key idea to consider here is that human beings are individuations of the superconscious mind. Humans were created in the "image" of God with the same prerogatives; that is, we are a depository of God's creative power on a minor scale, meaning that although we are "individuations," we are also integral aspects of that superconscious mind with the capacity for creation. The whole universe and everything in it is a single entity; there is no separateness. The other notion that needs to be kept in mind is that the only way we can have contact with the superconscious mind is through the subconscious mind.

The universal subconscious mind manifests itself in physical reality as vibratory energy; everything exists as reality due to the manifestation of this energy. The universal subconscious mind is the "prime matter," or fabric, of reality. The entire universe and everything within it at all levels and dimensions are direct expressions of the universal mind, which is infinite; it is conscious and intelligent life power. It may act as a blind force when it is not properly and constructively channeled by humankind.

The above considerations support the notion that the purpose of life is to create for the betterment of humanity and the expansion of consciousness. According to Jung, God needs humankind in order to achieve a greater level of consciousness. Unfortunately, the power that dwells in individuals to create their reality has been diminished by social programming and social indoctrination. Regrettably, most of the time, human behavior is the result of automated stimulus and response to socially domesticated patterns. Thus, the power of Now is to consciously create upcoming events, not to attempt to dwell in the illusion of the present moment. The Now as a static present moment means inaction—relinquishing one's creative power. However, the magic of tomorrow amounts to fashioning upcoming events with our thoughts and feelings in the present moment, right here, right now. This process is the very basis of how each person creates their own reality. Every single thought, as energy, directly and instantly influences the quantum field, causing quanta, in the form of energy, to arrange themselves into a localized, observable event.

The word "now" is a metaphorical term to indicate the ongoing "present moment." In absolute terms, there is no such thing as now. It is not possible to pinpoint the Now in the unfolding process of time and say, from here starts the past and from there starts the future. As soon as one marks the line, now turns into the past, and the future becomes now. As my personal friend Julio Miguel says, "As soon as one finishes saying now, it became past." In relative terms, it can be said that there is only an everlasting flowing of the future into the present and the present becoming the past. Thus, the power of Now is really about seizing the present to create the future. That is, the power of the present moment is the awareness to create now.

In passing, it should be mentioned that a very influential German existential philosopher, Martin Heidegger (1889–1976), in his book *Being and Time* (1927), considers *time* to be a fundamental factor in his ontological elucidations about human authenticity. According to Heidegger, human existence is historical and humans tend to see the world in the sense of the future; that is, humans usually see the world in term of possibilities, such as future options, aspirations, projects, and hopes.[12] Professor of philosophy Robert C. Solomon, of the University of Texas at Austin, in his audio courses on existentialism, asserts, "The future and the past define the present."[13] From these statements, it can be deduced that time is a basic element for human existence.

In the chronological scheme of things, the Now does not exist, because time is an aggregation of moments of quanta that constantly flows, similar to a river, which consists of multiple drops of water. We are usually aware of something when it has already gone; there is always a becoming and an ending in everything.

In an altered state of mind such as that produced by powerful meditation or induced by *ayahuasca* or hallucinogenic drugs, a person can go beyond space and time and experience nonspatial perceptions, where there is no time; but unfortunately, at the end of the session, the subject has to come back to the body and take care of daily business.

Our physical bodies are confined in time and space. Physical/spatial time and psychic/spiritual time are completely different realities. We live in parallel universes, and the closest to us is the physical one where our bodies exist. We use our bodies and brains to manipulate physical reality.

Humans are instruments of a divine plan. As long we develop our consciousness, we become cocreators with the Creator. Humans' role is to be creators of their own personal realities, social environments, and circumstances for a better world. Jung, in his book *Answer to Job*, indicates that God needs humankind to unfold consciousness. God is expanding along with the development of human consciousness. According to Jung, "God is reality itself." God uses humankind for his own purposes. The inference from this is that humanity's role in this universe is to be a conscious cocreator with the Supreme Being.

Most people are unaware of their creative power and inadvertently relinquish their power to random happenings; this is similar to the situation of a boat in the ocean should the captain abandon command of it to luck. In this case, people's destiny is left to the mercy of others for the creation of their own reality. When humans do not deliberately create their reality and experiences, they passively accept things imposed by the mass media, untested accepted common social beliefs, and so on.

The unstated irrational beliefs that dwell in the subconscious mind usually hinder the crystallization of our goals and dreams. This is why the concept of "psychological or personal congruence" is important. I understand psychological or personal congruence as an agreement or harmonious relationship between the conscious and subconscious desires. Goals and desires in life become reality when there is no contradiction between them. Desires expressed as clear thought-forms quickly come together in the physical plane when the individual gets into vibrational harmony with what he or she desires. Everything an individual experiences is a direct result of the person's thoughts and of the vibrational harmony between the conscious and subconscious minds; this applies equally to positive, negative, or neutral experiences.

This is why it is very important to examine one's habitual state of mind to identify what kinds of ideas actively run there. The act of reprogramming our subconscious has been called "paradigm shift" and involves replacing all negative and self-defeating beliefs in the subconscious with a new set of uplifting and positive ones, such as success, perfect health, desires fulfilled, and so on. For this to be done, a person must bypass the filters of the conscious mind in order to reprogram the software running below human awareness. The subconscious mind is docile to suggestions; that is to say, it never questions anything given, whether as a hint or indirectly; this procedure is similar to the placebo and nocebo effects.

However, and this is very important to consider, the subconscious will not accept any direct demands, coercion, or pressure. It will accept only suggestions or hints and will quickly oppose any direct demands. The Emerald Tablet, an ancient short al-chemical treatise, describes the secret of this process in cryptic words: "Thou shalt separate the earth from the fire, the subtle from the gross, suavely, and with great ingenuity." This is why the key of the matter—conveying an idea to the subconscious mind—has to be done in an indirect manner via suggestions.

The conscious mind, that is, our everyday waking mind, is heavily influenced by the materialistic demands of the false ego most of the time; it filters and logically analyzes everything presented to it, allowing only thoughts and ideas that are consistent with the belief system of the individual.

The power of beliefs has been called the Law of Life. I call it the template of one's destiny. There are some beliefs so ingrained and rationalized in our minds that we take them for granted and implicitly consider them to be part of our "normal" outlook on life. These hidden beliefs control our lives and create our external conditions. One's character is the sum of all one's thoughts and attitudes, whether correct or incorrect. Some people are willing to improve their circumstances but unwilling to honestly explore their core beliefs and correct the negative ones. They therefore remain bound to self-defeating beliefs and consequently perpetuate and replicate the same circumstances and situations over and over again.

The power of concentration is verified by quantum mechanics, which says that a concentrated thought shapes quantum energy. This confirms the assertion that the physical universe is indeed immaterial. Furthermore, quantum physics holds that *external circumstances are susceptible to being changed by the attention of an observer.* That is, everything resides in the individual's mental attitude. Each person experiences a unique reality according to his or her level of awareness and spiritual maturity.

Goddard provides a metaphysical explanation of this concept when he states, "The world moves with motiveless necessity. By this is meant that it has no motive of its own, but is under the necessity of manifesting your concept, the arrangement of your mind, and *your mind is always arranged in the image of all you believe and consent to as true*"[14] (italics in original). Humans give direction and purpose to this magical energy. Quantum mechanics affirms that reality is fluidic in nature; when something, a quantum, is not observed by humans, it exists only in a formless or latent state of probabilities. It is consciousness through the human brain that shapes or transforms this universal energy into myriad forms.

In summary, my fundamental proposition is that the point of power is to create in the *present moment*. If we do not use the present moment to create our future, others will create it for us, meaning our creation will be based on the ideas of other people and the mass media and the like. Attempting to stop the flow of life under the concept of "Now" results in a passive attitude and relinquishing of the power to have active control over one's life.

In the physical realm, there is no such thing as now because reality swiftly unfolds all the time. The concepts of time and space are intrinsically connected to each other; where there is no time, there is no space. Expressed in a different way, when the element of time is eliminated, there is no physical realm (space). If time and space are eliminated, one is out of tridimensional reality, existing in another dimension in an everlasting now (without a corporeal body). The fact that one's body occupies a fragment of space means one is subject to time.

Imagination is a powerful mental instrument for creation; deliberate creation begins with clear-cut pictures in the mind. Creation is first conducted in the mental plane and then crystallizes in the physical plane through our emotions and feelings. However, it is important to remember that the inner self that dwells in each individual is the *only* true creator.

Interesting enough, Napoleon Hill called the faculty of "creative imagination" the "sixth sense." He asserts that those who know how to use it are the ones who succeed in every life enterprise. The difference between an ordinary human and those who are healthy, wealthy, and prosperous are those who use the capacity of creative imagination. He further indicates that the faculty of creative imagination "is the direct link between the finite mind of man and Infinite Intelligence." Hill explains:

This sixth sense is "Creative Imagination." The faculty of creative imagination is one which the majority of people never use during an entire lifetime, and if used at all, it usually happens by mere accident. A relatively small number of people use, with deliberation and purpose aforethought, the faculty of creative imagination. Those who use this faculty voluntarily, and with understanding of its functions, are genii.[14]

Properly speaking, human imagination is the creative power of the higher self dwelling in humans. Mental images supported by beliefs and determination are the most powerful elements for creation. Through imagination, one gives shape to thought-forms and captures quantum energy. One can manifest one's heart's desire through the use of imagination. Nothing is impossible when it comes to imagination, and that capacity is innate to anyone. The power of imagination is unlimited, and one can accomplish whatever one wants in life as long as it is aligned with good deeds.

Again, humans, through the power of our imagination, create our own reality. More accurately, the higher self, who dwells in every human being, creates this reality according to human decisions. The vibrational attunement expressed in feelings and emotions coagulates the thought-forms into physical form. Neville agrees with this statement when he affirms the importance of "the knowledge that your creator is the very self of yourself."[15]

Case asserts that the place of humankind "in the scheme of things is to act as a transformer of energy." That is, humankind is the transformer of the electromagnetic energy available to anyone, and this transformation means creation. As Case further indicates, this "force flows <u>through</u> you to whatever you give your full measure of attention. Nothing can withstand the mental force of one who has mastered the art of concentration"[16] (underline in original).

I confess it took me some time to grasp the real meaning of Case's definition regarding *concentration*. He writes, "CONCENTRATION IS THE COLLECTION AT A CENTER, OR FOCUS, OF UNITS OF FORCE. These units are always units of the LIFE POWER."[17] He also defines "*attention*" as the "<u>means</u> which enables you to concentrate units of mental energy." He further advises, "Never forget that you are directing a <u>real force</u> when you practice concentration"[18] (capital letters and underline in original).

The self-conscious is the creator and transformer of one's reality. Thoughts are vibratory energy and have the power to impact the vibrations of the objects and circumstances around a person. Thomson Jay Hudson postulated that the subconscious is the medium for any psychic phenomenon that takes place. Indeed, the subconscious mind has been regarded by occult psychology since ancient times as an etheric ocean present in the entire world, a view confirmed by the Law of Conservation of Energy. This physical law states that "the sum total of energy in the universe is constant." Thus, "energy is all that is." This electromagnetic energy takes shape in myriad forms in the whole universe.

Finally, I should mention the well-known author Deepak Chopra, who stresses, in his writings, humans' creative capacity. He openly declares in his *Book of Secrets*: "The one reality has already revealed a deep secret: *Being a creator is more important than the whole world.*"[19] He further stresses this idea in his latest work, *You Are the Universe: Discovering Your Cosmic Self and Why It Matters* (2017), coauthored with physicist Menas C. Kafatos: "We are creators of reality living in a conscious universe that responds to our minds."[20] As a matter of fact, the whole book revolves around the thesis that the universe exists because of human consciousness.[21]

CHAPTER 13

The Qabalah and the Quaternity Principle

IN THE OCCIDENTAL world, Socrates was the first philosopher who articulated, in the Philebus dialogue, the notion that all things extant in the universe can be categorized into four divisions.[1] This can be understood as the tetrad composition of physical and metaphysical things; it is called the quaternity principle or *the rule of four*. This theory has been prevalent in Occidental religions and in metaphysical, gnostic, and esoteric literature, as will be explained hereafter. The quaternity principle seems to be the cornerstone of both the Jewish Kabbalah and the Hermetic Qabalah. Indeed, it can be said that the philosophical, esoteric, and theological literature of Western thought rests on the tetrad, or fourfold, structure of things; this is conspicuously found in Jewish sacred scriptures and the New Testament, as well as in philosophical and psychological literature. In Jungian psychology, the quaternity principle is regarded as the archetypical foundation of the human psyche.

The quaternity principle can be verified in the world's four cardinal directions; the four seasons; the four classical elements: fire (plasma), water (liquid), air (gas), and earth (solid); in psychology, the four temperaments of classic personality: sanguine, choleric, melancholic, and phlegmatic; and so forth. The quaternity principle expresses symbolically in the structure of the world and mirrors the nature of divine mystery. In esoteric numerology the quaternity means unity, as the four first digits of our numeral system return to one as follows: $1 + 2 + 3 + 4 = 10$, which by theosophical reduction comes back to one ($1 + 0 = 1$).

Moreover, in the New Testament, there are four Gospels and four evangelists; in the Old Testament, Ezekiel's vision consists of four creatures; and so on. The fundamental teaching of Buddhism is based on the Four Noble Truths, the fourth of which is the Eightfold Path. Buddha had an encounter with four entities: a sick man, an old man, a dead man, and a monk. The tetrad configuration of things seems to be common in religions such as Buddhism, Judaism, and Christianity.

Moreover, the Hebrew name given to the God of Israel, YHWH (wrongly translated as Jehovah or Yahweh), is composed of four Hebrew letters, for this reason, it is called the Tetragrammaton. In addition to *YHWH*, there are three other divine names mentioned in the Bible, each composed of four letters: *AHIH* (Eheyeh), meaning "I Am"; *ADNI* (Adonai), meaning the LORD; and *AGLA*, a Hebrew acronym for the phrase "Atah Gibor Le-olam Adonai," meaning "Thou art mighty forever, LORD." Hence, the quaternity principle is evidenced twice in this case, as there are four divine names each consisting of four letters (or four Tetragrammatons).

Nevertheless, most of the renowned Western occultists and esoteric writers regard the name (YHWH), commonly rendered as Yahweh or Jehovah, as the fundamental Tetragrammaton; they regard it as the most powerful and sacred word of the Western mystery tradition; it is also considered the master key to open the secrets of Freemasonry, Hebrew Kabbalah, the Hermetic Qabalah, and so forth. I think this is an overreaching statement that is based on medieval folklore, coming through Éliphas Lévi, who is considered to be the father of the modern "Western mystery tradition."

The above statement is taught as an axiom by the most respectable and authoritative scholars on these subjects as well as by the

Esoteric Order of the Golden Dawn. For instance, a highly respected scholar on Hermetic Qabalah and Tarot wisdom states, "The highest name of God, which is the Tetragrammaton, rendered in the West as both Jehovah and Yahweh, is the secret pattern behind the four elements."[2] He further indicates in a subsequent paragraph: "The secret of the Tetragrammaton is the basis for the elemental attributes of the Minor Arcana in the Tarot."[3] This is exactly what all the commentators and writers on the Western mystery tradition hold as truth. In addition, it should also be added, the Tetragrammaton: Yahweh is also applied to the quaternity composition of the Tree of Life, the four worlds or planes of existence of Qabalah, and so on.

However, I will argue that this is an unfounded hypothesis. My thesis is that all those classifications based on the four Hebrew letters that make up the name Yahweh are nothing other than the divisions based on the quaternity principle, or fourfold division of things. I will further argue that either name—Ehyeh, Yahweh, Adonai, or AGLA—can be chosen as the superior Tetragrammaton, because all of them are composed of four Hebrew letters. Even the magical name "Abracadabra," which starts and ends with the Hebrew letter Aleph, can be regarded as a Tetragrammaton. According to the Qabalist David A. Hulse, the word "Abracadabra" is "defined as the Word of Four or Fourfold Word."[4]

I advance the thesis that the sacred name *Ehyeh* seems more appropriate to be considered the fundamental Tetragrammaton, because it is the real name of God and because it starts with the Hebrew letter Aleph, which is the first letter of the sacred Hebrew alphabet. Aleph (bull or ox Hebrew) is "symbol of creative energy, and of the vital principle of living creatures."[5] Indeed, Aleph is the emblem of the ongoing unfolding of the life power; meanwhile, the word "Yahweh" starts with the letter Yod, which represents an open hand or a phallic symbol.

I further disagree with the notion that the ancient mysteries have been preserved in magical codes or magical alphabets and there is a secret knowledge encrypted in them, of which only those selected by or initiated into secret societies are entitled to partake. I have already argued elsewhere that "most of the so-called secrets are in plain sight for those who know how to look for them and have developed their inner resources."[6]

This notion of "mystery" and "secret knowledge" coming down from ancient cultures has been demonstrated to be a fallacy. One example is the huge upset in the occult and esoteric tradition when the founders of "Esoteric Order of the Golden Dawn" claimed having the privileges to establish that organization in 1888, based on the existence of a mysterious *Cipher Manuscript*. They also claimed to be in contact with a Germanic secret society that had a direct lineage from an existing medieval Rosicrucian order of the seventeenth century, which was instituted by the mythical and legendary Christian Rosenkreuz. All these allegations were demonstrated, beyond any shadow of a doubt, to be fallacies fabricated by the founders of the Golden Dawn.[7] Nevertheless, one cannot deny the tremendous influence of this organization in all areas of occult, esoteric, and metaphysic literature.

Returning to our discussion, after this short and interesting digression, in the field of modern psychology the importance of the quaternity was shown by C. G. Jung, who found the quaternity principle to be a fundamental theoretical symbol extant in the collective unconscious. Regarding this, Jungian psychologist Edward F. Edinger says:

> One of Jung's major discoveries is the psychological significance of the number four as it relates to the symbolism of psychic wholeness and the four functions. The significance of the quaternity is basic to his whole theory of the psyche, both as regards its structure and its developmental goal, the individuation process.[8]

Indeed, Jung regarded the quaternity as the most important symbol, even more important than the trinity. He considered the quaternity to be an archetype of almost universal occurrence. According to Jung, "the quaternity is the *sine qua non* of divine birth and, consequently, of the inner life of the trinity."[9] Moreover, the quaternity forms the "archetype of wholeness" and can lead to the discovery of God within. Jung asserts:

> Since a God identical with the individual man is an exceedingly complex assumption bordering on heresy, the "God within" also presents a dogmatic difficulty. But the quaternity as produced by the modern psyche points directly not only to the God within, but to the identity of God and man.[10]

In Catholic dogma, the concept of the Holy Trinity holds that God exists in three different persons: the Father, the Son, and the Holy Spirit; that is, one God in three divine persons. It follows that God, although he is part of the Father, the Son, or the Holy Ghost, is above and beyond all of them. This implicitly means there are four divine persons: God personified in the Father, in the Son, and in the Holy Spirit.

Furthermore, Jung asserts, "Contrary to the dogma, there are not three, but four aspects. It could be easily be inferred that the fourth represents the devil."[11] This position could be harmonized with the theory of "absolute monism," the oneness of life. In Hinduism, this is expressed in the Advaita Vedanta, which holds the metaphysical and theological view that all is One—God manifests in all his creation.

On the other hand, according to the dialectic method of reasoning, which is of paramount importance in the development of Occidental thought, the trinity entails quaternity in a dialectical discourse, as follows: a *thesis* always implies an *antithesis*, and these two get resolved in a *synthesis*. The synthesis becomes a *new thesis* at another level, making a quaternity, and the dialectical process or reasoning continues ad infinitum. The new thesis, or quaternity, marks the transition from one stage to another, on a higher level. Thus, the dialectic method explains the fourfold nature of physical and nonphysical phenomena in the universe. According to the dialectical perspective, the structure of physical and nonphysical things can be classified in four stages or categories.

This is better understood numerically:

THESIS	ANTITHESIS	SYNTHESIS	NEW THESIS (Quaternity)
1	2	3	4
4	5	6	7
7	8	9	10
10 (return to unity)	11	12	13
13 and so on			

According to theosophical addition and reduction, every numeral of two or more digits is always reduced to a single digit as follows: The number 10 is reduced to 1 (1 + 0 = 1); 11 is reduced to 2 (1 + 1), 12 = 3, 13 (1 + 3) = 4, and so forth. The quantity 2345 is reduced to number 5, because 2 + 3 + 4 + 5 = 14, and in turn 14 = 1 + 4 = 5.

The Jewish Kabbalah, which originated with the prophet Ezekiel's vision, describes a dramatic vision of a chariot-like object and four living beings resembling a lion, an ox, a man, and an eagle. Ezekiel describes them as follows: "Their faces looked like this: Each of the four had the face of a man, and on the right side each had the face of a lion, and on the left the face of an ox; each also had the face of an eagle" (Ezekiel 1:10, NIV). John the Apostle had a similar vision, recorded in Revelation 4:6–7 (NIV): "In the center, around the throne, were four living beings, and they were covered with eyes, in front and behind. The first living being was like a lion, the second was like an ox, the third had a face like a man, the fourth was like a flying eagle." Later esoteric and metaphysical authors have attributed these four beings to the four Gospels of the New Testament: Mark = ox, Matthew = lion, Luke = man, and John = eagle.

An ancient Hermetic adage declares that humankind (the microcosm) is the epitome or reflection of the universe (the macrocosm). Expressed in a slightly different way, there is an intimate relation between the cosmos and the human psyche.[12] According to the Hermetic Principle of Correspondence expressed in the Emerald Tablet, "that which is Above, is as that which is Below. That which is Below, is as that which is Above to perform the miracle of the One BEING" (capitalization in original). This is verified by the fourfold Qabalistic composition of the universe and by the fourfold constitution of humans described below.

In Qabalah it is taught that there are four worlds, or planes of existence, which are the emanations of the life power through successive stages; they are as follows:

1. **Atziluth,** or the Archetypal world, is the world of emanations, or sefirot, the highest of the four worlds. This realm consists of the first triad (or the three highest sefirot) of the Qabalistic Tree of Life: Keter, Hokhmah, and Binah.
2. **Briah,** or the Creative world, the second triad, is known as the realm of ideas. This is a world of abstract intellect. The realm of Briah is composed of the following three sefirot of the Qabalistic Tree of Life: Hesed, Din/Gevurah, and Tiferet.
3. **Yetzirah,** or the Formative world, the third triad, corresponds to the astral plane, or the collective unconscious, also known as the *anima mundi* (world soul). It is the world of thought-forms. Yetzirah is composed of the three lower sefirot of the Tree of Life: Netzah, Hod, and Yesod.
4. **Assiah,** or the Material world, is the plane of the actual physical forms that affect our corporeal senses. It is the realm of effects. It is also known as the pendant sefirah (singular). Only one sefirah of the Qabalistic Tree of Life, Malkut, belongs to this plane.

In summary, according to the Qabalistic tradition, the four worlds, or planes of existence, at the macrocosm level are the Archetypical world, the Creative world, the Formative world, and the Material world. These have their correspondences at the microcosm level with the Spiritual plane, the Mental plane, the Astral plane, and the Corporeal body. Therefore, a human being, in metaphysical terms, is understood as a replica or reflection of the whole universe.

1. *The Spiritual plane* is considered to be the root of consciousness and the innermost essence of the soul. The

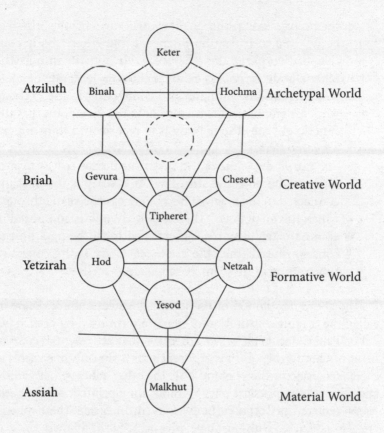

The Qabalistic Tree of Life

spiritual body allows us to experience abstract forms of human manifestation. It is not subject to time and space and is devoid of any physical form.

2. *The Mental, or Intellectual, plane* is the body of intellectual consciousness perceived by pure awareness, which opens realms of experience not bounded by space and time.

3. *The Astral, or Etheric, plane* is a template, a matrix for the physical body, which is an exact duplicate of it. It is believed that the "physical atoms, molecules and cells arrange

themselves according to the structure of the ethereal body."[13] For clarification purposes, the etheric body consists of two parts: the *etheric double* and the *aura*.[14] The etheric body, or energy body, is the conglomerate of energies surrounding humans and connecting to the external world. Metaphysical teachings hold the viewpoint that the function of the etheric body is to receive and transmit energy impulses.

4. *The Corporeal plane* is the instrument that serves to manipulate the objective universe. This body is intrinsically connected to the ethereal body, and it is the vessel through which life force flows. The corporeal body is composed of approximately fifty trillion cells, each cell being a unit of consciousness. Thus, the corporeal body is the collective functioning of these microscopic units (cells).

The above description of the four centers can appropriately be called the "occult constitution of man," a term used by French occultist Paul C. Jagot (1889–1962), because they are essential components of a human being. The corporeal body is the only one visible to the naked eye; however, behind it lie the other spheres that vitalize and support the physical one. Without the Spiritual, Mental, and Astral centers, the Corporeal body would disintegrate. These spheres are also associated with the quaternity principle as follows:

The Spiritual sphere: intuitive and transcendental knowledge.
The Mental sphere: rational and theoretical thinking.
The Astral, or Etheric, sphere: vitalizes and gives emotional impetus.
The Corporeal body: vegetative conductor.

The graphic below attempts to illustrate symbolically the fourfold constitution of human beings. Although the corporeal body is the only one visible, there are three invisible energy fields that are intrinsically connected to the visible one. The depiction of the four

Yod=Leo — *The Spiritual plane*

Hch=Eagle — *The Mental plane*

Vav=Aquarius (water) — *The Astral plane*

Heh=Taurus (bull) — *The Corporeal plane*

Symbolic Tetrad

Fourfold Constitution of Human Beings[15]

creatures of Ezekiel's vision is used to represent the four spheres that we have described above.

The Holy Grail sought in faraway lands is symbolized by the symbolic tetrad indicating that humans need to realize their inner constitution and their relationship with the universal forces. There is an intimate relationship between the universe—the

macrocosm—and humans—the microcosm. We live in an oce-
anic vibratory energy that responds to the command of our
thoughts and emotions; usually we are not aware of it. A metaphor
will clarify this idea: a fish that lives deep in an ocean of water is
not aware of it until it is pulled out of the ocean.

The Law of Attraction says thoughts have magnetic power of attraction; the focus of attention will cause one to manifest the things
one seeks to experience, when a person takes action toward the
manifestation. Therefore, whether one's focus of attention is on what
one desires or on what one lacks, one will experience more of those
things to which one gives attention. Although awareness selects reality on the mental plane, it is feelings and emotions that attract it
into manifesting on the physical plane. Emotion is energy in motion
that moves things into one's reality or out of it. According to Abraham's teaching, one attracts only those things with which one is
in emotional resonance. Positive emotions attract positive things,
events, and people while negative emotions attract negative ones.
With a lack of emotional resonance, a probable event would be
hindered from manifesting.

Negative anticipation, which is the feeling of expecting something full of doubts and insecurity, can deter the crystallization of
the upcoming desire. This is because the person is broadcasting
his or her fears and anxiety to the universe, and in agreement to
the Law of Attraction, events will manifest according to those
fears and not according to what the individual really desires. This
is because the anxiety for the goal to happen becomes frozen by
the constant awareness of it. That is, constant expectation pre-
vents the desired image from being fully submitted to the subconscious mind. Thus, the key here is to set one's intention and then
detach it from conscious awareness in the assurance that the goal
aimed for will come to pass sooner or later.

Thus, once a person formulates a clear-cut thought-form, it
should be submitted to the subconscious and allowed to do the
work. The conscious mind chooses or selects the options, but it is the
subconscious mind that does the work of manifesting into actualities. A desired goal held in constant conscious awareness means that
it has not been fully submitted to the subconscious mind. One thing

to bear in mind is that the Law of Attraction works through the subconscious level and not through conscious awareness; that is why the act of detachment with confidence is extremely important. It allows the subconscious to do its work without interruption. Keeping the desired goal in constant doubtful awareness is interfering with the work of the subconscious mind.

CHAPTER 14

The "I Am" and the Power of the Lost Word

Don't you know that you yourselves are God's temple
and that God's Spirit dwells in your midst?
—1ST CORINTHIANS 3:16 (NIV)

Our human task now is to wake up and recognize ourselves
as parts or aspects of God-as-Nature and behave accordingly.
—ELISABET SAHTOURIS[1]

THE TRADITIONAL CHRISTIAN concept of God is dualistic; it attributes the origin of good to God and the origin of evil to the devil. According to this conception the good God is always fighting against the bad deity; they are in eternal conflict, each sometimes winning and other times losing. These above notions have led to absurd ideas such as "There is no God," or "God is dead," and so forth. This cannot be further from the truth. There is only ONE God, creator of good and evil. This may sound like a blasphemy or sacrilege for some radical fundamentalists; however, I encourage them to read their Holy Bible. "Know therefore this day, and consider it in thine heart, that the LORD he is God in heaven above, and upon the earth beneath: there is none else" (Deuteronomy 4:39, KJV). Moreover, in previous pages I have quoted Isaiah 45:7,[2] which says there is only one God, author of good and evil in the world.

In *The Book of Tokens*, a treatise of inspirational meditations on the Hebrew alphabet received by Paul F. Case from the Inner School, the meditation on the Hebrew letter Ayin says:

And I am Prince of Darkness
As well as King of Light.
Shall there be anything Wherein
I, the Lord of all, have no dominion?
They see crookedly who know this not,
And in their deluded minds
They divide my nature,
Setting the Kingdom of Light
Over against the Realm of Darkness,
And thus making two gods.[3]

In addition, most of the sacred texts of the major world religions affirm that God is the only doer. For instance, Oriental philosophy, exemplified by Vedanta, clearly indicates that One God is the creator of everything good and evil. In Chapter 9 of the most sacred Hindu treatise, the Bhagavad Gita, Krishna, the supreme Hindu God, explains to the hero Arjuna that Krishna is the only one who creates, preserves, and destroys the entire universe.

German mystic Jacob Boehme elaborated on this issue as well. How could a good God have created a world so full of suffering and evil? How could the wrathful God of the Old Testament be reconciled with the God of love of the New Testament? Boehme devoted himself to meditation, intense Bible reading, and fervent prayers for a certain time; finally, he experienced revelations in 1600 and in 1610. In a state of overwhelming religious ecstasy, he had a vision into the inner heart of Nature and God. His explanation was that God consists of divine love and divine wrath. How could it be otherwise? There is only one God, and there is no opposite power against him.

Georg Hegel seems to have been strongly influenced by Boehme's mystical writings; Hegel considers that Divine Providence is working through history.[4] Furthermore, Hegel regards the philosophy of history as theodicy. The theory of theodicy is based on theological principles that seek to justify by reasonable means the existence of evil in the world. Hegel sees the concept of evil as part of the process in history itself. Hegel's thesis of theodicy is formulated in the introduction to his book *The History of Philosophy*, whereby he acknowledges that history can be seen as a theodicy, "a justification of the ways of God." He further states, "But even regarding History as the slaughter-bench at which the happiness of peoples, the wisdom of States, and the virtue of individuals have been victimized—the question involuntary arises—to what principle, to what final aim these enormous sacrifices have been offered."[5] Lack of space does not allow me to further elaborate on this issue.

Many Christians may have pondered the question of how a loving God would allow the atrocities that happened in the concentration camps during World War II. Initially, the fathers of the Catholic Church were well acquainted with God's dual nature. C. G. Jung in his preface to *Answer to Job* wrote, "Clement of Rome taught that God rules the world with a right and left hand, the right being Christ, the left Satan. Clement's view is clearly *monotheistic*, as it unites the opposites in one God."[6]

The American Qabalist Paul F. Case shed further light on this mystery. He wrote that the "Bible says that God is love, but it also speaks of God's wrath."[7] He further affirmed that a highly evolved spiritual teacher (probably his spiritual master) told him that both love and hate are root emotions, which are also spiritual. Consequently, "all other emotions and desires take on the character of either one or the other."[8] Hate is oriented to separation/involution, and love tends to union and evolution—return back to the source. This is the most coherent theory I have found to explain the apparent contradictions of life. Consider that, according to the Hermetic Principle of Polarity, love and hate are extremes of the same emotion. There are NOT two deities; there is only ONE that creates, maintains, and destroys everything in this universe.

Furthermore, Boehme suggested that God could have no knowledge of himself except by revealing himself through his creation. He viewed God as unconscious, adding that God is awakening, and he needs humans to become aware of him. According to this notion, God is gaining awareness along with humankind. Later on, philosophers Hegel and Jung stated the same idea. Humankind is an instrument for this process of unfoldment of consciousness; and this is done through all good and bad events throughout human history. Hence, the awakening of consciousness is the unfolding of the universal consciousness for both God and humankind.

Following Boehme, Jung wrote, "Existence is only real when it is conscious to somebody. That is why the Creator needs conscious man even though, from sheer unconsciousness, he would like to prevent him from becoming conscious."[9] God had the desire for self-expression and self-realization and needed humans as an instrument to achieve those goals. We should keep in mind that God lives in every human being.

The need to experience every kind of emotion and feeling can be verified by humans' endurance even in the worst situations of life. Psychiatrist Viktor Frankl, after he was liberated from the Auschwitz concentration camp, published a book in Germany entitled *The Unconscious God*.[10] The book discusses the relation between psychology and religion and posits that there is an unconscious sense of religiosity in the human subconscious mind. Interesting enough, Jung had already postulated this idea of the existence of an "authentic religious function in the unconscious"[11] in his Terry Lectures in 1937, which were later published as *Psychology and Religion*.

Frankl's work constitutes an existentialist perspective. He was in several concentration camps and witnessed many atrocities and the suffering of his people; he observed that people who survived these unbearable conditions were those who had religious hope and a strong desire to live. Frankl concluded that there is an unconscious spirituality in humans. In his words: "There is, in fact, a religious sense deeply rooted in each and every man's unconscious depths."[12] To this, it should be added that God goes through all this suffering along with humans. There is only one God, who dwells in all humanity.

Jung equates God with the universal unconscious and says that God is waking up alongside humankind's unfolding of consciousness. Jung was profoundly troubled by the biblical book of Job. Why was a pious, humble, and honest man treated as if he were the most evil man in the world? Job was stripped of all his wealth as well as his wife, family, and friends, and he was inflicted with the worst illness on the earth.

Jung's book *Answer to Job* is an interpretation of the Hebrew-Christian scriptures from a gnostic viewpoint. In that sense, it is a response to Yahweh's behavior in the Old Testament. Jung postulates that Yahweh is an unconscious deity who has two sons, Satan and Jesus. Satan's role here is similar to that of a prosecutor; Yahweh listens to the accuser and, because of it, inflicts unbearable suffering on the righteous and innocent Job. The blameless Job hopes that justice will be done. Indeed, Jung (who, incidentally, had a profound and thorough knowledge of both the Old and New Testaments) comes into this scenario and wrote this book as if he were *Job's defense attorney.*

Jung argues that the demiurge Yahweh, who created this world *ex nihilo* (out of nothing), lacked self-reflection and wanted to become a man in order to gain self-awareness; in Jung's own words, "[Yahweh's] consciousness seems to be not much more than a primitive 'awareness' which knows no reflection and no morality." For Jung, "morality presupposes consciousness."[13] In this respect, "Job stands morally higher than Yahweh."[14] Jung further asserts that "the naïve assumption that the creator of the world is a conscious being must be regarded as a disastrous prejudice which later gave rise to the most incredible dislocation of logic."[15] Jung also mentions the prophet Hosea, who was commanded by God to take a wife who would become a prostitute as an example of God's relationship with Israel. To this it can be added Yahweh's threats to the chosen people if they don't obey his rules: "My anger will be aroused, and I will kill you with the sword; your wives will become widows and your children fatherless" (Exodus 22:24, NIV).

Interesting enough, American evolutionary biologist Elisabet Sahtouris, in her scientific paper mentioned earlier, pointed out that consciousness is not local but everywhere, and this "Consciousness has been given different names by many cultures."[16] The striking touch is given by Sahtouris with her statement "All-That-Is God Source is perceived as I-Am from the perspective of the local consciousness."[17]

Along these lines, Jung has stated that God is in a process of awakening and needs man in this process; Sahtouris says almost the same thing in other words: "Our universe appears to be a learning universe." She adds, "Our learning universe implies a *learning God*—God learning to know the nature of Self through exploring its possibilities and learning to reflect on that Self." She further urges humans to consider themselves to be the "creative edge of God."[18]

Another important issue that Jung discusses in *Answer to Job* is the Christian doctrine of redemption. The implication is that the whole of Christian theology is centered in the doctrine of redemption, whereby humans are considered sinful by nature. The underlying message is that humans need a redeemer, a savior. Jung infers, "Consequently, the work of salvation is intended to save man from the fear of God."[19]

Moreover, Jung questions the concept of atonement, calling it unnecessary payment. He describes the torture of Jesus Christ on the cross "to appease the father's wrath." Jung additionally indicates that "Yahweh has a tendency to employ such means as the killing of the son and the first-born in order to test his people's faith."[20] Indeed, Exodus 22:29 (NIV) states, "Do not hold back offerings from your granaries or your vats. You must give me the firstborn of your sons."

Jung also states that "man is the mirror which God holds up before him, or the sense organ with which he apprehends his being."[21] According to Jung, God is expanding along with the development of human consciousness.[22] Incidentally, Jung also indicates that "God is reality itself."[23] God uses humanity for God's own purposes. These statements seem sacrilegious at first glance, but this small book, *Answer to Job*, from wherein these quotations were taken, is considered by Jungian scholars to be one of the most profound theological books in modern history.

I indicated earlier that the central issue of Jung's book *Answer to Job* is how to deal with the time-honored dilemma of good versus evil. Why is there evil in the world? Why is there injustice on the earth? Why did Job have to suffer so much when he was a righteous man? Because Satan is the accuser and the prosecutor, Jung finds that Yahweh is not conscious of himself, that God is awakening from an unconscious state to a conscious condition, and that God needs humans in this process of awakening.[24] Jung's pivotal idea is that humans' existence is important for God to develop a greater level of awareness and to become conscious of his dark side.[25] In short, Jung's main thesis is that consciousness develops out of unconsciousness through a series of stages of awareness—a process represented by the ego's emergence, as the ego consciousness gradually differentiates itself from nature, which is in a state of unconsciousness.[26] The life power begins experiencing its primordial unconsciousness and, in the course of its existence, gains greater awareness and autonomy as it evolves.

Madame Blavatsky also asserted that the "Logos (God) and Satan are one."[27] Incidentally, regarding this problem of good and evil, I wrote an essay entitled "The Adversary and the Redeemer," which is included in my book *Beyond Conventional Wisdom* (2006); in it I point out the unity of God as the sole creator of everything in the world including good and evil.[28] I also quote the prophet Isaiah, who gave a conclusive statement about this dilemma in the following terms:

> [5]I am the LORD, and there is none else, there is no God beside me: I girded thee, though thou hast not known me:

> [6]That they may know from the rising of the sun, and from the west, that there is none beside me. I am the LORD, and there is none else.

> [7]I form the light, and create darkness: I made peace, and create evil: I the Lord do all these things. (Isaiah 45:5–7, KJV)

The same idea is expressed in the Eastern religion exemplified by the Bhagavad Gita; Krishna (Godhead of Hindu religion) is the doer of good and evil. There are not two supreme Gods, only one. Modern science is "rediscovering the wheel" or, better to say, it is verifying ancient occult knowledge. For instance, the Hermetic treatise named *The Kybalion*, which reportedly summarizes ancient Egyptian and Greek knowledge, states that the universe is mental. Furthermore, many occult writers such as Madame Blavatsky and Qabalist Paul F. Case talk about the life power as consciousness that encompasses the entire universe, saying that matter and thoughts consist of the same substance or mental stuff, being different only in the level of vibration. Investigative journalist Lynne McTaggart recapitulates recent scientific discoveries in her book *The Field: The Quest for the Secret Force of the Universe,* where she describes the existence of an all-inclusive energy field connecting man and matter, which she calls the "zero point field." This notion would suggest a connection between matter and mind. Expressed in other words, everything is consciousness. Scientist Sahtouris encapsulates this idea as follows: "All are One."[29]

Now we are in a good position to search for the "lost word" that will lead us to the concept of the union with the Divine Source and empower us as sons and daughters of the living God. Since ancient times, many mystical and religious traditions have claimed the existence of a "secret" that would open the doors to wisdom, power, and wealth. This myth persisted in the Middle Ages; esoteric and occult schools of the time propounded the existence of a magical and all-powerful "word" that would give the possessor supernatural powers and wisdom; he or she would be capable of performing all sorts of miracles and even raising the dead. I contend that the allegory of a mystical, all-powerful word was part of the medieval occult lore without any substantiation, which I will attempt to demonstrate hereafter.

Some esoteric schools such as Freemasonry claim that the magical word was lost; the whole journey and advancement through the Masonic degrees (either York or Scottish Rite) is based on the belief that there once existed a secret word, and the quest in this fraternity is to find that lost word. From the time the aspirant is initiated into Freemasonry, the spiritual goal, along with that of perfecting the candidate's personality, is the quest for that lost word. This is in essence the whole narrative of Freemasonry.

The above account is only an allegory, a myth; it is nevertheless conducive to the perfection of the candidate's personality and elevation of the sense of brotherhood and fraternity of human beings. Every time the aspirant is advanced in the Freemasonry ladder, the candidate is given only substitutes for the lost word. In modern parlance, it can be said that the candidate receives only a *password*, which serves as a signifier to be acknowledged in the Freemasonry ranking-degree system. Thus, the lost word in Freemasonry is nothing but a password for advancement in the Masonry hierarchy.

Some writers on occult and esoteric matters, such as Éliphas Lévi, postulated that the lost word is the Tetragrammaton (YHWH). They argue that this word was given by the Elohim (literally translated as "the Gods") to Moses at the burning bush incident. Reportedly, the Divinity also revealed to Moses the proper pronunciation of the word "YHWH." However, this hypothesis lacks substantial veracity, becoming merely a myth of medieval lore and superstition.

The truth of the matter is that the word given to Moses was a verb—a living, creative power. The truly and duly initiated into the mysteries of life have alluded that the lost word is not something given by anybody, but is the conscious realization of a divine truth that dwells in the hearts of humans. And that can be achieved only when the candidate has developed his or her inner awareness to recognize this. Therefore, I conceive the lost word, or verb, to be the symbol of *divine truth,* which is the statement "*I Am Who I Am.*" Hence, the entire narrative of the lost word and the passwords given in the esoteric and occult schools are components of the allegorical narrative, which represents a search for the indwelling God in humans. This cannot be conveyed to the candidate by words; the aspirant has to find it by him- or herself.

Maybe for that reason, it has been indicated time and again that one cannot disclose spiritual teachings to people who are not ready to grasp them, because they can be misunderstood and the revealer of the divine truth subjected to mockery. Jesus expressed this concern in the following statement: "Do not give what is holy to the dogs; nor cast your pearls before swine, lest they trample them under their feet, and turn and tear you in pieces" (Matthew 7:6, KJV). That apprehension is still valid nowadays.

The real secret is plain and simple; precisely for that reason, many people don't get it. To communicate this "secret" to the spiritually unprepared would be a sacrilege because it would be misunderstood and subject to derision. The secret word can be appreciated and venerated only when the candidate becomes spiritually and mentally fit for it.

For instance, how many would really appreciate the first sentence of the Builders of the Adytum's (BOTA) "Pattern of the Trestleboard," which asserts: "All the power that ever was or will be is here now."[30] How many would really grasp Jesus Christ's statement, which complements the aforementioned quotation: "The Kingdom of Heaven is in you." This point cannot be stated more clearly. Only those who are ready will grasp its true significance.

The true meaning of the journey in the Freemasonry schools is—as its name suggests—to become masons, or builders, of the Inner Temple and to work hard in polishing the rustic stone into a perfect cubic one. The stone is the candidate's personality; he has to work on himself to be prepared to listen to the inner voice and then he will receive this revelation in his heart—the lost word will be found there, in the inner shrine.

Plato taught that the divine "logos," or "word," was the representation of God. The Apostle John said the same thing at the opening of his famous Gospel, when identifies the word with God. In other terms, the search for the lost word is the search for the inner self—the "I AM," which is truly the name of God (Exodus 3:14, NIV).

One of the most important spiritual events in the Pentateuch is Moses's encounter with the Divine in Moreb Mountain (the mountain of God). We read in the Bible that Moses stood up before the burning bush and asked the Elohim [meaning, literally, "the gods"], "What is your name?" The Elohim replied: *Ehyeh Asher Ehyeh*, "I AM WHO I AM. This is what you are to say to the Israelites: '"I AM" has sent me to you'" (Exodus 3:14, NIV). In the following verse, Exodus 3:15, the Elohim give Moses a substitute name, (in English, *YHWH*), commonly rendered as *Yahweh* or *Jehovah*. He added the second name, indicating that it would be the name to remember for eternity. Here is the verse:

> God also said to Moses, "Say to the Israelites, 'The LORD, the God of your fathers—the God of Abraham, the God of Isaac and the God of Jacob—has sent me to you.' This is my name forever, the name you shall call me from generation to generation."

It follows that both names make clear references to the verb "to be." This is a clear indication that both names "I Am who I Am" and YHWH (Yahweh) denote the verb "to be" or "existence." However, the verb "Yahweh" has been traditionally used as a proper name.

Confusion arose in the initial translation of the Bible from Hebrew and Latin into English, when the Hebrew characters were rendered as "Jehovah" or "Yahweh." Future versions of the Bible continue the same mistake. However, contemporary translations of the Bible render the four Hebrew consonants (YHWH) as "*Lord God*," which is more acceptable because the four Hebrew consonants YHWH are unutterable as a word, as it has no vowels. Some scholars believe that the name "Jehovah" or "Yahweh" is a hybrid form derived by combining the Latin letters *JHVH* with the vowels of "*Adonai*." The word (YHWH) can only be vibrated letter by letter; for this reason, it is believed that its meaning is to indicate that the nature of reality is vibration.

An occult interpretation of the word YHWH (Yod-Heh-Wav-Heh) could be as follows: The first Hebrew consonant, "Yod," is associated with a male phallus, or Adam. The three remaining consonants make the word "Heva" or "Heve" (HWH), which refer to the female uterus, or Eve. Thus, the name Jehovah or Yahweh (YHWH) is an allusion to an androgynous deity—that is, a being that contains male and female components.

This is confirmed by the fact that Genesis 1:27 (KJV) states: "God [Elohim] created man in his own image, in the image of

God created he him; male and female created he them." From this passage, one can infer that the Elohim created humankind as androgynous, of both sexes (male and female). Afterward, this androgynous being was separated into male and female, as indicated in the following biblical passage: "And the rib, which the LORD God had taken from man, made he a woman, and brought her unto the man" (Genesis 2:22, KJV).

The same assertion can be made for the name Elohim, which is plural for "gods." Theologian Rabbi Arthur Green acknowledges the plural connotation of this word. He further states that "*Elohim* is also occasionally used in the sense of 'great one,' referring to a respected human authority."[31] As per the Bible, the Elohim created Adam and Eve. The word "Elohim" is composed of two Hebrew words. The first letter (הא) means El (God), masculine; the rest of the letters, "Eloah," mean Goddess, feminine.

Furthermore, the Garden of Eden was not in the physical world but in another realm; in other words, the Garden of Eden was located in another dimension—on the sefirah (singular) called Yesod (Foundation) of the Tree of Life. The famous Fall of Man refers to the descent of Adam and Eve from the sefirah Yesod (Foundation) to the sefirah Malkhut (Kingdom), which is the physical world.

Perhaps the reason for the substitute name given to Moses is the fact that Ehyeh ("I Am") is the most secret name and should not be misused. This is verified by the third commandment that God inscribed on two stone tablets and gave to Moses on Mount Sinai; it specifies the following prohibition: "You shall not misuse the name of the LORD your God, for the LORD will not hold anyone guiltless who misuses his name" (Exodus 20:7, NIV).[32]

I question the long-standing belief in the occult, esoteric, and Qabalistic traditions that regard the word "Yahweh" (YHWH) as the sacred Tetragrammaton and ascribe extraordinary powers to this name. Those who hold this position argue that it is the key word to unlock all the ancient mysteries, including the arcana of Qabalah. However, in addition to YHWH (Yahweh) there are other names of the Hebrew Divinity indicated in the Bible, such as: El Shaddai, El, Elohim Gebor, Yahweh Zabaoth, and so on.

Nevertheless, the reasoning behind the choice of the name YHWH as the most secret and almighty name was never convincingly explained. Bear in mind that word "YHWH" (Yahweh) is the name given to the jealous, irascible, and unforgiving deity who, according to the Bible, selected the Israelite tribe as his only chosen people, leaving the rest of humankind to be considered the gentiles.[33] Yahweh never claimed to be a universal God; he was the enemy of the Egyptians and other tribes of the time. It was customary in ancient times for most Middle Eastern tribes to have their own protector gods.

According to occult authorities (Éliphas Lévi, Gérard Encausse (Papus), Case, Goddard, and others), the word "YHWH" is the only divine Tetragrammaton. The existence of four divine names composed of four Hebrew letters, Tetragrammatons, notably Yahweh or Jehovah (YHWH), Ehyeh (AHIH), Adonai (ADNI), and AGLA, has already been mentioned. Consequently, there are four Tetragrammatons (quaternity names) in the Bible, which are the expression of the quaternity principle.

It seems that this misinterpretation started with Éliphas Lévi, who has misled the occult and esoteric writers mentioned above as well as the magicians of the Esoteric Order of the Golden Dawn. Case mentions that "the Bible ascribes peculiar power to [YHVH], and tradition says that to pronounce it is to possess a key to all wisdom."[34] Furthermore, occult writers allege that its correct pronunciation was lost after the destruction of the Second Temple. However, there is no conclusive argument to validate that statement.

I would advance the thesis that the name "Ehyeh" ("I Am"), rather than "YHWH" (Yahweh), is the innermost sacred and powerful name of God for the following reason: the Divinity identified first as Ehyeh Asher Ehyeh—I Am Who I Am—(Exodus 3:14). In the following verse, the Divinity gave a substitute name (Yahweh) to be remembered for future generations. The New International Version of the Bible has an interesting footnote on the verse Exodus 3:15, which states that "the Hebrew for LORD (YHWH) sounds like and may be related to the Hebrew for 'I Am' in verse 14." Therefore, the two names are the same; the translators of the New International Version do not consider the word "Yah-weh" to be different from "Ehyeh."

Furthermore, Ehyeh ("I Am") is the innermost name of the first sephirah of the Qabalistic Tree of Life; from it everything visible and invisible unfolds. As well-known occult writer David Allen Hulse has indicated, "To know God's true name is to know God." Well, I think that we are now in a position to say that we do know the name of God: "I Am" is the name of God. "Yahweh" is only a substitute name.

The above argument is validated by Rabbi Arthur Green; he opens the first chapter of his book *Ehyeh* as follows: "Kabbalah teaches that *Ehyeh*, or 'I shall be,' is the deepest, most hidden name of God. It begins with the Hebrew letter *Aleph*, which indi-cates the future tense."[35]

Moreover, I have already discussed in a previous book that the Hebrew names Ehyeh and Yahweh are not nouns but verbs mean-ing "*to be*" or "existence." They both make reference to "one exis-tence"—a being in eternal unfolding. This statement is verified by contemporary Jewish scholars such as Rabbis Arthur Green and David A. Cooper, and others.

In this regard, the great Qabalist Paul Foster Case back in 1920 emphatically stated that the word "Yahweh" or "Jehovah" is not a name but a verb. He wrote:

The master-key to the Hebrew wisdom is the "name" translated "Lord" in the Authorized Version of the Bible,[36] and "Jehovah" in the revised versions. It is not really a name at all, but rather a *verbal, numerical and geometrical formula*. In Roman letters cor-responding to Hebrew it is spelled IHVH.

This is a noun form derived from a Hebrew verb meaning "to be." Correctly translated, it means "That which was, That which is, That which shall be." THAT, not HE. Thus, it is a perfect verbal symbol for the One Reality—for that Something which has always subsisted behind all forms in the eternity of the past, for that Something which really is behind all the appearances and misun-derstandings of the present, for that Something which will be the foundation for all the changing forms of life-expression in the eternity to come.[37] (Bold and italics added.)

Rabbi Green, teacher of Jewish mysticism, further states: "The timeless God allowed the great name YHWH to be conjugated, as though to say: *'Ehyeh. I am tomorrow'*"[38] (italics in original). The implication of this transliteration suggests that God, the Almighty, is in fact the very essence of existence and a truly eternal state of Being. Green goes on to say: "God is Being. The four letters of the Name, taken in reverse order spell the word H-W-H-Y meaning existence." The name contains past, present, and future.

It has been postulated in these pages that the Hebrew names for God YHWH and AHEH are verbs in motion. The mystery of the Judeo-Christian tradition is based on the key word—the lost word of the Freemasons, the magnum opus of the alchemists, the verb that was made flesh, the light at the beginning of the world's creation, and so forth. All of these are labels for a two-word "I Am." Indeed, "I Am" is the lost word for those who are not yet spiritually awakened.

The above is also confirmed by John the evangelist when he solemnly opened his Gospel, "*In principio erat Verbum et Verbum erat apud Deum et Deus erat Verbum*" (John 1:1, Latin Vulgate). This is the rendering from Greek into Latin. Thus the correct translation into English should be "In the beginning was the Verb, and the Verb was with God, and the Verb was God," rather than the commonly accepted translation, "In the beginning was the Word, and the Word was with God, and the Word was God" (NIV). Notice this indication that the "Verb was God." Hence, the "Verb" is the universal consciousness. Rabbi David A. Cooper encapsulates this idea in the title of his book *God Is a Verb*. Furthermore, Hermetic Qabalah holds the viewpoint that in the beginning was the "Thought." Stated in other words, in the beginning, the Verb was a *thought* expressed in a sound, AUM (thought in vibration), and the sound was the beginning of creation. This idea is held as truth in the Hindu philosophy.

In contrast to the label Yahweh, which is given to a vengeful, irascible, and jealous deity who cares only for one nation, the designation Ehyeh ("I Am") is the name of the living God who dwells in the heart of every human being.

Jesus Christ, being a Jew and a strict follower of the teachings of the Torah (Jewish law or tradition) *never called God by the name of Yahweh or Jehovah*, but by the title Father. Incidentally, the name *"Father"*—the primordial Yod—is ascribed to the second sefirah on the Qabalistic Tree of Life. Jesus usually uttered, "I and the Father are one" (John 10:30, NIV). "That all of them may be one, Father, just as you are in me and I am in you. May they also be in us so that the world may believe that you have sent me" (John 17:21, NIV). Thus, Jesus regarded the name of God to be *"Father."* He taught his apostles to pray using the name "Our Father." He further stated: "Go instead to my brothers and tell them, 'I am ascending to my Father and your Father, to my God and your God'" (John 20:17, NIV). Incidentally, Jesus clearly admonished his apostles, "And *call no man your father on earth, for you have one Father, who is in heaven*" (Matthew 23:9, NIV).

Moreover, the use of the name "I Am" is recorded in the Gospel of John repeatedly. Indeed, in this Gospel are found the "I am" statements that Jesus made during his public mission. The following verses are from the New International Version (NIV). Jesus stated, "I am the bread of life" (6:35 and 6:48); "I am the light of the world" (8:12); "I am the good shepherd" (10:11); "I am the door" (10:7); "I am the resurrection" (11:25); "Before Abraham was I am" (8:58); "I am the true vine (15:1); "I am the way, and the truth and the life. No one comes to the Father except through me" (14:6). This last statement can be fully grasped under the perspective of the Qabalistic Tree of Life. This is not the place to do such explanation, and lack of space does not allow me to further elaborate on it; suffice to say that Jesus Christ as sacrificed God is associated with the sefirah Tifaret located on the Middle Pillar. The verse John 14:6 gives a hint for those who are seeking enlightenment through the Qabalistic Tree of Life. The Middle Pillar is the "Path of the *Arrow"* or *straight path located at* the center of the Tree. Furthermore, Jesus said, "Anyone who has seen me has seen the Father" (14:9). There you are.

In the Gospel of John are recorded the words *"I Am"* (*Ehyeh*) as pronounced by Jesus about twenty-one times. Interestingly enough, the number twenty-one is the numeric value of *Ehyeh* in the Hebrew Gematria,[39] and it is a multiple of three and seven, both of which are fundamental numbers in the Bible. Furthermore, Jesus acknowledges that he does not do anything by himself; he asserts, "Don't you believe that I am in the Father, and that the Father is in me? The words I say to you are not just my own. Rather, it is the Father, living in me, who is doing his work" (14:10, NIV). "I am the resurrection and the life. He who believes in me will live, even though he dies; and whoever lives and believes in me will never die" (11:25–26, NIV). These verses seem to intimate a validation of the theory of incarnation.

Consciousness is all that is, and though it is expressed in an infinite series of levels, it is not divisional. There is no real separation or gap in the universal consciousness. "I Am" cannot be divided. No matter how a person conceives him- or herself, whether rich or poor, beggar or thief, the inner self will remain the same. At the center of manifestation, there is only one "I Am" manifesting in legions of forms and concepts of itself, and that is the "Ehyeh Asher Ehyeh," which is transliterated almost exactly as "I shall be."

The Divine Name, when it is rendered as "I shall be," is not limited by time and space. God cannot be restricted by time, thus, "I shall be" is the eternal becoming; nevertheless, it is the same in essence. The definition given by Orthodox rabbi Arthur Green about God's name (Ehyeh) entails careful consideration. "I shall be" means "I am becoming" eternally, an ongoing becoming. Furthermore, Rabbi Green's statement "I shall become whatever you want me to be" can be interpreted as the flow of the life force energy that is directed by human consciousness to create our own reality. He reiterates that God called himself "I shall be what I shall be."[40]

The following is worth reiterating—the words "AHIH" ("I Am") and "YHVH" (Yahweh or Jehovah) refer to a single verb—to *be*; a verb manifests in manifold forms and ways throughout human history. Neville Goddard equates God, or the "*I Am*," with consciousness.[41] It is the all-encompassing energy that pervades the whole universe, which scientists called the zero point field and both Jewish theologians and Hermetic Qabalists identify with the names of God Ehyeh and YHWH. Both names indicate a pure consciousness in a process of eternal unfolding, or "All-that-Is." There is nothing else besides It. It is all-encompassing energy pervading the whole universe.[42]

There is only one fountain of energy, which is consciousness—the universal "I Am." The second name of God given to Moses in the Bible is a substitute name used to throw dust into the eyes of the uninitiated or those not ready for spiritual understanding. Considered as verbs, AHIH ("I Am") is God's name in the future tense or in an act of becoming and YHWH (God) is the past-present-future. They are always unfolding into tomorrow; that is why ultimate reality is indefinable. Both names are verbs in motion. The Elohim told Moses through his names that he is the eternal present in motion; he cannot be limited by time or space. Both names describe the concept of *existence*—that is the ultimate reality. God cannot be comprehended or named with a temporal name, as he is indefinable. Saying "God is a Verb" indicates that God is immanently present and actively involved in the universe. He is not far away, remotely distant from his creation; he lives in his creation.

Interestingly, Green's statement *"Ehyeh is God as future"*[43] is being confirmed by contemporary science: physicists, biologists, epigeneticists, and other scientists in other fields of knowledge have arrived at the conclusion that the only reality is the life force, also known as light or consciousness, which is in an eternal process of becoming. There is nothing but consciousness; the verb "to be" is an infinite consciousness, in this case synonymous with existence.

Without a subject, there is no object—no awareness and no consciousness. This is why Descartes's statement "I think, therefore I am" is accurate. By saying "I think" (I have awareness, or consciousness), he then realizes that he is. One certain thing is that "I exist because of my awareness." Expressed in a slightly in different way, I know I exist because I am aware of my existence. The only real thing is consciousness, which is expressed as awareness. The ensuing proposition is that once one is aware of oneself, the next step is creation of one's own reality.

Interestingly enough, Edward F. Edinger, in his book *The Aion Lectures: Exploring the Self in C. G. Jung's Aion*, discusses this issue. He is accurate when he asserts that René Descartes discovered the ego in his "Discourse on Method." Edinger emphasizes that the Descartes expression *Cogito ergo sum* has been wrongly translated. "A better translation would be 'I am conscious, therefore I am,'" which appears to be an appropriate interpretation.

Metaphysically and scientifically (through quantum physics), it can be said that the only reality is consciousness—the zero point field, or zero point energy. Thus, to say, "I think, therefore I am aware" is similar to saying, "*To be aware is to be conscious.*" The subject and object are one in the metaphysical world, but in the physical, or tridimensional world, existence is manifested as a pair of opposites—the One, for the sake of manifestation, expresses itself as dual.

CHAPTER 15

An Existential Question: Who Am I?

You are God. You are the "I AM that I AM."
—NEVILLE GODDARD[1]

You will be like God, knowing good and evil.
—GENESIS 3:5, NIV

THE MOST MYSTERIOUS and striking passage in the Bible is found in the encounter of Moses with the Divinity in the burning bush incident. Moses asks him, "Who are you? What is your name?" Humans have been addressing to themselves the same questions since the dawn of civilization: *Who am I? Why am I here?* And the ancient injunction runs: "Man, know thyself; then thou shalt know the Universe and God."[2] All these questions lead to what is now known as existential philosophy. An occult writer stated that by knowing the name of God we will know God itself.

Existential philosophy, in addition to being concerned with finding the meaning of and a purpose in life, regards the essence of humans as an indispensable point for their philosophy. However, for some reason, they are unable to identify that the "essence" of humans is the "I Am," which should be the Archimedean point for existential philosophy. This notion is authenticated by Christian Kabbalah and Hermetic Qabalah, which regard "I Am" as the supreme essence of human beings.

Existentialism further advocates that people should be responsible for their lives and make choices based on their experiences, beliefs, and outlook on life. The issue with this is that, in contemporary modern societies, most humans have been domesticated and programmed to have a herd mind. People in power or those who have access to the mass media and education impose their beliefs, values, and ideas; this handicaps individualism and free choice, making individuals alienated as they become part of a huge materialistic and consumerist society in which the main demands are to satisfy false sensorial needs rather than to nurture their inner being. In this way they became dehumanized and find life meaningless, with the ensuing problem of suicidal ideations. This predicament has become an increasing issue in modern industrialized and consumerist societies.

This may be because mainstream philosophy, psychology, and sociology usually neglect what can be called the invisible world, which is the origin for everything that is seen in the objective world. The invisible world consists of the universal life force that pervades the entire universe. The human brain, through thoughts, feelings, and emotions, gives shape to this universal life power, or consciousness, to become actualized as objective things. Both worlds are real, and they are in a symbiotic relationship. Furthermore, the two worlds are subject and object together and form the one identity. Thus, there are three things that we should take into consideration:

1. Everything visible or invisible has its counterpart to form the unity.
2. The world is an intentional, driven universe.
3. The universal intention aims toward self-expression and self-fulfilling consciousness.

This life power is alive, intelligent, and self-directed. This is confirmed by the theory of phenomenology, which states that we live in an intentional, driven world and that intention is directed to the development of the universal consciousness. Every human being contributes, in some way or another, to this expansion. In that way, the universal consciousness is getting more aware of itself and developing into unlimited horizons.

Coming back to our ontological and time-honored question: Who are you? Let's first ponder the following biblical passage:

³ When I consider your heavens,

the work of your fingers, the moon and the stars,

which you have set in place,

⁴ what is mankind that you are mindful of them,

human beings that you care for them?

⁵ You have made them a little lower than the angels [Elohim]

and crowned them with glory and honor.
(Psalm 8:4–5, NIV).

In verse five, "You have made them a little lower than the angels," the correct translation should be "You have made them a little *lower than the gods.*" This has been acknowledged in the NIV version of the Bible, where there is a footnote to that effect.

This takes us back to the burning bush incident and to the enigmatic statement "I Am Who I Am." In this expression lies the core issue of existentialism and "the secret of secrets" in plain sight for the Occidental Mystery Tradition. The Divinity told Moses indirectly that the "I Am" is your inner self. Your inner self, who always envisions self-liberation and higher self-fulfillment, is sending you to experience your potentiality as a human being. In similar circumstances, we usually feel powerless and incapable of achieving a huge task, but if we believe in ourselves and have self-confidence in the inner self, most likely we will accomplish the task, or at least we will get very close to it. The underlying message here is that the Divinity is telling Moses indirectly, "You have the power to do it." Incidentally, we should always remember that *"I*

Am" *is the name of God,* who is always with us, no matter what; it is the power of God dwelling within us.

The identity crisis arises when we identity the "I Am" with externals such as our bodies, thoughts, or emotions. Or when we define the "I Am" by our social status, or by our names, social categories, or social roles such as "I am a psychologist, or I am a carpenter, or I am a poor man, I am smarter, and so forth. All those external labels do *not* define our inner selves. They are merely labels of comparison with other human beings; instead they create a sense of separateness and competitiveness. Sad to say, most people search for that divine power in faraway lands and places when the most secret mystery is in plain sight and very close to us. Some don't believe this because they think it is too simple. The masters of life (sages and initiates) don't want to overemphasize this truth; they prefer that everyone should find the message for himself or herself, and that way they will value it.

Metaphysical tradition ascribes to the Greek philosopher Pythagoras the expression: "Know thyself and thou shall know the mysteries of God and the universe."[3] Socrates, one the greatest philosophers of the Occidental world, took this injunction as his personal motto. Indeed, to "know thyself" is a sine qua non condition for reaching Christ consciousness or Buddha's state of enlightenment. In passing it should be mentioned that Pythagoras was very familiar with the teachings of Oriental and Occidental occult and Hermetic philosophies. He traveled around the ancient world learning from all the branches of mysticism. Reportedly he was initiated into the Egyptian, Babylonian, and Chaldean Mysteries.[4]

The injunction "Man, know thyself" is the master key for self-development and self-transformation. Proper understanding of this proverb leads to discovery of the philosophers' stone of the alchemist and to the meaning of existence.

It is interesting to analyze the Oracle of Delphi to better understand the message of this adage, "Know thyself." In ancient Greece, people used to come to the temple of Apollo to ask the spirit of Apollo for advice concerning their lives. The process was more or less as follows: people's questions were addressed to Pythia, the priestess, or medium, who channeled the spirit of Apollo. Pythia would pronounce her prophesies while the priests wrote them down and translated them to the people. The temple's walls were inscribed with words of wisdom received by Pythia, such as "Know thyself," "Nothing in excess is good," and the like.

Chaerephon was Socrates's close friend; he once consulted the Oracle of Delphi and asked, "Is there was any person in the world wiser than Socrates?" The oracle answered: "No man is wiser than Socrates." Chaerephon pleasantly conveyed the oracle's pronouncement to Socrates. But Socrates in his modesty did not take that assessment for granted. Therefore, he decided to test himself with other people who were considered the wisest and most intelligent of the time. After questioning the wisest men of Greece, Socrates found that people boasted about their knowledge; that attitude hindered them from being able to acquire further knowledge. In addition, their pride eroded some of their wisdom, as they lacked humility. Hence, *humility* was the most significant characteristic of wisdom. Socrates found the true meaning of the Oracle of Delphi was not that he was the most intelligent person in the world, but that, among other humans of that time, he *was the wisest man because he was aware of his own ignorance.* From this the Socratic saying "I know that I know nothing" is derived. In fact, the wisest people on earth are probably the most humble ones.

Socrates's attitude and example are the right approach to gaining wisdom. This is the beginning of learning—becoming aware of our ignorance in the infinite sphere of wisdom; adopting a humble attitude and recognizing that our own ignorance is the beginning of wisdom.

Socrates was an authentic philosopher, a philosopher who loved and sought wisdom per se, not to gain money or fame. The common characteristic of Jesus Christ and Socrates is the evidence that they did not leave any writings; however, their knowledge and example have profoundly impacted the entire universe. Ironically, both were unjustly sentenced to death for their teachings, which, paradoxically, are still prevalent in modern times.

Jesus's spiritual teachings were preserved by his apostles, while Socrates's philosophical teachings were recorded in the form of dialogues by his disciple Plato, in which most of the conversation is directed by Socrates and other personages, not by Plato. Thus, the problem has been to determine which ideas belong to Socrates and which to Plato. This concern has already been verbalized by G. W. Hegel in his *Lectures on the History of Philosophy*.

The thing that I find ironic is the fact that Hegel, a philosopher who is considered extremely difficult to understand, complains that Plato's writings are difficult to comprehend. Hegel finds a solution to that impasse, indicating that Plato merely exposes the philosophy of Socrates and other early sophists and philosophers.[5] He further affirms that philosophy in general is one and is developed sequentially by succeeding philosophers. Thus, according to Hegel, philosophy should be considered to be a continuation of previous philosophers, as evolvement or development of the "idea." As per Hegel, Plato's philosophy is the summary and continuation of all Greek philosophical speculation before him, which has been expressed in what is called Platonism and Neo-Platonism. Hegel concludes, "Plato does nothing more than explain the doctrines of earlier philosophers; and the only particular feature in his representation of them is that their scope is extended."[6] In that sense, Platoism should be considered the systematic body of Greek knowledge, and not necessarily belonging to Plato himself.

The late British author Alan Alford (1961–2011) had a persuasive theory about the forty-two volumes of dialogues ascribed to Plato. As per Alford, some scholars are of the opinion that several dialogues were lost over time; if that is the case, there were more than forty-two dialogues. Alford expressed the same concern as Hegel: "It is virtually impossible to tell if a certain idea belonged to Socrates or to Plato. Where does Socrates's philosophy end and Plato's begin?"[7] It should also be considered that there are some ideas belonging to the participants on the dialogues, and those resulted from the discussions of the disciples of Socrates.

For instance, the theory of *anamnesis* (Greek for "recollection" or "reminiscence") was propounded by Socrates in two dialogues:

"Meno" and "Phaedo." According to Socrates, what we call learning is actually recollection of facts that we possessed before incarnation into human form. However, academia gives the credit for this to Plato, when it is Socrates who is the one talking in the two dialogues. I understand that Plato (and many Socrates and Plato students) wrote the dialogue, but Socrates is the one who is formulating this concept.

According to the theory of anamnesis, there are certain basic ideas, innate beliefs, and knowledge in the mind before we are incarnated in this world. Thus, under this theory, learning is understood as remembering knowledge that was once ours before we were born. Socrates's explanation is that the human soul knew these things before it was born, so that learning these things is really just a matter of recollecting them. This has been acknowledged by philosophers such as Descartes and others, who argued that certain concepts and knowledge could not have been acquired from sensory experience in this life but are inherent to some human beings. As contemporary examples, one can mention the cases of Phineas P. Quimby, father of the New Thought movement, and José Silva, founder of the Silva Method; the first attended school for only about three weeks and the second never stepped into a classroom. Both of them were self-taught. The interesting thing is that their teaching and theories have deeply influenced modern American society.

So why is it that we don't remember that we are extensions of the Divine Source? Why we don't recall the innate knowledge we had before we were born? The explanation I posit is that for some reason we forget our divine origin as well as the knowledge and wisdom we had at the moment of birth, and then we conduct our lives hypnotized by the mechanical causation of the external world, dismissing the priority of the internal world. In this way, we put the carriage before the horse. We humans suffer from amnesia syndrome since we threw out of the Garden of Eden—womb of the mother—in psychological terms.

Returning to our discussions, as per Alford, modern scholars recognize that many of "Plato's works" were not actually written by Plato himself but by other Socratic and Platonic writers; this seems a reasonable thesis, considering the extensive writings extant without counting the lost works. In fact, of the "forty-two" books mentioned above, modern scholars believe that "between thirteen and sixteen volumes should be attributed to '*the school of Plato*' rather than Plato per se."[8] Another thing to keep in mind is that most of the Platonic ideas were indelibly influenced by Socrates. Alford concludes his assessment as follows:

> My own feeling is that Plato personally authored just three books: *Timaeus, Critias* and *Laws* (the latter being unpublished at the time of his death in 347 BC). In my opinion, all of the other books, including the famous treatise *Republic* which acts as a direct prelude to *Timaeus, Critias* and *Laws*, were authored by other Socratic writers, with the credit later being given to Plato as the founder of the Academy for philosophical studies of this kind."[9]

Much credit has been given to Plato as author of the dialogues, dismissing the role of Socrates, who was one of the greatest thinkers of the past. Plato himself described Socrates as "the wisest and justest man of that time."

The injunction that Socrates selected as his motto: "*Man, know thyself*," has a profound message. Only a rigorous analysis of ourselves that unmasks our own shortcomings and defects impels us to improve ourselves and become better. And this act of discovering who we really are leads us to inquire what or who the *Self* is. Answering this question is the real purpose of humankind on planet Earth.

In his many freestanding essays found online, Neville Goddard states that our true identity is "I Am Awareness," which is synonymous with consciousness. He further states "Awareness is my Father,"[10] and "'I AM' is pure awareness, and this awareness is omnipresent, omniscient, and omnipotent. The 'I AM' is the thinker and feeler through our thoughts and emotions."[11] From this, it can be inferred, if the other names of God are consciousness and awareness, the individual awareness is the localized consciousness.

Indeed, awareness provides the ability to handle things while they are happening. The more aware a person is, the more the person is able to consciously direct his or her creation. When there is no awareness, there is no element directing the power of consciousness. Since awareness is the highest level of consciousness, nothing can come into our lives until we are aware of it. To say, "I am awareness," is similar to saying, "I am consciousness." Incidentally, Descartes's famous statement "I think, therefore I am" indicates the act of awareness as a condition of being. It recognizes that *I exist because I am aware.*

In preceding pages, the real meaning of the names of the biblical God has been expounded. Many people do not realize that they are using the name of God ("I Am") on a daily basis, and we are not aware of its profound and powerful meaning. Isn't it a paradox and a sacrilege when we diminish that magical name and spend most of our time feeling powerless? Although these concepts have been stated previously, it is important to repeat them so they can sink into the collective mind.

I confess that I was unable to really grasp the mystical meaning of this for most of my life because I was indoctrinated by my Christian education and by conventional wisdom. After many years of disappointment and tribulation from seeking the truth in the wrong places, I finally was able to realize that the truth and the Divinity are closer than my nose.

Hence, my long quest to find ultimate reality and the role of humans on this planet boils down to the ancient proverb inscribed on the forecourt of the Temple of Apollo at Delphi: "Man, know thyself, and thou shall know the universe and its gods." This is complemented by the Cartesian statement "I think, therefore I am." It is the capacity for self-inquiry that makes humans aware of their existence. The ensuing axiom is the name of God: "I am that I am." These are the cornerstones of Occidental philosophy and are intimately interrelated.

The introspection of knowing oneself takes us to the axiom "I am who I am," meaning Eternal Becoming. "I Am" is the feeling of permanent awareness. Thus, the *statement of being* "I Am Conscious" indicates that the act of thinking is an inherent condition of awareness. The only thinker is the "*I Am*"; awareness is the basis of being.

To be is to exist. This axiom is composed of a subject and a verb, which denotes that the subject is in the process of awareness. The very center of consciousness is the feeling of "I Am." In this context, the words "I Am" and "consciousness" are synonymous. The original consciousness (the original Verb) is the creative principle of life.

In Jungian psychology, there are three parts of the Self: the conscious mind, the unconscious mind, and the ego. The Self is the sum total of the psyche; it embraces both consciousness and the subconscious. The Self is the center of the totality of the psyche (soul) that contains the drive toward fulfillment and individuation. According to Jung, the ego is the center of the field of consciousness, the part of the psyche where our conscious awareness resides, our sense of identity and existence. The ego is a small portion of the Self; it is the agent that organizes "our thoughts, feelings, senses, and intuition, and [regulates] access to memory. It is the part that links the inner and outer worlds together, forming how we relate to that which is external to us."[12]

Westerners seek to affirm the ego as a means of awareness and of conquering the physical realm, while in the East, the goal is to dissolve or eliminate the ego. Hindu teachers usually illustrate this with the salt-and-water story. They say if a grain of salt is thrown into water, it will dissolve, and that grain of salt will no longer exist. This is exactly the purpose of their spiritual practices: the dissolution of the ego into the Atman (universal soul).

The ego should not be confused with the words "I Am," which are central to the selfhood of humans. The "I Am" uses the physical body and its psychological components to manipulate the physical world. The "I Am" is synonymous with the "self."

The most radical teaching of Buddha is his declaration that there is no such thing as the ego. For Buddha, the ego is not real; it is only an illusion. Buddhism seeks to eliminate the ego to eradicate selfishness. For Western individuals, whether religious or secular, the ego is real, as has been demonstrated above. Selfishness can be transformed into altruism, but one needs the ego as a tool to accomplish this. In other words, the ego is needed to create either selfish greed or justice in love.

In metaphysical terms, consciousness is the only reality; it is the only cause and effect of the phenomena of life. What appear to be circumstances, conditions, and even material objects are the products of one's own consciousness. Consequently, one's reality and social environment are not separate from oneself and cannot be regarded as existing separately. The individual and his or her personal world are one. The external world is the mirror of the internal world. Therefore, in order to change the external world, or the "objective appearance of things," one must change the subjective world; the patterns held in our subconscious minds have to be changed. And each individual is the only one who can do that.

Thus, instead of asking who one is, one should ask oneself who one is not.

A Metaphysical Answer: You Are a Magician

All the power that ever was or will be dwells in you;
whoever tells you otherwise is a liar.
—ALBERT AMAO SORIA

Be still, and know that I Am God.
—PSALM 46:10 (KJV)

BELIEVE IT OR not, you are a magician in your own right. Whether we want it or not, *we are all magicians.* We can use magical words such as "Abracadabra" ("I create as I speak") or the magical name "Ehyeh" ("I Am") to create our own reality and social environment. One is a "white magician" if one's acts and thoughts are of kindness, love, understanding, compassion, and spreading positive ideas and behaviors for the betterment of humankind. One is a "black magician" if one dwells on negative thoughts, nurses feelings of resentment and envy, dwells on hate and selfish greed, and sees the world under negative paradigms. Although these concepts are nothing new, it is time for modern humankind to fully grasp this truth.

What makes it black or white magic is *the intention.* As Madame Blavatsky has accurately stated, "For it is the motive, *and the motive alone*, which makes any exercise of power become black, malignant, or white, beneficent Magic."[1]

The fluidic nature of reality has already been demonstrated. Every moment, wanted or not, we are creating; that is universal law. In this eternal process of becoming, one as a magician shapes and gives form to the flowing life force called consciousness, or the zero point field.

The external observed reality results from an intermingling of creations by myriads of people, most of whom are creating semiconsciously according to their subconscious patterns. As a magician, one has been creating one's own reality and social environment since birth. Every person has the power to change or transform his or her reality if he or she does not like it.

Before proceeding, we need to define what we understand as "magic." In the Middle Ages, the word "magic" alluded to enchantment—a sense of power, of creating things at will. The term "magic" has been abused and has come to mean a hoax or trickery, used for negative purposes.

In general terms, we can distinguish three kinds of magic: (a) fictional magic, which includes ancient legends and fairy tales; (b) stage magic, performances by professional conjurers for the purpose of entertaining the public with tricks and incantations that appear real; and finally, (c) creative magic, which can be defined as the innate capacity of a human to create his or her personal reality. This last statement may sound difficult to believe; however, it is absolutely true. One of the purposes of this chapter is to demonstrate how powerful a magician each person really is, and that magic—the power of creation—resides within each individual.

I understand "*personal reality*" to mean the particular social environment of a specific individual derived from the individual's personal attitude toward life and others, his or her belief system (religious, philosophical, political, cultural, etc.), prejudices, and level of awareness. Based on these premises, each person designs his or her reality or personal world, which is usually different from that of other humans.

The magnum opus of occultism and alchemy is the mastery of ourselves, or perfect self-control. However, until that is achieved, we cannot attain spiritual fulfillment. In spite of external appearances, one has to feel in control of oneself. The conditions and events of one's life are one's mental children, formed from the moldings of one's subconscious impressions. They are made in the image and likeness of one's innermost feelings and may reveal aspects that are lodged in one's subconscious mind.

The creative process is first imagining and then believing the state imagined. One should always imagine and expect the best. The world cannot change until we change our conceptions of ourselves first: "As within, so without." Thus, the magic of tomorrow is being the conscious creator of one's reality and environment, right now.

People are only what one believes them to be. No matter what the problem is, no matter where it is, no matter whom it concerns, a person has no one to change but him- or herself, and one has neither opponent nor helper in bringing about that internal change. We have nothing to do but convince ourselves of the truth that we can manifest our dreams and desires. As long as we succeed in convincing ourselves of the reality sought, results will follow to confirm that belief (faith).

Many spiritual authors have acknowledged the power of human beings; for instance, writer Marianne Williamson accurately indicated, "Our deepest fear is not that we are inadequate. Our deepest fear is that we are powerful beyond measure. It is our light, not our darkness, that most frightens us."[2]

Reaching this level of spiritual awareness and putting into practice the psychological principles outlined here are indispensable elements in transforming oneself and one's destiny. All one needs to do is follow the principles explained above, such as regaining one's inner power, creative visualization, affirmations, proper breathing, and healthy nutrition. The first thing is to accept responsibility for the present situation, let go of the past, forgive oneself and others, and reassess one's options for the future according to one's real mental, intellectual, and physical capabilities. These steps will allow everyone to regain control over his or her life and circumstances. It is important to be kind and patient with oneself. Patience as a method of persistence is a valuable virtue, and it will be of great use toward achieving one's goals. One of the purposes of this book is to set each person free from all self-imposed limitations. However, we have to love ourselves first and feel rich in spirit to attract more love, wealth, and prosperity.

One very important element is honest introspection to determine what holds one back and what stumbling blocks or psychological resistances are in one's way. It is important to identify the psychological determinants that are running in one's subconscious mind. Is it a sense of inferiority, lack of determination, powerlessness, past traumatic events, or unrecognized inner conflicts? What are the factors that are hindering a person in reaching his or her goals in life?

The esoteric and occult traditions generally hold the viewpoint that reality consists of four major realms: the gross, the subtle, the causal, and the spiritual. The *gross realm* is the realm of the material body, the world we can see with our physical senses in the waking state. The *subtle realm* is the field of the mind and its displays, which we can see in a vivid form in the dream state and in certain states of meditation. The *causal realm* is the landmark of pure, formless consciousness, unlimited and unbounded, radically free and radically full. The causal realm is experienced by everybody in deep, dreamless sleep (which is pure formlessness without an object), but it yields its final secrets only when it is entered with full consciousness. The *spiritual*, or *numinous*, realm is something we can attain in certain profound meditative states, various types of satori or initial awakening, and vastly expanded states of boundless consciousness. All these are subtle states of consciousness.

The problem usually arises when one gets stuck identifying with the "false created identity" as we indicated before. This false identity overshadows the real Self and becomes enmeshed with the illusory world, or the "maya." Most of the time, the subconscious mind (which has been conditioned and programmed with ideas and wrong beliefs acquired during our upbringing) is the engine (main motivator) that propels our personality.

We already noted the importance of discrimination, that is, the capacity to distinguish the real from the false, to question everything as to its real value, and to discern the illusory world from the real one. The faculty of discrimination allows each person to distinguish between the mirage of glamorous illusion and the world of manifestation. It is this discriminatory power that helps one avoid false prophets, cults, and myths that entrap those seeking spiritual and esoteric knowledge. At this point, we should be aware that the real healer is our inner being, to whom all credit should be given.

To summarize, there is a tremendous power latent within each human being that can be tapped with discipline, prayer, concentration, and meditation. There is no guru, teacher, healer, or anyone else who can liberate us from bondage to the external, sensorial world. The individual alone is the solution to all of his or her problems.

Jesus has taught that the same divine Father dwells in every human being; thus we all have the same divine Father. He also taught that humans can do things similar to those he did (John 14:12, NIV). So what is holding you back? Why don't we all exercise our divine rights? The problem is that we have been brainwashed since we were children and maybe even in previous lives, with erroneous ideas that we are powerless. In other words, we have been indoctrinated most of our lives with the single idea: "We are not good enough."

Buddha's famous last exhortation to his disciple before his death was "Work out your own salvation. Do not depend on others."[3] The staggering thing is that we find similar advice in the Bible, which says, "Work out your own salvation with fear and trembling" (Philippians 2:12, KJV). Ironically, this verse is overlooked by fundamentalist Christian ministers for their own convenience. The truth of the matter is that nobody is able to save anybody; one has to save oneself. Here we come back to the notion of self-reliance.

Although we should work out our own "salvation," we still need spiritual assistance in our spiritual unfoldment. At this point, it is appropriate to mention again the old saying "God helps those who help themselves," which conveys the idea very well. Therefore, to get an extra push or assistance to tread the path of return, one needs what has been called "providential help"; that is, divine intervention in the most difficult moments of our lives. Most people consider this "help" luck or a miracle.

To get this help, intense and honest prayer is extremely important. Israel Regardie, a well-known esoteric and occult writer, quoted the following spiritual adage: "Inflame thyself with prayer"[4]; this is an effective step in invoking not only spiritual protection, but also assistance in our spiritual evolution. Thus, invoke the God Flame of love and peace to elevate your mind to the Divine. The real identity is reached when we achieve union with our higher self.

Thus, it seems appropriate to close with an ancient prayer that summarizes the message of this book. The prayer's name is "Invocation to the Flame." It should be kept in mind that when we pray, we pray to the inner self ("I Am") that dwells in each of us. Jesus has given us the key for it: "But when you pray, go into your room, close the door and pray to your Father, who is unseen. Then your Father, who sees what is done in secret, will reward you" (Matthew 6:6, NIV).

Since early times the fire has been venerated as the symbol of the Divinity throughout all civilizations and religions of the world. The fire flame represents the inner light that burns in every human being. It is the symbol of the inner spark as well as of light and divine love. The flame is the symbol of the beginning of creation, of the sun, which keeps alive every creature on the face of the universe. It is the burning bush in the book of Exodus, and the flame that animates human beings. Let's keep the Divine alive in the flame of the burning bush, with our prayers and candles, and lamps in every sacred place.

The ancients used to sit around the fire pit and stare in a contemplative disposition, which led them into altered states of mind. The flame waves always invoke in people's minds the mystery of the unfathomable one. In the Bible we read that the Divinity appeared to Moses as a burning bush. In the Incan culture, they used to celebrate the "fire ceremony," which was traditionally held on or around a full moon and a new moon, as means of purification and atonement. In India, the fire was known as Agni, the Fire God. The Upanishads, one of the most sacred books of the Hindu tradition, states:

O Agni, O Fire God, lead us along the

Right path so that we can enjoy the fruits of

Our divine actions."[5]

The following is a beautiful ancient prayer expressed in a way of invocation; it summarizes the spiritual message of this book:

INVOCATION TO THE FLAME[6]

I call upon thee, O living God, radiant with
    Illuminating Fire!
O Unseen Parent of the Sun,
pour forth Thy light-giving power and energize
Thy Divine Spark.
Enter into this Flame and let it be
    agitated
by the breaths of Thy Holy Spirit!
Manifest Thy Power and open for me the
    Temple
of the Almighty God which is within this Fire!
Manifest Thy Light for my regeneration,
and let the Breadth, Height, Fullness
and Crown of the Solar Radiance appear!
And may the God within shine forth!

Amen.

Notes

Introduction

1. "self-help," Dictionary by Merriam-Webster, https://www.merriam -webster.com/dictionary/self-help.
2. The Law of Attraction is discussed in detail in my book *Healing Without Medicine: From Pioneers to Modern Practice* (Wheaton, IL: Quest Books, 2014).
3. Napoleon Hill, *Think & Grow Rich* (New York: Fall River Press, 2012), ix.

Chapter 1: Overview of the Self-Help Movement

1. Steven Starker, *Oracle at the Supermarket: The American Preoccupation With Self-Help Books* (New Brunswick, NJ: Transaction Publisher, 2008), 2.
2. Ibid., ix.
3. Ibid., 1.
4. Ibid.
5. Ibid., 2.
6. Steve Salerno, *Sham: How the Self-Help Movement Made America Helpless* (New York: Crown Publishers, 2005), 25–26.
7. Ibid., 8.
8. Ibid.
9. Ibid., 3.

10. Napoleon Hill, *Think and Grow Rich* (New York: Fall River Press, 2012), xi.
11. Caroline Fraser, *God's Perfect Child: Living and Dying in the Christian Science Church* (New York: Henry Holt & Company, 1999), 13.
12. "Poorest U.S. Presidents," Investopedia, http://www.investopedia.com /slide-show/poor-us-presidents/.
13. "William Holmes McGuffey: An American Educator," Encyclopedia Britannica, www.britannica.com/biography/William-Holmes-McGuffey.
14. Starker, *Oracle at the Supermarket*, 16.
15. Quoted in Starker, *Oracle at the Supermarket*, 17.
16. "*The Little Engine That Could*," *Wikipedia*, https://en.wikipedia.org/wiki /The_Little_Engine_That_Could.
17. Ibid.
18. Micki McGee, *Self-Help, Inc.: Makeover Culture in American Life* (New York: Oxford University Press, 2005), vii.
19. Éliphas Lévi (1810–1875) is the father of the modern revival of occult science in the Occidental world.
20. "Self-Help, Inc.—About the Author," Self-Help, Inc.: Makeover Culture in American Life, http://www.selfhelpinc.com/author.html.
21. McGee, *Self-Help, Inc.*, 195.
22. Ibid., 24.
23. Tom Tiede, *Self-Help Nation: The Long Overdue, Entirely Justified, Delightfully Hostile Guide to the Snake-Oil Peddlers Who Are Sapping Our Nation's Soul* (New York: Atlantic Monthly Press, 2001), 15, 18.
24. Barbara Ehrenreich, *Bright-Sided: How the Relentless Promotion of Positive Thinking Has Undermined America* (New York: Metropolitan Books, 2009), 8.
25. Ibid., 11.

CHAPTER 2: OVERVIEW OF POSITIVE THINKING

1. Mitch Horowitz, *One Simple Idea: How Positive Thinking Reshaped Modern Life* (New York: Crown Publishers, 2014), 8.
2. Ibid., 10.
3. Ibid., 7.
4. Anne Harrington, *The Cure Within: A History of Mind-Body Medicine* (New York: W. W. Norton & Company, 2008), 33.
5. Ibid., 153.
6. Ibid., 136.
7. Ibid., 126.
8. Ibid., 137.

9. Refer to my book *Healing Without Medicine*.
10. A wealth of information on Emerson's writings can be found at the following website: http://www.emersoncentral.com/selfreliance.htm.
11. Edward F. Edinger, *Ego and Archetype: Individuation and the Religious Function of the Psyche* (New York: G. P. Putnam's Sons, 1972), 107.
12. "Truth is a Pathless Land," J. Krishnamurti Online, http://www.jkrishnamurti.org/about-krishnamurti/dissolution-speech.php.
13. Horowitz, *One Simple Idea*, 79.
14. "Warren Felt Evans," http://warrenfeltevans.wwwhubs.com/.
15. Horowitz, *One Simple Idea*, 81.
16. Napoleon Hill, *Think and Grow Rich* (New York: Fall River Press, 2012), 1.
17. "The Life of Ernest Holmes," Science of Mind Archives, http://www.scienceofmindarchives.org/about-the-archives/about-ernest-holmes.
18. Ibid.
19. Mitch Horowitz, *Occult America: The Secret History of How Mysticism Shaped Our Nation* (New York: Bantam Books, 2009), 94.
20. See Harrington, *The Cure Within*, 120. Refer also to Horowitz, *Occult America*, 95.
21. Harrington, *The Cure Within*, 119.
22. Norman Vincent Peale, *The Power of Positive Thinking: A Practical Guide to Mastering the Problems of Everyday Living* (New York: Touchstone, 1980), 212. Also in e-book version, at http://www.makemoneywithpyxism.info/joinstevehawk.com/PowerOfPositiveThinking.pdf.
23. Harrington, *The Cure Within*, 119–120.
24. "Peale 33 Degree Mason Proof," online at http://www.theforbidden knowledge.com/hardtruth/norman_vincent_peale33.htm.
25. Peale, *The Power of Positive Thinking*, 66.
26. Tom Tiede, *Self-Help Nation: The Long Overdue, Entirely Justified, Delightfully Hostile Guide to the Snake-Oil Peddlers Who Are Sapping Our Nation's Soul* (New York: Atlantic Monthly Press, 2001), 21.
27. Regarding Rhonda Byrne's book and video *The Secret*, scientist Robert L. Park has this to say. "The great champion of *The Secret*, who single-handedly made it a runaway best-seller, is Oprah Winfrey, the queen of day-time television. . . . [B]y featuring *The Secret* twice on her popular daytime talk show, Oprah guaranteed it would be a huge financial success." Robert L. Park, *Superstition: Belief in the Age of Science* (New Jersey: Princeton University Press, 2008), 126.
28. Harrington, *The Cure Within*, 119.

29. M. Scott Peck, *The Road Less Traveled: A New Psychology of Love, Traditional Values, and Spiritual Growth* (New York: Simon & Schuster, 2003), 6.
30. Peck, *The Road Less Traveled*, 277–278.
31. Ibid.
32. Tom Tiede, *Self-Help Nation*, 15.
33. Ibid., 15–16.
34. Ibid., 15.
35. Peck, *The Road Less Traveled*, 311.
36. Tiede, *Self-Help Nation*, 224.
37. Mitch Horowitz, "All You Can Be: Why Positive Thinking Matters," *Quest* (Winter 2016), 16.

CHAPTER 3: MAKING SENSE OF SELF-HELP AND POSITIVE THINKING

1. Ralph Waldo Emerson's "Self-Reliance," http://www.emersoncentral. com/selfreliance.htm.
2. Mitch Horowitz, *One Simple Idea: How Positive Thinking Reshaped Modern Life* (New York: Crown Publishers, 2014), 4. Also his article "All You Can Be: Why Positive Thinking Matters," *Quest* (Winter 2016), 16.
3. Richard Wiseman, *The "As If" Principle: The Radically New Approach to Changing Your Life* (New York: Simon & Schuster, 2012), xi.
4. Steven Starker, *Oracle at the Supermarket: The American Preoccupation With Self-Help Books* (New Brunswick, NJ: Transaction Publisher, 2008), 173.
5. Ron Rhodes, "Anthony Robbins and the Quest for Unlimited Power," Spiritual Counterfeits Project, http://www.scp-inc.org/publications /journals/J2202/Rhodes.htm.
6. Albert Ellis, *Overcoming Resistance: Rational Emotive Therapy with Difficult Clients* (New York: Springer Publishing, 1985), 147.
7. See also "The Chief of Sinners," http://www.evangelicaloutreach.org /worst-of-sinners.htm.
8. Refer to my book *Healing Without Medicine*.
9. See the interesting essay by Marie Ziemer McCarthy, "Calvin, Milton, & the Fall of Man." Free online PDF version can be found at http://www .bu.edu/av/core/journal/xxiv/McCarthy.pdf. See also the Belgic Confession at https://www.crcna.org/welcome/beliefs/confessions/belgic-confession.
10. Max Weber in his remarkable book *The Protestant Ethic and the Spirit of Capitalism* advanced the idea that the rise of modern capitalism was attributable to Protestantism, particularly Calvinism.

11. Mitch Horowitz, *Occult America: The Secret History of How Mysticism Shaped Our Nation* (New York: Bantam Books, 2009), 87.
12. Ibid., 87.
13. Anne Harrington, *The Cure Within: A History of Mind-Body Medicine* (New York: W. W. Norton & Company, 2008), 126, 135.
14. Horowitz, *One Simple Idea*, 3.
15. Horowitz, "All You Can Be," 15.
16. Ibid., 17.
17. Refer to the chapter entitled "New Thought and the Law of Attraction" in my book *Healing Without Medicine*.
18. Esther and Jerry Hicks, *Ask and It Is Given: Learning to Manifest Your Desires* (New York: Hay House, 2004), 15.
19. Someone who believes in reincarnation would say that Walter W. Atkinson is one of the masters who channel through Esther Hicks. The teachings of "Abraham" are very similar to the ones of Atkinson. Incidentally, modern scholars have ascribed the authorship of *The Kybalion* to Atkinson, who wrote this treatise under the pen name "The Three Initiates."
20. Hicks, *Ask and It Is Given*, 15.
21. Horowitz, *One Simple Idea*, 4. See also his article "All You Can Be," 16.

CHAPTER 4: THE FALLACY OF THE "POWER OF NOW"

1. The dialectic is a scientific discipline that considers the universe and everything in it to be in an eternal process of transformation and becoming. For more, refer to my book *Beyond Conventional Wisdom* (Bloomington, IN: AuthorHouse, 2006).
2. Eckhart Tolle, *The Power of the Now: A Guide to Spiritual Enlightenment* (Novato, CA: New World Library, 1999), 3, 4.
3. Ibid., 5.
4. Ibid., xiv.
5. Ibid., 8.
6. Stanislav Grof, "Psychology of the Future: Lessons from Modern Consciousness Research," http://www.stanislavgrof.com/wp-content /uploads/pdf/Psychology_of_the_Future_Stan_Grof_long.pdf. Refer also to his book with the same title.
7. Ibid.
8. Tolle, *The Power of Now*, 12.
9. Ibid., 13.
10. Ibid., 15.
11. Ibid., 12.

12. Ibid., 15.
13. Ibid.
14. Ibid., 18.
15. Ibid., 22.
16. Ibid., 16–17.
17. Ibid., 23.
18. Ibid., 5.
19. Paul Foster Case: "Introduction to Tarot" 1:7; Builders of the Adytum (BOTA) lessons by correspondence. Builders of the Adytum (BOTA) is a Qabalisitic organization founded by Paul F. Case. They send lessons to their members. This note makes reference to the lesson "Introduction to Tarot," lesson 1, page 7. This is the conventional way that they identify the Correspondence Lessons. Lately, former members of this organization have published much of the Correspondence Lessons in several books such as the *Wisdom of Tarot: The Golden Dawn Tarot Series*, which has been noted in the bibliography. There are some lessons that have not been published, as the one quoted here.
20. C. G. Jung, *Memories, Dreams, Reflections,* ed. Aniela Jaffe, trans. Richard and Clara Winston (New York: Vintage, 1989), 304.
21. Jung, *Memories, Dreams, Reflections*, 319.
22. Pamela B. Paresky, "What is Reality?" *Psychology Today*, https://www.psychologytoday.com/blog/happiness-and-the-pursuit-leadership/201510/what-is-reality.
23. Tolle, *The Power of Now*, 52.
24. Lee Pulos, "The Future Creates the Present—NOT the Past!" Adventures in Learning, http://drpulos.com/blog/the-future-creates-the-present-%E2%80%93-not-the-past/.
25. "The Neuropsychology of Self-Discipline," YouTube video, https://www.youtube.com/watch?v=-wcn2EbOIbQ.
26. Von Braschler, *7 Secrets of Time Travel* (Rochester, VT: Inner Traditions, 1982), 5.
27. Ibid., 4.
28. Ibid., 25.
29. L. Ron Gardner, *Beyond the Power of the Now: A Guide to, and Beyond, Eckhart Tolle's Teaching* (USA: Vernal Point Publishing, 2012), 8.
30. Ibid.
31. Ibid., 8.
32. Ibid.
33. Ibid.
34. Ibid., 9.

35. Ibid.
36. Ibid.
37. Ibid., 8.
38. Arthur Green, *Ehyeh: A Kabbalah for Tomorrow* (Woodstock, Vermont: Jewish Light Publishing, 2004), 5.
39. Ibid., 5.
40. "Galactic Year," Wikipedia, https://en.wikipedia.org/wiki/Galactic_year.
41. Refer to the Amazon website: http://www.amazon.com/gp/pdp/profile /A3NH00FP22PTR5/ref=cm_cr_pr_pdp.
42. Andrea Sachs, "Channeling Ram Dass," *TIME* 161, no. 16, April 21, 2003, 79. Also at http://content.time.com/time/magazine/article /0,9171,1004693,00.html.

Chapter 5: The "As If" Principle and the Power of Assumption

1. Paul F. Case, Correspondence Lessons, *Tarot Fundamentals* 20:3.
2. Refer to Wiseman's books: *59 Seconds: Change Your Life in Under a Minute* and *The "As If" Principle: The Radically New Approach to Changing Your Life*.
3. Ibid., 236–237.
4. Neville Goddard, *The Power of Awareness* (USA: Pacific Publishing Studio, 2010), 9.
5. Goddard, *The Power of Awareness*, 10–11.
6. Ibid., 10.
7. Ibid., 54.
8. Hill, *Think and Grow Rich*, 42.
9. For further information refer to my book *Healing Without Medicine*, 108–109.
10. Lee Pulos, "The Future Creates the Present—NOT the Past!" Adventures in Learning.
11. Quoted in Ibid.
12. Ibid.
13. Wiseman, *"The As If" Principle*, xi; repeated in the book's conclusion, 235, 236.
14. Ibid., 214.
15. Ibid.

Chapter 6: Self-Help and Therapeutic Suggestions

1. Refer to my book *Healing Without Medicine*.
2. Quoted by William W. Atkinson, *Suggestion and Autosuggestion* (Hollister, MO: YogeBooks, 1909), 62–63.

3. Norman Cousins, *Anatomy of an Illness as Perceived by the Patient* (New York: W. W. Norton & Company, 1979), 50–51.

4. Lolette Kuby, *Faith and the Placebo Effect: An Argument for Self-Healing* (Novato, CA: Origin Press, 2001), 2.

5. Ibid., 30.

6. Cousins, *Anatomy of an Illness*, 52.

7. Lissa Rankin, *Mind Over Medicine: Scientific Proof That You Can Heal Yourself* (New York: Hay House, 2013), xv.

8. Ibid., xiii.

9. Refer to my book, *Healing Without Medicine*, 177.

10. Atkinson, *Suggestion and Autosuggestion*, 47. Free online PDF version can be found at http://www.yogebooks.com/english/atkinson/1909suggestion.pdf.

11. Del Hunter Morrill, "The Power of Suggestion," http://www.hypnocenter.com/articles/the-power-of-suggestion.

12. Ibid.

13. Harriet Hall, "Does Religion Make People Healthier?" *Skeptic* 19, no. 1, 2014, 8.

14. Refer to my book, *Healing Without Medicine*, 171–172.

15. Hall, "Does Religion Make People Healthier?" 8.

16. Anne Harrington, *The Cure Within: A History of Mind-Body Medicine* (New York: W. W. Norton & Company, 2008), 135.

17. Atkinson, *Suggestion and Autosuggestion*, 61.

18. Ibid.

19. Ibid., 62.

20. Ibid., 57.

21. Ibid., 58.

22. See Willa Cather and Georgine Milmine, *The Life of Mary Baker G. Eddy and the History of Christian Science* (Lincoln, NE: University of Nebraska Press, 1993); also refer to my book *Healing Without Medicine*.

CHAPTER 7: CHRISTIAN SCIENCE AND COLLECTIVE SUGGESTION

1. Adam Crabtree, "Animal Magnetism, Early Hypnotism, and Psychical Research, 1766–1925," http://www.esalen.org/ctr-archive/animal_magnetism.html.

2. Caroline Fraser, *God's Perfect Child: Living and Dying in the Christian Science Church* (New York: Henry Hott & Company, 1999), 15.

3. Harriet Hall, "Faith Healing: Religious Freedom vs. Child Protection," *Skeptical Inquirer*, July/August 2014, 42.

4. *75 Books by Women Whose Words Have Changed the World*, https://www.utm.edu/staff/jimnance/bestbooks/newbery/seventy five.htm.

5. National Women's Hall of Fame, https://www.womenofthehall.org /inductee/mary-baker-eddy/.

6. Those interested in learning more about this topic should visit the website: https://exchristianscience.com.

7. Fraser, *God's Perfect Child*, 417.

8. "Dr. John M. Tutt," Mary Eddy Baker Institute. https://mbeinstitute.org /author/tutt-dr-john-m/author-john-m-tutt-index.html.

9. Ibid.

10. John M. Tutt, "The Role of a Practitioner," *Christian Science Sentinel*, June 12, 1965, http://sentinel.christianscience.com/shared/view /20mkoky1rnm.

11. The Bookmark, "Dr. John M. Tutt." http://thebookmark.com/dr-john -m-tutt/.

12. Mary Baker Eddy Science Institute, "Dr. John M. Tutt." https://mbeinstitute .org/author/tutt-dr-john-m/author-john-m-tutt-index.html.

13. Fraser, *God's Perfect Child*, 26.

14. Martin Gardner, *The Healing Revelations of Mary Baker Eddy: The Rise and Fall of Christian Science* (New York: Prometheus Books, 1993), 145–158.

15. Quoted in Ibid., 52.

16. Willa Cather and Georgine Milmine, *The Life of Mary Baker G. Eddy and the History of Christian Science* (Lincoln, NE: University of Nebraska Press, 1993), 118.

17. Tim Challies, "The False Teachers: Benny Hinn," https://www.challies .com/articles/the-false-teachers-benny-hinn/; also Leo Igwe, https://www .csicop.org/sb/show/benny_hinn_healing_crusade_ends_in _controversy.

18. Kuby, *Faith and the Placebo Effect*, p. 113.

19. Cather and Milmine, *The Life of Mary Baker G. Eddy*.

20. Mary Baker Eddy, *Miscellaneous Writings 1883–1896* (Boston: First Church of Christ, Scientist, 1924), ix.

21. Mary Baker Eddy, *Science and Health with Key to the Scriptures* (Boston: First Church of Christ, Scientist, 1971), 600.

22. Fraser, *God's Perfect Child*, 419.

23. Lolette Kuby, *Faith and the Placebo Effect: An Argument for Self-Healing* (Novato, CA: Origin Press, 2001), 5.

24. Ibid., 267.

CHAPTER 8: EXPLORING A SCIENTIFIC
RATIONALE OF SELF-DECEPTION

1. Norman Cousins, *Anatomy of an Illness as Perceived by the Patient* (New York: W. W. Norton & Company, 1979), 29.
2. Robert L. Park, *Superstition: Belief in the Age of Science* (New Jersey: Princeton University Press, 2008), 57.
3. Mary Baker Eddy, *Science and Health with Key to the Scriptures* (Boston: First Church of Christ, Scientist, 1971), 157.
4. Mary Baker Eddy, *Unity of Good and Other Writings* (Boston: Trustees under the Will of Mary Baker Eddy, 1919), 31.
5. Harriet Hall, "Faith Healing: Religious Freedom vs. Child Protection," *Skeptical Inquirer*, July/August 2014, 42.
6. John M. Tutt, "The Role of a Practitioner," *Christian Science Sentinel*, June 12, 1965, http://sentinel.christianscience.com/shared/view/20mkoky1rnm.
7. "persuasion," Thesaurus.com, http://www.thesaurus.com/browse/persuasion.
8. Quoted in Joseph Murphy, *The Power of Your Subconscious Mind* (Radford, VA: Wilder Publications, 2007), 60.
9. Martin Gardner, "The Healing Revelations of Mary Baker Eddy," *Kirkus Reviews*, https://www.kirkusreviews.com/book-reviews/martin-gardner/the-healing-revelations-of-mary-baker-eddy/.
10. Ibid.
11. Mary Baker Eddy, "Malicious Animal Magnetism," *The Christian Science Journal*, February 1889. Also at http://www.endtime.org/library/mbe/mam.html.
12. Lolette Kuby, *Faith and the Placebo Effect: An Argument for Self-Healing* (Novato, CA: Origin Press, 2001), 268.
13. Caroline Fraser, *God's Perfect Child: Living and Dying in the Christian Science Church* (New York: Henry Holt & Company, 1999), 14.
14. Ibid., 14, 435–444.
15. Ibid., 88.
16. Ibid., 21.
17. Ibid., 63.
18. Ibid.
19. Ibid.
20. Ibid., 51.
21. Ibid., 88.
22. Ibid., 14.
23. Ibid., 438.
24. Ibid., 441.

25. Ibid., 441.
26. Ibid., 442.
27. Ibid., 445.
28. Ibid., 372.
29. Ibid., 443.
30. Martin Gardner, "The Healing Revelations of Mary Baker Eddy," *Kirkus Reviews*.
31. Fraser, *God's Perfect Child*, 60.
32. Martin Gardner, *Mary Baker Eddy: The Rise and Fall of Christian Science* (New York: Prometheus Books, 1993), 145.
33. Ibid., 145–146.
34. Ibid., 172.

CHAPTER 9: RELIGION AND PLACEBO HEALING

1. Lolette Kuby, *Faith and the Placebo Effect: An Argument for Self-Healing* (Novato, CA: Origin Press, 2001), 7.
2. Henry F. Ellenberger, *The Discovery of the Unconscious: The History and Evolution of Dynamic Psychiatry* (New York: Basic Books, 1970), 53.
3. Ibid.
4. Harriet Hall, "Scientology's War on Medicine," *Skeptic* 18, no. 3, 2013, 9.
5. Scientology Handbook (Tools for Life), http://www.scientologyhandbook .org/.
6. Steven Starker, *Oracle at the Supermarket: The American Preoccupation With Self-Help Books* (New Brunswick, NJ: Transaction Publisher, 2008), 171.
7. Glove Eddy (aka Mary Baker Eddy), *Christian Healing, A Lecture Delivered at Boston* (Cambridge, MA: John Wilson and Son, 1905), 12. Also at https:// books.google.com/books?id=71EZAAAAYAAJ&pg=PA12&dq=Mind+as+ the+only+curative+principle&hl=en&sa=X&ved=0ahUKEwiZ6eODqvz RAhVBWGMKHTurBB4Q6AEIMTAE#v=onepage&q=Mind%20as %20the%20only%20curative%20principle&f=false.
8. Mary Baker Eddy, *Miscellaneous Writings, 1883–1896* (Boston: First Church of Christ, Scientist, 1896), 348.
9. Mary Baker Eddy, *Science and Health with Key to the Scriptures* (Boston: First Church of Christ, Scientist, 1971), 156.
10. Martin Gardner, *The Healing Revelations of Mary Baker Eddy: The Rise and Fall of Christian Science* (New York: Prometheus Books, 1993), 21.
11. Eddy, *Science and Health*, 370.

CHAPTER 10: FAITH HEALING AND MASS SUGGESTION

1. Joseph Murphy, *The Power of Your Subconscious Mind* (Radford, VA: Wilder Publications, 2007), 13.
2. Dustin White, "Becoming a Faith Healer: An Insider's Look at the Business of Revealed Religion," *Skeptic* 19, no. 1, 2014, 18.
3. Ibid.
4. Rita Swan, "Victims of religion-based medical neglect." http://children shealthcare.org/?page_id=132.
5. Mary Baker Eddy, *Science and Health with Key to the Scriptures*, (Boston: First Church of Christ, Scientist, 1971), 584. See also Mary Baker Eddy, *Unity of Good and Other Writings* (Boston: Trustees under the Will of Mary Baker Eddy, 1919), 31–43.
6. Eddy, *Unity of Good*, 9–10.
7. Ibid.
8. Mary Baker Eddy, *Miscellaneous Writings, 1883–1896* (Boston: First Church of Christ, Scientist, 1896), 249.
9. Refer to Matthew 9:27–31 and Mark 8:22–30.
10. R. Barker Bausell, *Snake Oil Science: The Truth about Complementary and Alternative Medicine* (New York: Oxford University Press, 2007), 275.
11. Edzard Ernst, "A New Blog on Alternative Medicine. Why?" http://edzardernst.com/2012/10/a-new-blog-on-alternative-medicine-why/.
12. Interested readers are also referred to the interesting articles, "Faith Healing," written by family doctor Harriet Hall in the magazines *Skeptic* 18, no. 3, 2013; *Skeptic* 19, no. 1, 2014; and *Skeptical Enquirer* 38, no. 4, 2014.

CHAPTER 11: THE MENTAL UNIVERSE

1. Three Initiates, *The Kybalion: A Study of The Hermetic Philosophy of Ancient Egypt and Greece* (Chicago: The Yogi Publication Society, 1940), 46.
2. Elisabet Sahtouris, "A Scientist's Thoughts about Redefining our Concept of God," 1999, http://www.sahtouris.com/pdfs/DefiningGod.pdf.
3. Richard C. Henry, "The Mental Universe," *Nature* 436, no. 29, July 7, 2005.
4. Paul F. Case, *The Book of Tokens: Tarot Meditations* (Los Angeles, CA: Builders of the Adytum, 1989), 31.
5. Paul F. Case, *Wisdom of Tarot: The Golden Dawn Tarot, Series 1* (Laguna Niguel, CA: Rosicrucian Order of the Golden Dawn, 2009), 72.

6. I understand by the name Qabalah the Hermetic Qabalah, which is product of the Western renaissance and occult revival.

7. Peter Baksa, "The Zero Point Field: How Thoughts Become Matter?" HuffPost, October 3, 2011, http://www.huffingtonpost.com/peter-baksa /zero-point-field_b_913831.html.

8. Herbert Spencer, *Principles of Sociology*, vol. 2 (New York: D. Appleton & Company, 1884), 843. Also online at https://archive.org/stream /principlessocio38spengoog#page/n8/mode/2up.

9. Insistent rumors have been circulating in esoteric and occult group discussions on the Internet indicating that the authors of *The Kybalion* were William Walter Atkinson, Paul Foster Case, and Michael Withy, head of the Esoteric Order of the Golden Dawn in America. Further investigation reveals that in 1908, the year of the first edition of this book, Paul F. Case and Michael Withy did not know each other yet because Withy was still living in Australia; therefore, that hypothesis is unfounded.

10. Author Philip Deslippe has identified Atkinson as the author of this pseudonymous work; see the introduction to *The Kybalion: The Definitive Edition* (New York: TarcherPerigee, 2011); also Horowitz, *Occult America*, 210.

11. Stanley Sobottka, "A Course in Consciousness," Chapter 26. Very short summary, http://faculty.virginia.edu/consciousness/home.html.

12. Henry, "The Mental Universe," online at http://bj2.netsh.com/bbs/83260 /messages/8692.html; also at http://henry.pha.jhu.edu/The.mental .universe.pdf.

13. Ibid.

14. Refer to my book, *Beyond Conventional Wisdom*, 144.

15. Dion Fortune, *The Mystical Qabalah* (York Beach, ME: Samuel Weiser, 1984).

16. Copenhaver, Brian, "Giovanni Pico della Mirandola," *The Stanford Encyclopedia of Philosophy* (Fall 2016 Edition), Edward N. Zalta (ed.), https://plato.stanford.edu/archives/fall2016/entries/pico-della -mirandola/.

17. Quoted in Robert Wang's books *The Qabalistic Tarot: A Textbook of Mystical Philosophy* (York Beach, ME: Samuel Weiser, 1983), 24, and *The Rape of Jewish Mysticism by Christian Theologians* (Columbia, MD: Marcus Aurelius Press, 2001), 31.

18. Stephen Prothero, *Religions of the East: Paths to Enlightenment* (Boston: Boston University, Modern Scholar Recorded Books, 2005).

19. Edward F. Edinger, *The Aion Lectures: Exploring the Self in C. G. Jung's "Aion"* (Toronto: Inner City Books, 1996), 22.

CHAPTER 12: THE WILL TO CREATE

1. Esther and Jerry Hicks, *Ask and It Is Given: Learning to Manifest Your Desires* (New York: Hay House, 2004), 11.
2. Ontology is a branch of metaphysics that studies the nature of being, our existence, and reality in general.
3. C. G. Jung, *Memories, Dreams, Reflections*, ed. Aniela Jaffe, trans. Richard and Clara Winston (New York: Vintage, 1989), 256.
4. Refer to Atkinson's book *Thought Vibration: The Law of Attraction in the Thought World* (Chicago: New Thought Publishing Company, 2008).
5. Esther and Jerry Hicks, *Ask and It Is Given*, 3–4.
6. Ibid., 4–5.
7. Refer to my book, *Healing Without Medicine*, 108.
8. Refer to C. G. Jung, *The Collected Works, Psychology and Religion: West and East*, translated by R. F. C. Hull (New York: Bollingen Foundation, 1958).
9. Refer to my book, *Healing Without Medicine*, 198.
10. Bob Proctor, "How to Develop Your Higher Mind's Faculties Paradigm Shift," https://www.youtube.com/watch?v=E7coTmkkLS4.
11. Paul F. Case, *Wisdom of Tarot*, 136. *Tarot Fundamentals*.
12. Robert C. Solomon, *No Excuses: Existentialism and the Meaning of Life*, Virginia: The Teaching Company, The Great Courses (audio lectures), 2000.
13. Ibid.
14. Hill, *Think and Grow Rich*, 133–134.
15. Neville Goddard, *The Power of Awareness* (USA: Pacific Publishing Studio, 2010), 6.
16. Ibid., 110.
17. Case, *Introduction to Tarot*, 1:7.
18. Case, *Wisdom of Tarot*, 33.
19. Ibid.; also in Correspondence Lessons, *Tarot Fundamentals* 5:2.
20. Deepak Chopra, *The Book of Secrets* (New York: Harmony Books, 2004), 27. Emphasis in original.
21. Deepak Chopra and Menas C. Kafatos, *You Are the Universe: Discovering Your Cosmic Self and Why It Matters* (New York: Harmony Books, 2017), 4.
22. Ibid., 2–3.

CHAPTER 13: THE QABALAH AND THE QUATERNITY PRINCIPLE

1. Jong Hwan Lee, "The Fourfold Distinction in the Philebus and Plato's Grand Project," *Journal of General Philosophy* 1, no.1, March 2014, dl6 .globalstf.org/index.php/jphilo/article/download/123/120.
2. David Allen Hulse, *The Key of It All: An Encyclopedic Guide to the Sacred Languages and Magical Systems of the World*, Book Two: *The Western Mysteries* (St. Paul, MN: Llewellyn Publications, 1996), xiv.
3. Ibid.
4. Ibid., cii.
5. Paul Foster Case, *Wisdom of Tarot*, 24.
6. Refer to my book *Healing Without Medicine*, 3.
7. Among other sources, refer to Ellic Howe, *The Magicians of the Golden Dawn: A Documentary Story of a Magical Order, 1887–1923* (York Beach, ME: Samuel Weiser 1984). Also refer to Hulse, *The Key of It All*, Book Two, 270–271.
8. Edward F. Edinger, *Ego and the Archetype: Individuation and the Religious Function of the Psyche* (New York: G. P. Putnam' Sons, 1972), 179.
9. C. G. Jung, *The Collected Works, A Psychological Approach to the Dogma of the Trinity*, trans. R. F. C. Hull (New York: Bollingen Foundation, Inc., 1958), 73.
10. Jung, *The Collected Works, Psychology and Religion*, 60–61.
11. Ibid., 61.
12. *The Birth of a New Consciousness and the Cycles of Time* (Bloomington, IN: AuthorHouse), 2016.
13. Anonymous, "The Spiritual Layers of Man," www.soul-guidance.com /houseofthesun/spirituallayers.htm.
14. "The Different Bodies of Man," www.plotinus.com/subtle_bodies_copy.htm.
15. Adaptation of Paul C. Jagot diagram, *Ciencia Oculta y Magia Practica* (Barcelona, Spain: Iberia Editorial, 1982), 9.

CHAPTER 14: THE "I AM" AND THE POWER OF THE LOST WORD

1. Sahtouris, "A Scientist's Thoughts," 1999, http://www.sahtouris.com /pdfs/DefiningGod.pdf.
2. "I form the light, and create darkness: I make peace, and create evil: I the LORD do all these things" (Isaiah 45:7 KJV).

3. Paul F. Case, *The Book of Tokens: Tarot Meditations* (Los Angeles, CA: Builders of the Adytum, 1989), 148.

4. Georg Wilhelm Friedrich Hegel, *The Philosophy of History*, preface by Charles Hegel, trans. J. Sibree (Mineola, NY: Dover Publications Kitchener, Inc., 1956), 13. Also at http://www.efm.bris.ac.uk/het/hegel /history.pdf.

5. Hegel, *The Philosophy of History*, 21.

6. C. G. Jung, *Answer to Job*, trans. R. F. C. Hull (Princeton, NJ: Princeton University Press, 1973), xi.

7. Paul F. Case, *Lessons on Tarot Fundamentals* 15:2, also in Case, *Wisdom of Tarot*.

8. Ibid.

9. Jung, *Answer to Job*, 10.

10. Viktor E. Frankl, *The Unconscious God: Psychotherapy and Theology* (New York: Simon and Schuster, 1975), 9.

11. C. G. Jung, *The Collected Works, Psychology and Religion: West and East*, translated by R. F. C. Hull (New York: Bollingen Foundation, 1958), 6.

12. Frankl, *The Unconscious God*, 10.

13. Jung, *Answer to Job*, 10.

14. Ibid., 43.

15. Ibid., 21.

16. Sahtouris, "A Scientist's Thoughts."

17. Ibid.

18. Ibid.

19. Ibid., 54.

20. Ibid., 56.

21. Quoted in Edward F. Edinger, *The Creation of Consciousness: Jung's Myth for Modern Man* (Toronto: Inner City, 1984), 58.

22. Refer to Ibid.

23. Jung, *Answer to Job*. Also quoted by Edinger, *Creation of Consciousness*, 68.

24. Refer to Jung, *Aion: Researches into the Phenomenology of the Self* and *Answer to Job*, among other works.

25. Jung, *Answer to Job*.

26. See Edward F. Edinger's books *The Creation of Consciousness* and *The New God-Image: A Study of Jung's Key Letters Concerning the Evolution of the Western God-Image* (Wilmette, IL: Chiron, 1996).

27. H. P. Blavatsky, *The Secret Doctrine*, Theosophical University Press Online Edition, vol. 2, 515, http://www.theosociety.org/pasadena/sd /sd-hp.htm.

28. Refer to my book *Beyond Conventional Wisdom*, 195–210.
29. Sahtouris, "A Scientist's Thoughts."
30. BOTA's "Pattern of the Trestleboard," https://bota.org/resources/index .html.
31. Arthur Green, *Ehyeh: A Kabbalah for Tomorrow* (Woodstock, Vermont: Jewish Light Publishing, 2004), 84.
32. Indeed, one who diminishes and misuses the "I Am" is subject to its consequences.
33. "Gentile" is defined as "in general all nations except the Jews." (Bible Study Tools dictionary, http://www.biblestudytools.com/dictionary /gentiles/).
34. Paul F. Case, *An Introduction to the Study of the Tarot* (originally published in New York, 1920), 8.
35. Green, *Ehyeh*, 3.
36. The "Authorized Version" means the King James Version.
37. Paul F. Case, *The Tarot: A Key to the Wisdom of the Ages* (Los Angeles, CA: Builders of the Adytum, 1990), 3.
38. Green, *Ehyeh*, 5.
39. The Hebrew alphabet is alphanumeric, similar to Latin; based on it, Qabalists assign a numerical value to a word or words based on the addition of their letters/numbers.
40. Green, *Ehyeh*, 37.
41. Neville Goddard, "CONSCIOUSNESS IS WHO I AM," http://www .iamawareness.com/.
42. Green, *Ehyeh*, 5.
43. Ibid.

CHAPTER 15: AN EXISTENTIAL QUESTION: WHO AM I?

1. Neville Goddard, *The Power of Awareness* (USA: Pacific Publishing Studio, 2010), 109.
2. "Pythagoras," Wikiquote, https://en.wikiquote.org/wiki/Pythagoras.
3. http://blog.meditation-presence.com/know-thyself/.
4. http://www.sacred texts.com/cso/sta/sta15.htm.
5. Georg W. Hegel, *Lectures on the History of Philosophy*, trans. by E. S. Haldane and Frances H. Simson, vol. 2 (Lincoln and London: University of Nebraska Press, 1995), 12.
6. Ibid., 14.
7. "Plato's Biography," Alan Alford official website, http://www.eridu.co.uk /Author/atlantis/plato.html.

8. Ibid.
9. Ibid.
10. Neville Goddard, "My Father," http://realneville.com/text_archive
    -pdf.htm.
11. Goddard, *The Power of Awareness*, 5.
12. "The Jungian Model of the Psyche," *Journal Psyche*, http://journalpsyche
    .org/jungian-model-psyche/.

EPILOGUE: A METAPHYSICAL ANSWER:
YOU ARE A MAGICIAN

1. H. P. Blavatsky, *Practical Occultism* (Wheaton, IL: The Theosophical
   Publishing House, 1999 [1948]), 11.
2. Marianne Williamson, *A Return to Love: Reflections on the Principles of A
   Course in Miracles* (New York: Harper Collins, 1992), 190–191.
3. "Gautama Buddha," *Wikipedia*, https://en.wikiquote.org/wiki/Gautama
   _Buddha; also at "Buddha Quotes," http://www.buddhist-tourism.com
   /buddhism/buddha-quotes.html.
4. Israel Regardie, *Foundations of Practical Magic: An Introduction to
   Qabalistic, Magical and Meditative Techniques* (Great Britain: Aquarian
   Press, 1982), 153.
5. Sri Chinmoy, *Commentaries on the Vedas, The Upanishads, and the
   Bhagavad Gita: The Three Branches of India's Life-Tree* (New York: AUM
   Publications, 1996), 117.
6. The source of this beautiful invocation is from an unidentifiable
   metaphysical magazine.

Bibliography

Amao, Albert. *Beyond Conventional Wisdom: Essays for Personal Self-Evaluation*. Bloomington, IN: AuthorHouse, 2006.

———. *The Birth of a New Consciousness and the Cycles of Time*. Bloomington, IN: AuthorHouse, 2016.

———. *Healing Without Medicine: From Pioneers to Modern Practice*. Wheaton, IL: Quest Books, 2014.

Atkinson, William Walker. *Mind-Power: The Secret of Mental Magic*. Hollister, MO: YogeBooks, 1912.

———. *Suggestion and Autosuggestion*. Hollister, MO: YogeBooks, 1909.

———. *Thought Vibration: The Law of Attraction in the Thought World*. Chicago: New Thought Publishing Company, 2008.

Bausell, R. Barker. *Snake Oil Science: The Truth about Complementary and Alternative Medicine*. New York: Oxford University Press, 2007.

Braschler, Von. *7 Secrets of Time Travel: Mystic Voyages of the Energy Body*. Rochester, VT: Destiny Books, 2012.

Case, Paul Foster. *The Book of Tokens: Tarot Meditations*. Los Angeles, CA: Builders of the Adytum, 1989.

———. *The Early Writings*. Volume 1. Laguna Niguel, CA: Fraternity of the Hidden Light, 2008.

———. *The Early Writings*. Volume 2. Covina, CA: Fraternity of the Hidden Light, 2008.

———. *The Name of Names*. Los Angeles: Builders of the Adytum, 1981.

———. *The Secret Doctrine of the Tarot*. Los Angeles: Rosicrucian Order of the Golden Dawn, 2009.

———. *The Tarot: A Key to the Wisdom of the Ages*. Los Angeles: Builders of the Adytum, 1990.

———. *Wisdom of Tarot: The Golden Dawn Tarot, Series 1*. Laguna Niguel, CA: Rosicrucian Order of the Golden Dawn, 2009.

Cather, Willa, and Georgine Milmine. *The Life of Mary Baker G. Eddy and the History of Christian Science*. Lincoln, NE: University of Nebraska Press, 1993.

Chopra, Deepak. *The Book of Secrets: Unlocking the Hidden Dimensions of Your Life*. New York: Harmony Books, 2004.

——— and Menas Kafatos. *You Are the Universe: Discovering Your Cosmic Self and Why It Matters*. New York: Harmony Books, 2017.

Cooper, David A. *God Is a Verb: Kabbalah and the Practice of Mystical Judaism*. New York: Riverhead, 1997.

Cousins, Norman. *Anatomy of an Illness as Perceived by the Patient*. New York: W. W. Norton & Company, 1979.

Dolby, Sandra K. *Self-Help Books (Why Americans Keep Reading Them)*. Chicago: University of Illinois Press, 2008.

Dunne, Claire. *Carl Jung, Wounded Healer of the Soul*. New York: Parabola, 2000.

Edinger, Edward F. *The Aion Lectures: Exploring the Self in C. G. Jung's Aion*. Toronto: Inner City, 1996.

———. *The Creation of Consciousness: Jung's Myth for Modern Man*. Toronto: Inner City, 1984.

———. *Ego and the Archetype: Individuation and the Religious Function of the Psyche*. New York: G. P. Putnam's Sons, 1972.

———. *The New God-Image: A Study of Jung's Key Letters Concerning the Evolution of the Western God-Image*. Wilmette, IL: Chiron, 1996.

Eddy, Mary Baker. "Malicious Animal Magnetism." *The Christian Science Journal* (February 1889). www.endtime.org/library/mbe/mam.html.

———. *Miscellaneous Writings 1883–1896*. Boston: First Church of Christ, Scientist, 1924.

———. *Science and Health with Key to the Scriptures*. Boston: First Church of Christ, Scientist, 1971.

———. *Unity of Good and Other Writings*. Boston: Trustees under the Will of Mary Baker Eddy, 1919.

Eddy, Glove (aka Mary Baker Eddy). *Christian Healing, A Lecture Delivered at Boston*. Cambridge, MA: John Wilson and Son, 1905.

Ehrenreich, Barbara. *Bright-Sided: How the Relentless Promotion of Positive Thinking Has Undermined America*. New York: Metropolitan Books, 2009.

Eliade, Mircea. *Myth and Reality: Religious Traditions of the World*. Prospect Heights, IL: Waveland, 1998.

Ellenberger, Henry F. *The Discovery of the Unconscious: The History and Evolution of Dynamic Psychiatry*. New York: Basic Books, 1970.

Ellis, Albert. *Overcoming Resistance: A Rational Emotive Therapy Integrated Approach, 2nd ed.* New York: Springer Publishing, 2002.

Fortune, Dion. *The Mystical Qabalah.* York Beach, ME: Samuel Weiser, 1984.

Frankl, Viktor E. *The Unconscious God: Psychotherapy and Theology.* New York: Simon and Schuster, 1975.

Fraser, Caroline. *God's Perfect Child: Living and Dying in the Christian Science Church.* New York: Henry Holt & Company, 1999.

Gardner, L. Ron. *Beyond the Power of Now: A Guide to, and Beyond, Eckhart Tolle's Teachings.* USA: Vernal Point Publishing, 2012.

Gardner, Martin. *The Healing Revelations of Mary Baker Eddy: The Rise and Fall of Christian Science.* New York: Prometheus Books, 1993.

———. *Mary Baker Eddy: The Rise and Fall of Christian Science.* New York: Prometheus Books, 1993.

Goddard, Neville. *The Power of Awareness.* USA: Pacific Publishing Studio, 2010.

Green, Arthur. *Ehyeh: A Kabbalah for Tomorrow.* Woodstock, VT: Jewish Lights Publishing, 2004.

Greenhouse, Lucia, *fathermothergod: My Journey Out of Christian Science.* New York: Crown Publishers, 2011.

Hall, Harriet. "Does Religion Make People Healthier?" *Skeptic* 19, no. 1 (2014).

———. "Faith Healing: Religious Freedom vs. Child Protection." *Skeptical Inquirer* (July/August 2014).

———. "Scientology's War on Medicine." *Skeptic* 18, no. 3 (2013).

Harrington, Anne. *The Cure Within: A History of Mind-Body Medicine.* New York: W. W. Norton & Company, 2008.

Hegel, Georg Wilhelm Friedrich. *Lectures on the History of Philosophy.* Volume 2. Translated by E. S. Haldane and Frances H. Simson. Lincoln, NE, and London: University of Nebraska Press, 1995.

Hegel, Georg W. F. *The Philosophy of History.* Mineola, NY: Dover Publications, 1956.

Henry, Richard C. "The Mental Universe." *Nature* 436, no. 29 (July 7, 2005). http://henry.pha.jhu.edu/The.mental.universe.pdf.

Hicks, Esther and Jerry. *Ask and It Is Given: Learning to Manifest Your Desires.* New York: Hay House, 2004.

Hill, Napoleon. *Think and Grow Rich.* New York: Fall River Press, 2012.

Horowitz, Mitch. "All You Can Be: Why Positive Thinking Matters." *Quest* (Winter 2016).

———. *Occult America: The Secret History of How Mysticism Shaped Our Nation.* New York: Bantam, 2009.

———. *One Simple Idea: How Positive Thinking Reshaped Modern Life.* New York: Crown Publishers, 2014.

Howe, Ellic. *The Magicians of the Golden Dawn: A Documentary Story of a Magical Order, 1887–1923.* York Beach, ME: Samuel Weiser 1984.

Hulse, David Allen, *The Key of It All: An Encyclopedic Guide to the Sacred Languages and Magical Systems of the World*, Book Two: *The Western Mysteries*. St. Paul, MN: Llewellyn Publications, 1996.

Jagot, Paul C. *Ciencia Oculta y Magia Practica*. Barcelona: Iberia Editorial, 1982.

Jung, C. G. *Aion: Researches into the Phenomenology of the Self*. Translated by R. F. C. Hull. Princeton, NJ: Princeton University Press, 1978.

———. *Answer to Job*. Translated by R. F. C. Hull. Princeton, NJ: Princeton University Press, 1973.

———. *The Archetypes and the Collective Unconscious*. Translated by R. F. C. Hull. London: Routledge, 1996.

———. *Collected Papers on Analytical Psychology*. New York: Moffat Yard, 1917.

———. *The Collected Works, Psychology and Religion: West and East*. Translated by R. F. C. Hull. New York: Bollingen Foundation, 1958.

———. *Man and His Symbols*. New York: Anchor, 1978.

———. *Memories, Dreams, Reflections*. Translated by Richard and Clara Winston. New York: Vintage, 1989.

Kuby, Lolette. *Faith and the Placebo Effect: An Argument for Self-Healing*. Novato, CA: Origin Press, 2001.

McGee, Micki. *Self-Help, Inc.: Makeover Culture in American Life*. New York: Oxford University Press, 2005.

McTaggart, Lynne. *The Field: The Quest for the Secret Force of the Universe*. New York: Harper, 2008.

Murphy, Joseph. *The Power of Your Subconscious Mind*. Radford, VA: Wilder Publications, 2007.

Park, Robert L. *Superstition: Belief in the Age of Science*. Princeton, NJ: Princeton University Press, 2008.

Peale, Norman Vincent. *The Power of Positive Thinking*. New York: Touchstone, 1980.

Plaut, W. Gunther, ed. *The Torah: A Modern Commentary*. New York: Union of American Hebrew Congregations, 2005.

Peck, M. Scott. *The Road Less Traveled*. New York: Simon & Schuster, 2003.

Prothero, Stephen. *Religions of the East: Paths to Enlightenment*. Boston University: Modern Scholar Recorded Books, 2005.

Rankin, Lissa. *Mind Over Medicine: Scientific Proof That You Can Heal Yourself*. New York: Hay House, 2013.

Regardie, Israel. *Foundations of Practical Magic: An Introduction to Qabalistic, Magical and Meditative Techniques*. England: Aquarian Press, 1982.

Salerno, Steve. *Sham: How the Self-Help Movement Made America Helpless*. New York: Crown Publishers, 2005.

Solomon, Robert C. *No Excuses: Existentialism and the Meaning of Life*. Virginia: The Great Courses (audio lectures). The Teaching Company. 2000.

Spencer, Herbert. *Principles of Sociology*. Volume 2. New York: D. Appleton & Company, 1884.

Starker, Steven. *Oracle at the Supermarket: The American Preoccupation With Self-Help Books*. New Brunswick, NJ: Transaction Publishers, 1989.

Stauth, Cameron. *In the Name of God: The True Story of the Fight to Save Children from Faith-Healing Homicide*. New York: St. Martin's Press, 2013.

Tarnas, Richard. *Cosmos and Psyche: Intimations of a New World View*. New York: Penguin, 2006.

———. *The Passion of the Western Mind: Understanding the Ideas That Have Shaped Our World View*. New York: Harmony, 1991.

Three Initiates. *The Kybalion: A Study of the Hermetic Philosophy of Ancient Egypt and Greece*. Chicago, IL: The Yogi Publication Society, 1940.

Tiede, Tom. *Self-Help Nation: The Long Overdue, Entirely Justified, Delightfully Hostile Guide to the Snake-Oil Peddlers Who Are Sapping Our Nation's Soul*. New York: Atlantic Monthly Press, 2001.

TIME. *Secret Societies (Decoding the Myths and Facts of History's Most Mysterious Organizations)*. New York: TIME Books, 2010.

Tolle, Eckhart. *The Power of Now: A Guide to Spiritual Enlightenment*. Novato, CA: Namaste Publishing and New World Library, 1999.

Tutt, John M. "The Role of a Practitioner." *Christian Science Sentinel* (June 12, 1965). https://sentinel.christianscience.com/shared/view/20mkoky1rnm.

Wang, Robert. *The Qabalistic Tarot: A Textbook of Mystical Philosophy*. York Beach, ME: Samuel Weiser, 1983.

———. *The Rape of Jewish Mysticism by Christian Theologians: How the Modern Occult Movement Grew Out of Renaissance Attempts to Convert the Jews*. Columbia, MD: Marcus Aurelius Press, 2001.

Williamson, Marianne. *A Return to Love: Reflections on the Principles of A Course in Miracles*. New York: HarperCollins, 1992.

Wiseman, Richard. *59 Seconds: Think a Little, Change a Lot*. New York: Alfred A. Knopf, 2009.

———. *The "As If" Principle: The Radically New Approach to Changing Your Life*. New York: Simon & Schuster, 2012.

ONLINE RESOURCES

Alford, Alan. "Atlantis—Plato." The Official Alan Alford Website. http://www .eridu.co.uk/Author/author.html.

Anonymous. "Awareness Locks Reality and Emotions Attract It." http://www .remoteviewer.nu/?p=3816.

———. "The Different Bodies of Man." Soulmerging. www.soulmerging.com
/article/3237-the-four-bodies-of-existance.

———. "The Four Bodies of Existance." Soulmerging. www.soulmerging.com
/article/3237-the-four-bodies-of-existance.

———. "I Am." http://www.growthingod.org.uk/IAM.htm.

———. "The Spiritual Layers of Man." Soul-Guidance.com. www.soul
-guidance.com/houseofthesun/spirituallayers.htm.

Bedard, Moe. "Letter 'G' in Freemasonry Signifies Gnosis." Gnostic Warrior.
http://gnosticwarrior.com/g.html.

Friesen, J. Glenn. "Jung and Western Mysticism." http://www.members.shaw
.ca/cgjung/Individuation.html.

Lilla, Jenna. "Quaternity and Divinity: Symbol of God within." On
Self-awareness. https://jennalilla.org/2013/01/17/quaternity-and-divinity/.

Paresky, Pamela B. "What is Reality?" *Psychology Today*. https://www
.psychologytoday.com/blog/happiness-and-the-pursuit-leadership/201510
/what-is-reality.

Pulos, Lee. "The Future Creates the Present—NOT the Past!" Adventures
in Learning. http://drpulos.com/blog/the-future-creates-the-present
-%E2%80%93-not-the-past/.

Sahtouris, Elisabet. "A Scientist's Thoughts about Redefining our Concept of
God." 1999. http://www.sahtouris.com/pdfs/DefiningGod.pdf.

Sobottka, Stanley. "A Course in Consciousness." http://courseinconsciousness
.org/.

Index

About the Author

Albert Amao Soria, is a graduate of the National University of San Marcos, in Lima, Peru. He holds a PhD in sociology, and is a social theorist and cultural critic. He lectures widely on metaphysical subjects. He is national speaker for the Theosophical Society in America. Mr. Amao has written on metaphysics, New Thought philosophy, and Hermetic Qabalah, and is the author of several books including *Healing Without Medicine* (Quest Books, 2014) and *The Dawning of the Golden Age of Aquarius* (AuthorHouse, 2012). He is the founder of the Center for Spiritual Self-Development and is available for lectures upon request. Mr. Amao can be contacted by e-mail at Stgermain777@gmail.com. For further information, visit http://www.albertamao.com.